IBM
VS.
JAPAN

Also by Robert Sobel:

The Origins of Interventionism
The Big Board: A History of the New York Stock Market
The Great Bull Market: Wall Street in the 1920s
Panic on Wall Street: A History of America's Great Financial Disasters
The Curbstone Brokers: The Origins of the American Stock Exchange
Conquest and Conscience: The United States in the 1840s
The Age of Giant Corporations
Amex: A History of the American Stock Exchange
Machines and Morality: The United States in the 1850s
Money Manias: Eras of Great Speculation in American History
For Want of a Nail . . .: If Burgoyne Had Won at Saratoga
The Entrepreneurs: Explorations Within the American Business Tradition
Herbert Hoover at the Onset of the Great Depression
N.Y.S.E.: A History of the New York Stock Exchange
The Manipulators: America in Media Age
Inside Wall Street
The Fallen Colossus: The Crash of the Penn Central
They Satisfy: The Cigarette in American LIfe
The Last Bull Market: Wall Street in the 1960s
The Worldly Economists
IBM: Colossus in Transition
ITT: The Management of Opportunity
The Rise and Fall of the Conglomerate Kings
*Car Wars: The Untold Story of the Great Automakers and the Giant Battle
    for Global Supremacy*

IBM
VS.
JAPAN

The struggle for the future

Robert Sobel

STEIN AND DAY / *Publishers* / New York

First published in 1986
Copyright © 1986 by The New York Times Syndication Sales Corporation
All rights reserved, Stein and Day, Incorporated
Designed by Louis A. Ditizio
Printed in the United States of America

STEIN AND DAY/*Publishers*
Scarborough House
Briarcliff Manor, N.Y. 10510

Library of Congress Cataloging-in-Publication Data

Sobel, Robert, 1931 Feb. 19–
  IBM vs. Japan.

  Bibliography: p.
  Includes index.
  1. IBM.   2. Computer industry.   3. Computer industry—
United States.   4. Computer industry—Japan.   I. Title.
II. Title: IBM versus Japan.
HD9696.C64I4885 1986   338.4'7004   85-43058
ISBN 0-8128-3071-7

For Murray, Marsha, Margot,
and Sean Henner

CONTENTS

In the world information processing market, we have to respect IBM. We are like the hunter who approaches the lion with a rifle in hand. Suddenly the beast kneels down. "Are you afraid?" the hunter asks. "No," the lion replies, "I'm just praying before eating."

—a Fujitsu executive

INTRODUCTION

There can be no doubt that the concept of computing originated either in the Near East or Europe, depending upon how far back you want to go. But for all practical purposes the modern information processing industry has been dominated by Americans. Just as the turn-of-the-century American boy supposedly was born with an instinct for fiddling around with horseless carriages, so modern Americans celebrate the "computer freak," "space cadet," or "hacker," depending upon whether one admires or ridicules those whose waking hours are devoted to staring at video screens, developing software, and preparing to create machines that will challenge those of the leader: International Business Machines. Or they dream of working for the firm alternately known as "The Armonk Monster" or "Big Blue" (for the location of its home office in the first instance and the color of lettering for its logo in the second).

IBM is on everyone's list of the top half-dozen or so best managed corporations. To outsiders it often appears as a monolith, a firm of clear-cut unity of purpose, led by individuals who rarely make missteps, and when they do, recover rapidly. For example, in early 1985 IBM announced the "suspension" of the contentious PCjr, a microcomputer whose sales would have made it a success by other standards, but not those of Big Blue. Earlier it had conceded errors in the keyboard and generously offered a free replacement to any earlier buyers, which proved a public relations coup. No one seriously believes IBM will ignore the home micro segment of the market. Rather, having made an error it went back to the drawing board, and at this writing it appears a new machine, perhaps to be known as PC III, will soon be offered to a waiting public.

Other firms in other industries age and become arthritic—U.S. Steel in basic metals, General Motors in automobiles, RCA in consumer electronics, and Xerox in copying machines come to mind—and concede ground to younger, more vigorous challengers. Not IBM, as its rivals, and investors, have come to know. On Wall Street IBM is known as the one stock that has been the star of bull markets since the 1920s.

The company is constantly engaged in the process of renewal so that it appears vigorous, youthful, and dynamic even as its revenues approach the $50 billion level. During the past six years IBM has invested over $15 billion on new facilities and equipment and $18 billion more on research and development. Senior vice president for finance and planning Allen Krowe has indicated that in the second half of the 1980s upward of $56 billion more will be invested. "The pace of our capital investment is, if anything, accelerating," he told a reporter.

Moreover, the product mix is changing. The factories will remain, turning out a wide variety of industrial products, telecommunications devices, and the like along with the familiar computers, but increasingly IBM will be known for its programs and services. In 1984 software of various kinds accounted for approximately 10 percent of revenues, and it appears the figure for 1985 will come in at around 11–12 percent. Management has set a goal of 35 percent growth in this area. Says Krowe, "Software may represent up to a third of our business [by the 1990s]."

Most industry observers expect IBM to expand at the rate of approximately 15–20 percent per annum for the foreseeable future, an amazing performance, comparable to seeing an elephant whizz by at 100 miles per hour. Yet the firm has done so in the past, and it would be unwise to expect less in the future. Should this happen, IBM would be a more than $200 billion concern before the end of this century.

IBM has made mincemeat of those domestic companies that have dared challenge it head-on, and the Europeans who have done so have fared no better. These competitors have signaled their defeat by going "the plug-compatible route," which is to say they have concentrated on manufacturing mainframes that can run IBM software, in effect telling customers that they have produced a better and less expensive IBM machine than has the Armonk

Monster itself. Even so their machines often are difficult to place; the industry rule of thumb is that you have a chance if your machine performs ten percent faster and is ten percent lower in price.

The only successes in the information processing field have gone to firms that made oblique assaults, concentrating on special markets and customers, content to live off IBM's leavings. RCA and GE, giants by anyone's standards, couldn't make it; Control Data, Digital Equipment, and Apple were start-up operations that took careful aim at a segment that IBM had ignored and were able to graduate to the big leagues before the response was mounted. They remain specialized firms, knowing that to lay down a challenge across the board would be disastrous.

Ironically, if these three firms, each positioned in a different segment of the market, could somehow come together and iron out their differences, they might offer a viable alternative to Big Blue. But the chances of that happening are nil. And even less can be anticipated from the Europeans; not a single company in the Common Market could present a challenge, and in fact most have difficulty coping with the IBM subsidiary in their countries.

It is commonly believed the Japanese possess the only entries left in the field. Fujitsu and Hitachi are given a chance at putting a dent into IBM's market share, though even these firms concede the going will be tough. Optimists in Japan observe that if the likes of Canon, Minolta, Sony, Nippon Steel, Toshiba, and Toyota could take on such American giants as Eastman Kodak, Xerox, RCA, U.S. Steel, GE, and GM, so Fujitsu should be able to do as much with IBM. Japanese pessimists reply that this is a different ball game entirely, that IBM is a much leaner and tougher competitor than any of the others, and that if Fujitsu couldn't conquer IBM in its own domestic market without massive government help, it hardly can hope to do so in the export area.

The Japanese have three responses: partnerships with national firms whenever possible; the same kind of oblique response that worked for those few U.S. competitors that survived and grew; and the development of an entirely different approach toward information processing, which will make all IBM machines obsolete and in the end force the Armonk Monster to go into the plug-compatible business—turning out Fujitsu and Hitachi lookalikes.

Those who a few years ago considered the first approach to be the most viable now know of its limitations. The second is now being attempted, and with some success, especially in the area of computer peripherals and microcomputers. The third, the (to the author illusory) promise of the "Fifth

Generation Project," is the great hope of the future. In effect, Japan seems to this writer to be saying, "Today the PCM and micro, tomorrow the Fifth Generation!"

These issues provide the *leitmotif* for *IBM vs. Japan: The Struggle for the Future.* The book is divided into two parts. The first seeks to explain how IBM obtained its dominant position, exploring the firm's *élan,* how it operates, and the methods other American firms attempted either to defeat it or to find some *modus vivendi* with the Armonk Monster. In addition, there are discussions of how, when all else failed, IBM's rivals utilized American antitrust law in their struggles and why that path doesn't look promising for the future.

The second section deals with the European and Japanese computer industries, their strategies and experiences in dealing with Armonk. It opens with an analysis of the methods IBM used to obtain its dominant position in Europe and its strong one in Japan. I then go on to indicate paths the Japanese might take in their struggle against IBM, how they might capitalize on strengths and minimize weaknesses. The book concludes with a forecast of what seems likely to transpire in the information processing and distribution industry, which in all probability will become the world's largest sometime in the 1990s.

IBM
VS.
JAPAN

AT HOME

I

IBM: ORIGINS

The Beginning

It started with John Vincent Atanasoff, the son of Bulgarian immigrants, who was to data processing what Charles Duryea had been to cars.

Who is Charles Duryea? Why, the manufacturer of America's first motor car designed to be produced for use rather than as a mere curiosity. Duryea is all but forgotten today; ask the proverbial man-in-the-street who was the father of the horseless carriage and chances are he'll respond with a fast "Henry Ford." Now ask him who invented the computer, and most likely the answer will be a blank stare—or "Someone at International Business Machines."

Nonetheless, it was Atanasoff who deserves the credit. Born in 1903, he progressed up the educational ladder, obtaining a Ph.D. in theoretical physics from the University of Wisconsin, and during the Great Depression he taught that subject at Iowa State University at Ames. While there Atanasoff read about and then experimented with computing machines. With a small grant and the help of a graduate assistant, Clifford Berry, he produced the Atanasoff-Berry Computer (which he dubbed the ABC) in 1939. It was a crude, rickety device, which broke down regularly—not unlike Duryea's first buggy—but it was a beginning.

Late in 1940, Atanasoff attended a convention of the American Association for the Advancement of Science, where he was surprised to learn not only of interest in his work, but that others were also in the field. One of these was

John Mauchly, on the faculty at Ursinus College in Collegeville, Pa., who was creating a machine to do calculations for weather forecasting. The two men shared ideas and information, and the following summer Mauchly journeyed to Ames to witness the ABC in action and continue conversations with Atanasoff, after which he returned to Ursinus.

Atanasoff continued experimenting with the ABC and later founded an electronics company, the sale of which provided him with sufficient funds for the rest of his life. As a result of legal actions in 1968 (of which he wasn't a party, merely a witness) he received recognition for his contributions. But the story of the computer's development continued with Mauchly.

War was coming, and Mauchly felt he had a role to play in it. So in the summer of 1942 he enrolled in an electronics course at the Moore School of Engineering at the University of Pennsylvania. It was there that he ran into J. Presper Eckert, a graduate student in physics, and began an association out of which would emerge the first commercial computer firm. Together they designed and then built—with government financial assistance—the Electronic Numerical Integrator and Calculator, or ENIAC for short. The machine was a huge, complex affair, with 17,000 tubes, miles of wiring, and hundreds of electromechanical gears that, as one observer noted, when in action sounded like an army of knitting needles at work and was programmed via punched cards.

The ENIAC intrigued John von Neumann, a Hungarian-born mathematician at the nearby Princeton Institute for Advanced Studies, who even then had a considerable reputation, and he joined Eckert and Mauchly in further research. In time von Neumann came to dominate the group that sprang up between Princeton and the Moore School, not only due to his genius, but also to his uncanny knack of being able to extract research and development funds from the government and large corporations.

In any case, von Neumann was largely responsible for finding applications for ENIAC, which although it broke down frequently was useful in such important tasks as creating the first atomic bomb. He deserves credit for something else, too, which may in time appear even more significant. Von Neumann set down the rules—mapped the terrain, as it were—for how computers should be created and function. There was to be a mainframe, a memory, a programming unit, and peripherals by which information is fed into the machine and from which it is extracted. The computer would function in a serial fashion, one step at a time. Improvements would come— larger capacity and faster mainframes, larger memories that were more easily accessible than those original ones, highly complex programs, and more rapid entry and access methods. But the essentials of what in a few years would be known as the "von Neumann machines" (one was even dubbed the Jonniac) would remain the rule up to our time. Von Neumann even established the limitations of such machines, writing that while they would be capable of highly complex tasks, they would never be able to learn, to replace the human being. As far as he was concerned, "artificial intelligence" was a chimera. This is a point worth keeping in mind, for a major part of the Japanese challenge to American computer domination, the heart of this book, concerns just this principle.

To return to the subject at hand, during the war interesting work was also being done elsewhere and at other campuses, much of it initiated and coordinated by Colonel Paul Gillon of the Office of the Chief of Army Ordnance. Jay Forrester of the Massachusetts Institute of Technology was designing military computers. George Stibitz of Bell Telephone Laboratories, who before the war had probed the uses of computers in switching operations, was asked to adapt his ideas to military uses; by the time the war ended Bell had more patents in the field than all the others combined. And there were many others.

This was the beginning of interest in computers in the United States. To a lesser extent the British and Germans, too, were involved; indeed, they had been a distance ahead of their American counterparts before and during the war. German technicians were experimenting with computers even prior to Atanasoff, and one model, the Zuse 4, was used to assist in aircraft design in 1942. British scientist Alan Turing, a brilliant Princeton-educated mathematician, was playing a role in England similar to the one von Neumann played on the other side of the Atlantic, and, indeed, Turing had worked with von Neumann prior to the war. There were projects at the National Physics Laboratory in Teddington, at Cambridge, and at the University of Manchester, where scientists like John Wormersley, Douglas Hartree, and C. L. Comrie had developed computers prior to Eckert and Mauchly, and many of the ideas developed at Moore came from these researchers. All had high hopes for computers, but could not visualize an important need for them after the war. Hartree was one of the more optimistic; he thought the United Kingdom would require a dozen or so.

In 1939, a British team headed by Turing developed the crude Heath Robinson electronic computer at Bletchley and other machines followed. Later, a variant of this device was used to crack the German codes, and some computer historians deem this device to have been the first of its kind in the world. To them, it is clear that the honor of inception belongs to Great Britain and not the United States. A moot point, perhaps, because while the British possessed the intellectual capital they lacked its economic counterpart, and in any case those in charge understandably considered computers a military weapon and little else.

The scene now shifts to Radio Corporation of America, which under Chairman David Sarnoff had become one of the most innovative and imaginative firms in the electronic field. During the war, Jan Rajchman, a brilliant scientist at RCA, had developed a computer that automatically aimed large guns, but Sarnoff was not so much interested in entering the computer business as he was in a relatively new brainchild: television. He saw in the ENIAC-type machines a wonderful market for electronic tubes. And, if a small market did develop for computers—in laboratories, weather bureaus, and the military—perhaps it could form a small profit center for RCA. During the war, RCA developed an analog computer for the Navy, known as the Typhoon, which was not delivered, however, until after the fighting had ended. By then Sarnoff had also agreed to fund research on a new machine to be developed by von Neumann and others at the Institute for Advanced Studies, to be given the name of EDVAC (Electronic Discrete Variable Automatic Computer). EDVAC was completed five years later.

Enter IBM

Eckert and Mauchley elected to remain at Moore and work on their own. But not for long. The war was over and with it government-funded research on computers. The GI Bill of Rights had gone into effect, colleges and universities all over America were bulging with students, and Moore wanted the space being utilized by the computer project. So the two associates sought a new home for their research. This is where IBM entered the picture. It was not the firm's first encounter with computers; IBM had a hand in them prior to the war, an experience that had soured Chairman Thomas Watson on the whole idea.

James Bryce had been one of IBM's leading scientists in the 1930s and, more important, perhaps, was a man who had Watson's ear and respect. He had supported the work of IBM scientist Clair Lake and Columbia's Professor Wallace Eckert (no relation to J. Presper) who adapted tabulators and accounting machines to create a new device: the large, complex electromechanical calculator, for which the company had received applause and burnished its already considerable reputation. Scientists and engineers from all parts of the country arrived to see the machine in action, much to Watson's delight. One of these was a young Harvard graduate student, Howard Aiken, who wondered whether a calculator might be constructed that could perform according to preprogrammed instructions or, in other words, had a memory. Without knowing about the ABC and the work being conducted at the Moore School, Aiken had also grasped the essentials of the computer.

With IBM funding and considerable help from Lake, Aiken began designing his computer, the Automatic Sequence Controlled Calculator (ASCC, and later Mark I) in 1940, and it was ready for unveiling by 1943. A grand ceremony was planned at Harvard, with Watson expecting much of the glory to go to IBM. So he was shocked and disappointed when, at a press conference, Aiken tried to take all the credit. "I'm just sick about the whole thing," he screamed at Aiken. "You can't put IBM on as a postscript. I think about IBM just as you Harvard fellows do about your university." As Tom Watson, Jr., later said, "If Aiken and my father had had revolvers, they would both have been dead."

Bryce was convinced that there was a future at IBM for computers and was in contact with Eckert and Mauchly during the war. On learning they had to leave Moore, he invited them to the firm's Endicott, New York, headquarters to meet with Watson, who offered them jobs—but on calculators and in electronics. Watson wanted nothing to do with computers, in part due to the Aiken experience, but also because he did not believe there would be much of a market for them. But IBM was then developing its first electronic products, which were to be calculators for use as accounting machines, known as the 600 series. Not a little dismayed and hoping to interest some other firm in their machine, Eckert and Mauchly looked elsewhere.

There followed meetings with Burroughs, Addressograph-Multigraph, National Cash Register, and General Electric where Eckert and Mauchly were greeted with polite receptions and equally polite rejections. All the while, they worked on ENIAC, hoping to bring it into operation and so have something to show to potential investors. The machine was completed in 1945 and turned over to the Army, at which time the Moore administration renewed its requests for Eckert and Mauchly's departure. So they went and, lacking a sponsor, organized their own company, which was called Electronic Control Corporation. There they worked on a new machine, to be called the Binary Automatic Computer (BINAC), that featured a tape drive that replaced the cards. BINAC was ordered by their one and only customer, Northrop Corporation.

By then, computers had started to receive some press attention, and so had the two men. And they had a second customer: the Census Bureau awarded the firm a study contract for a new and improved machine. So, to capitalize upon this situation, the company's name was changed to Eckert-Mauchly Computer.

Help finally arrived from what at first appeared to be the third customer. American Totalizator manufactured the pari-mutuel machines used at most of the nation's racetracks. The Mun brothers, who owned the firm, knew little about the business and were content to permit it to be run by Henry Straus, a man of limited education but an intuitive feel for machines, whose instincts told him computers would do better than calculators in processing information at the tracks. Straus offered $500,000 for 40 percent of Eckert-Mauchly's stock, giving American Totalizator control of the nation's one and only computer company. He then funded development out of the parent company's meager cash flow, much to the chagrin of the Muns.

UNIVAC

Eckert and Mauchly's new machine—which was called UNIVAC (Universal Automatic Computer)—was supposed to be delivered in time to process the 1950 census, but in 1949 it seemed it would arrive late, and even then no one knew if it could do the job. Straus remained confident, however, keeping the Muns in line behind the project. But then he died in an airplane crash and the Muns, with little faith in or knowledge of computers, immediately searched for someone to take Eckert-Mauchly off their hands.

They found a buyer in James Rand of Remington Rand, a company that had started out in the 1920s as what might be described as an office machine conglomerate put together as much for speculative purposes as anything else, a not unusual occurrence during the Great Bull Market of that era. Rand himself was no great shakes as a businessman or manager; the role he most enjoyed was that of promoter and speculator. In 1920 he headed a smallish firm known as Rand Cardex, whose only important product was a well-received filing system. To join Cardex he brought in the likes of Dalton Adding Machine, Powers Accounting Machine, and the famous Remington Typewriter, hence the name of Remington Rand. By the 1940s it was the largest business machine firm in the world, not a great accomplishment since the industry was in its infancy. Still, RemRand posted sales of a shade less than $60 million in 1928, which was three times the sales of IBM. But it was a flabby, disorganized, and poorly managed operation, which showed in its low profitability: $6 million for RemRand, $5.5 million for IBM.

While typewriters were its most famous product, accounting machines might have been its most promising area—if Rand and his colleagues had had any vision at all. In the 1930s Powers was a big name in that small field, and would soon be even bigger in Europe. It had been created shortly after the turn of the century by James Powers, a shadowy, Russian-born figure of mechanical bent—he also invented a toothpick-cutting machine and a coin-operated photographic device—who worked in the Census Bureau during the 1900 count, which was done by leasing punchers, tabulators, and sorters designed by Herman Hollorith. Hollorith, also a Bureau employee, had incorporated himself in 1896 as the Tabulating Company.

The Powers machines not only were superior to Hollorith's, they were more economical, and Powers won the contract for the 1910 counting. Indeed, during the next few years Powers all but put the Tabulating Company machine out of business, in the end obliging Hollorith to sell out to Charles Ranlett Flint, a promoter, who united the company with a second firm, which manufactured time clocks, and a third whose business included a scale which also calculated the price of the item being weighed. Flint called his new company Computing-Tabulating-Recording, a name which was changed in 1924 to International Business Machines.

This was one of the more interesting ironies of American business history. In 1910, Powers had a head start on Tabulating Company, a lead which was lost in the 1930s; by then RemRand had slipped into second place behind IBM, with Burroughs breathing hard on its back in third. Now RemRand and IBM were about to undergo what almost amounted to a repetition of the earlier experience.

Just as Tom Watson had been urged by James Bryce to consider entering the computer field, so Jim Rand had been prodded by Arthur Draper, who at RemRand was charged with keeping a weather eye out for interesting new technologies and potential takeover candidates.

What Rand saw in Eckert-Mauchly Computer was a firm whose first Univac was a year from completion and would need another million dollars to bring on stream. But the company did have orders for six more—always assuming the Census Bureau's performed as promised. This was a time when it was generally assumed that the total world-wide market for computers was around a dozen or so. (Japanese and American supporters of supercomputer programs also note this when talking about the market for their huge machines, which in the late 1970s was assumed to be the same "dozen or so.")

Jim Rand's initial plans for computers are not known, for he rarely spoke of the matter, and never for publication. But in March 1950 he purchased all of American Totalizator's holdings in Eckert-Mauchly, plus those of others, giving Remington Rand 95 percent of the company's common shares. For their holdings, Eckert and Mauchly received $40,000 each, plus another $40,000 in patent royalties.

The first Univac was delivered in 1951, for a price of around $1 million, and was sufficiently impressive to result in additional orders, all from government agencies. Then, in 1953, General Electric purchased one of the machines and took delivery the following year, thus becoming the first corporate customer.

Meanwhile, in the United Kingdom research proceeded apace. But not its companion, development. More concerned with social welfare programs, the Labour government evinced little interest in funding computers. Nor was private enterprise, impoverished by the war, capable of anything more than gestures in that direction. Needless to say, the Germans were more concerned with digging their way out of the rubble, and no one then considered that the Japanese—without an electronic base and occupied by Americans—would ever get into the game. Down the list it went—France, Italy, the Netherlands, and so on—with no organized or, in most cases, even individual, efforts in that direction. Whether or not work on computers was taking place on the other side of what soon would be known as the Iron Curtain is unknown, but given the laggard performance in later years, it would appear doubtful. Even more so than the automobile and the airplane, in the early years (which is to say the first quarter of a century or so) the computer was to be the province of Americans.

By the late 1940s and early 1950s, others had joined RemRand in the field, at least on an experimental basis. They came, more or less, out of four streams. One was that of traditional business machine firms, which were looking at new product ideas to augment existing business (such as IBM, National Cash Register, Underwood, and Burroughs). The second was electronic-oriented companies eager to utilize expertise in a different product area (American Telephone & Telegraph, International Telephone & Telegraph, RCA, Westinghouse, and General Electric, who, satisfied with its Univac, was also exploring the technology). The third was defense contractors intrigued with products it might sell to the government (Northrop, Raytheon, Boeing, Douglas, Consolidated Vultee, and Lockheed). Finally, there was a host of smallish, young firms (usually headed by technicians), most of which were underfunded and inexperienced and soon to fall by the wayside, their names forgotten except by historians and those directly involved—Potter Instruments, Intelligent Machines Research, MacDonald Electronic, Telecomputing, and Engineering Research Associates.

Engineering Research Associates was one of the more interesting, important, and successful of the new operations. A St. Paul, Minnesota, based outfit, it was founded in 1946 by a group of naval officers who had worked with electronics during the war and was headed by William Norris, a bright, blunt, forceful engineer. ERA intended to develop a computer which might be used by Naval Intelligence. It started out with a research-and-development grant and contract to deliver such a system to the Navy. Out of this came the ATLAS I, which, under the terms of the arrangement, ERA was permitted to market to commercial clients, and which it did as the 1101—with modest success. Still, one of the 1101s was delivered in December 1950, shortly before the Census Bureau took delivery of the Univac, and so might be considered the first operational American computer. It was followed by the 1102 and the 1103, which were well-received. By 1952, ERA had sold more than 20 computers and had more personnel working on machines than RemRand; indeed, by some calculations, at this time ERA accounted for more than four out of every five computers in the United States.

All the above were reasons for Jim Rand to seek it out for a takeover. Norris hated the idea, but reluctantly agreed, in part because ERA was then being criticized for having obtained government contracts without competitive bidding and was in danger of costly legal action, but more so due to Rand's promises of bountiful financing and continued independence. In 1952 RemRand purchased ERA and merged it into the Eckert-Mauchly operation. But not without difficulty. Norris and Eckert and Mauchly clashed repeatedly over matters of theory, design, and authority, to the point where they worked at cross purposes. For a while there was virtually no contact between St. Paul and Philadelphia, with Rand apparently uninterested or unable to do anything about it.

It remains to be noted, however, that in the early 1950s RemRand was the unquestioned leader in the computer field, with the two most important and innovative units. This was a time when the very name Univac was becoming as much a generic expression for computers as Addressograph had been for addressing machines and Xerox later would be in copiers. More than one science and technology writer wondered when the industry would see "IBM's Univacs."

As far as Watson was concerned, the answer might well have been "never." The 600 series calculators were a huge success. In late 1950, while Eckert and Mauchly attempted to rush their Univac to the Census Bureau, IBM was shipping 600s at the rate of 40 a month, with an expanding backlog; a year later the number had risen to 100 per month. This was the sort of machine the firm's clients seemed to need, and Watson was not about to make an important foray into uncharted territory for a product which, if successful, might cut deeply into the sales of 600s.

It was a classic case of corporate myopia which, had the leaders at RemRand been more astute, would have given them a commanding position in what was to become the greatest growth industry of the second half of the twentieth century. While Mauchly and Norris found little to agree upon, both thought as much later on. RemRand had a "five year lead" over IBM in 1951, said the former, while Norris thought the firm "had a chance to take over the computer market." To which Saul Rosen, one of the leading historians of the computer, added that Univac I "was probably the best large-scale computer in use for data processing applications. Internally, it was the most completely checked commercial computer ever built. . . . Remington Rand was launched into the computer field with a product that was years ahead of any of its competitors."

To understand why IBM acted as it did, and why the company was able to first recognize and then compensate for its errors, one must first appreciate the company's origins, development, and outlook in the early 1950s.

Watson Sr.

That Tom Watson, Sr. was one of the most distinguished businessmen of this century is beyond debate, but he wasn't an original thinker, as, for example, Andrew Carnegie had been in steel, Alfred Sloan in automobiles, and Ray Kroc in fast foods. Rather, Watson was an adept practitioner of concepts that were developed by John H. Patterson—the founder of National Cash Register, the father of the modern business machine industry, the leading personality in NCR's home city of Dayton, and Watson's mentor. Watson became a NCR salesman in 1895, rose rapidly, and by 1913 was Patterson's number two man. Along the way, he absorbed the older man's philosophy.

Patterson was an irascible character who in 1884 purchased control of what would become known as "The Cash" for $6,500; by the time of Watson's arrival its owner had made it the leader in its field. NCR's registers did not incorporate the latest technology, and Patterson did not believe in pioneering. Rather, he relied upon a superior sales force, rebates, and aggressive merchandising to win customers.

At The Cash, Watson studied the training of sales personnel, this being Patterson's main concern. Patterson personally inculcated his beliefs into his sales force, listing goals in sets of five, for he had an eccentric fixation on that number, perhaps because he liked to tick items off on the fingers of one hand. There were five fingers, five senses, and, more important insofar as business was concerned, five kinds of money (gold, silver, copper, nickel, and paper) and five of fractional currency (half dollars, quarters, dimes, nickels, and pennies). Cash registers were set up to record a like number of transactions—cash sales, credit sales, purchases on account, bill collections, and money changing.

When feasible, Patterson divided states into five territories. When lecturing to his salesmen, he used flip cards—the kind Watson would later bring to Computing-Tabulating-Recording—and there inevitably would be five of these, each with lists of five points to be ingested. It was from Patterson that Watson get his first C-T-R slogan: "Read—Listen—Discuss—Observe—Think."

Patterson paid his salesmen well. Each had a guaranteed territory and even received commissions on unsolicited placements, quite unusual for the period. Patterson wanted his salesmen to look prosperous; it was not at all unusual for an NCR man to be sent to a nearby big city and told to outfit himself at company expense. He also wanted his salesman to appear uniform and hired the head valet at the Waldorf Astoria to write a booklet on the proper attire for the NCR contingent.

For those salesmen who exceeded their quotas, there was the Hundred Point Club. Members would receive bonuses and be the subject of writeups in the company journal—and the following year be assigned a higher quota. In a period when managers often resented their highly successful salesmen and tried to save money by cutting their commission rates, Patterson might reward salesmen by upping the cut. "If you can sell a million dollars a week," he told one of them, "we'll hire a brass band to take your commission to you." There was a reason for this: Patterson thought that individuals who had had a taste of luxury would work harder in order to maintain such a way of life.

Along with the stress on sales was a willingness to play hardball with competitors who dared invade his turf, often with superior machines. "The best way to kill a dog is to cut off his head," was the way Patterson put it. When a rival firm came out with a new machine, the machine would be bad-mouthed by NCR. To discourage purchases, Patterson would claim that he was readying a superior model to sell at a lower price. (In 1954, when IBM announced it was preparing computers to go against the Univacs, RemRand charged that Watson was up to his old NCR tricks.)

On at least one occasion, Patterson employed a more indirect approach. Using NCR funds, Watson established a sales outlet in New York known as Watson's Cash Register and Second Hand Exchange. Ostensibly independent of NCR, Watson would sell registers at prices geared to "knock out" the competition. That the Exchange did not show a profit was not the point; the object was to destroy rivals.

This led to charges of violation of the antitrust laws, and in 1910, Patterson, Watson, and other NCR executives were placed on trial. All were found guilty three years later, and Patterson and Watson were sentenced to fines of $5,000 each and a year in jail. They appealed, but before a new trial could be scheduled, Dayton was hit by a flood, and NCR provided relief, making the two men heroes. In 1915, the court of appeals found errors in the original verdict and the case was dropped.

Before then, however, Patterson and Watson had drawn apart. Some thought Patterson suspected that Watson was trying to hog the glory for the flood heroics, and it might have been that Patterson believed the younger man had tried to dissociate himself from the others during the trial, since he alone refused to consider plea bargaining. More likely was the fact that Patterson often tired of his fellow executives and fired them. "When a man gets to feel independent," Patterson used to say, "get rid of him."

Whatever the reason, Watson was ejected in 1914. According to his official biographers, he vowed revenge. "I've helped build all but one of those buildings," he said while taking one last look at The Cash. "Now I am going out to build a business bigger than John H. Patterson has."

Within less than a year, Watson was at C-T-R, employing Patterson's techniques in the new locale. In fact, the much discussed and imitated "IBM Man" of the post-World War II period was really a remake of the NCR Man of the turn of the century, of whom Thomas Watson was a prime example.

Computing-Tabulating-Recording

Computing-Tabulating-Recording was not much of a firm when Watson arrived. Little growth could be anticipated from the scales, and while time-clock sales rose during World War I (they were needed in the new factories), they fell soon after. Tabulating Company was another matter. Watson perceived possibilities with this product, though it was a lackluster second to Powers because it gobbled up punch cards on which was stored data by the gross. His was really a simple idea, pioneered by King Gillette, the safety-razor tycoon, who occasionally sold his razors at below cost, contenting himself to make large profits on blade sales. Watson would do the same. Revamping the sales force and modernizing the antique manufacturing facilities, he targeted insurance companies and railroads, slashing prices in order to win orders, and then made substantial profits on card orders. By 1918, C-T-R had 1,400 tabulators and 1,100 sorters leased to 650 firms, and was selling more than 100 million cards per month to feed the voracious creatures.

The newly christened IBM did well in the 1920s by renting machines to corporations. Watson purchased Ticketograph (a firm that printed rate schedules for factories, another repeat business) and Peirce Accounting Machines, which as the name indicates was also in the business machine field, manufacturing and selling a variety of them to banks and other financial institutions.

Watson had ideas in the accounting machine area, too. The Holloriths could be mastered in a matter of hours, but accounting machines could not. If he could place enough of his accounting machines, to be used by the young women who traditionally were their operators, the women would become "loyal" to them, and have to be retrained should the banks attempt to switch to another brand. The idea—which like that for cards was not really new, since Underwood had done the same with typewriters years before—worked, and by the early 1930s advertisements for "IBM operators" started appearing in newspapers around the country.

And there were similar IBM success stories during the interwar decades. One concerned Benjamin Wood, a Columbia University psychology professor who toyed with the idea of creating standardized multiple-choice tests, the questions on which would be answered by making small lead pencil marks in the proper place, after which they would be "read" by a machine in a fashion not unlike that of Watson's punch cards, and so be graded automatically. Wood took the idea to Watson, who instantly realized that not only would this be an interesting product, but one which would require large quantities of special forms, thus creating another dependable revenue stream. Out of this came the 805 test scorer, a machine that became standard in what turned out to be a relatively small field, but which also served to introduce IBM into the colleges and universities. Watson was particularly interested in Columbia, to which he donated millions of dollars of equipment in the 1930s and more

31

thereafter, and which later established the Thomas J. Watson Astronomical Computing Bureau in his honor. Watson even served on the Columbia board of trustees, and after World War II was instrumental in selecting Dwight Eisenhower as the school's president, an office which he rightly thought could prove a proper launching pad for a White House bid.

Of course, the Columbia connection paid dividends. As has been seen, collaboration between the firm and the university resulted in the development of the test scorer—and a stream of other machines came out of that school and others in the next decades. Watson was not the first to invent the "industrial-academic complex," but no one of his generation did more to develop or encourage such ties.

IBM did relatively well during the Great Depression of the 1930s. While corporate placements declined, after 1932 those for government increased sharply, as Franklin Roosevelt's New Deal agencies—especially Social Security—became prime customers for punchers, tabulators, and sorters. By the mid-1930s, IBM was selling more than 4 billion cards a year, at a price of $1.05 per thousand.

And the firm was evolving. Watson shucked off the scale operation and purchased Electromatic, which pioneered in the still-untested electric typewriter field. The machines cost around $250, more than twice as much as the mechanical Underwoods, and did not sell particularly well; by the end of the decade it accounted for only 6,000 placements a year, which was five percent of the typewriter market, but 100 percent of the electric segment. In time Underwood, Royal, Remington, and others would come out with their electric versions, but too late to crack IBM's grip, since in this area, as with accounting machines, operators trained on one electric were reluctant to try another. Moreover, the rival firms had difficulties with their sales forces, accustomed as they were to placing manuals, a matter which presented Watson with no problem.

With all of this, IBM seemed little more than a vigorous firm in a moderately growing industry. In 1938, Watson planned an impressive pavilion for the New York World's Fair scheduled to open the following year. A young reporter, Peter Drucker, asked his editor for permission to write a piece on the company and its plans. "Forget it," replied the editor. "We are not interested in a story on an unsuccessful company which as far as anyone can tell is never going to amount to much." Relating the story close to a half century later, Drucker noted that at that time Watson Sr. was 65 years old, and presumably close to the end of his career.

The editor was wrong on more than one count. The IBM of that period was innovating and growing, and it did not have difficulties financing research and development due to its expanding rental base, which brought in a steady and dependable cash flow to augment that from card sales. It got to the point where IBM might actually lose money on the first and second year rentals but recoup it in the third, while everything from then on out was pure profit. And all the while, the firm paid little in the way of taxes, since it was able to depreciate the machines that were on lease. For example, in 1939 IBM's gross earnings came to $11.2 million, on which it paid only $2.1 million in taxes. And during World War II, when taxes were increased sharply, the firm was able to expand rapidly due to its accounting procedures. In 1943, the firm's revenues rose to $139.4 million; pre-tax earnings were $37 million, and the post-tax figure was whittled down to $9.2 million. Yet IBM's net assets increased $33.6 million over the previous year's figure.

Not that IBM engaged in profiteering during the war. When the United States became a combatant, Watson organized the Munitions Manufacturing Corporation, which turned out ordnance of various kinds, on which a uniform low profit of 1.5 percent was obtained, and that placed in a fund for the survivors of IBMers killed in action. Watson froze his own salary and that of other leading executives and stood prepared to accept any assignment given by the War Department.

The government needed business machines of all kinds since the war created a huge bureaucracy and much paperwork, which meant that IBM's primary task was to churn out punchers, sorters, tabulators, and accounting machines. All the while, research continued on the aforementioned calculators, and toward the end of the war Watson directed the beginning of work on the Selective Sequence Electronic Calculator (SSEC), intended to be the largest, not only for that time, but for the foreseeable future as well. But this did not mean he had changed his mind regarding their scientific possibilities. Watson thought that one SSEC "could solve all the scientific problems in the world involving scientific calculations." Moreover, he believed none could be sold to commercial clients.

IBM was involved with computers as well, but, as indicated, in no serious way. Part of the reason was the firm's dedication to calculators, part the perceived limitations of the market, but also there was the lack of a competitive challenge within the rest of the industry. Recall that this was prior to RemRand's interest in Eckert-Mauchly, at a time when of the industrial companies only AT&T was devoting much time and funds to computers, and those for internal use. But there was one other factor. Watson turned 70 in 1944, and, though in sound mental and physical shape, he no longer sought challenges. Around this time, he remarked, "It isn't a hard thing to build up a business if you are willing to do a reasonable amount of work. The hard thing is to protect a business after you build it up." Hardly the words of a bold pioneer.

Fortunately for the firm, one was waiting in the wings.

Watson Jr.

"The company is in the family unconscious," Thomas Watson, Jr., once remarked, indicating that from the first he was wedded to IBM. Born in 1914, as a child he was taken on factory tours, attended company functions, and was always aware he was being groomed for a place at the firm. But in the 1930s, when he was shuttling between Brown University and Manhattan's more famous watering spots, it was by no means certain his would be the top slot. Tall and trim, motion-picture-star handsome, personable, with more than a touch of the playboy about him, Tom enjoyed socializing to the small hours, by which time he often was tipsy. This was a period when his father had rigid strictures against imbibing, a period when IBM's small French operation wasn't permitted to serve wine. In those days, IBMers were made to understand that alcohol and business didn't mix. Only soft drinks and juices were served at IBM banquets, and a period in the dog house and stern warnings from superiors could be expected for IBMers seen in a saloon. All of which was well known, and the subject of jokes bordering on ridicule.

There is every indication that Watson Sr. loved all four of his children and had a special affection for Tom, his eldest. Nonetheless, he was not about to turn the firm he created over to such an individual. No, Tom would join IBM, but as a salesman in the Wall Street area, where the machines were placed rather than sold. He spent some time on the job, but also skied in the winter, raced yachts in the summer, and flew private planes all year around. To those who knew him best, it was obvious Tom cared more about these pursuits than he did business.

Watson Sr. was sufficiently astute in such matters to realize the pressures that must have been building on the son of a founder, and gave Tom Jr. all the room he needed. Perhaps in time everything would work out well.

In the autumn of 1940, when Tom was a 26-year-old bachelor and a member of the New York National Guard (which he joined to get in more flying time), he was activated. Tom joined the Army Air Corps as a private, but soon he was an officer flying assignments as a transport pilot. He ferried planes to Britain once the United States entered the war and afterwards flew generals and political leaders to wherever they had to go; on one occasion he took Winston Churchill to Teheran, and on another he flew to besieged Moscow.

The war ended in 1945, and Watson returned to New York, but not to his old ways. The war had been a sobering experience. A quickly graying, mature individual by then, Watson married, settled down to raise a large family, and was rarely seen in nightclubs and then usually on business. And he finally gave a clear indication of making a serious career at IBM. "When I think of the difference in my general outlook now as against the 1937-1940 period," he told his father, "I am convinced that I am now at least 75 percent better equipped mentally to follow in your footsteps as I intend to do."

In January 1946, Tom was at a headquarters desk, where he was to undergo a crash course in how to be CEO of IBM, by then a firm with close to $120 million in revenues, profits of $18.8 million, and a long-term debt of a bare $30 million. He came to an enterprise which had become famous for its service and sales operations—indeed, in this period Watson Sr. remarked that if he had it all to do over again, he would have preferred to be sales manager than CEO of IBM, and earlier had admitted that "collecting salesmen is my hobby."

That Watson Jr. shared his father's general views but was more modern soon became obvious, even in small, symbolic things. For example, one day he arrived at the office wearing a striped shirt, a switch that reverberated throughout the firm, as employees followed his example, switching off occasionally from the IBM dark suit, white shirt uniform. Gradually, wines were permitted at IBM functions, and while the strictures against alcohol never fully disappeared, at least they were softened. But Watson Jr. could be every bit as harsh and demanding as his father. For example, in a speech at the firm he told a story drawn from the Danish philosopher, Sören Kierkegaard, about a kindly soul who fed a flock of wild ducks, which discouraged them from flying south for the winter. In time, they flew less and less. When the other ducks returned these would circle up to greet them but then head back to their feeding grounds on the pond. After three or four years, they grew so lazy and fat that they found difficulty in flying at all.

Kierkegaard drew his point—you can make wild ducks tame, but you can never make tame ducks wild again. One might also add that the duck who is tamed will never go anywhere any more. We are convinced that any business needs its wild ducks. And at IBM we try not to tame them.

The next day the story at headquarters was that Watson Jr. was having his office redecorated—with mounted wild ducks in various spots.

If their temperaments were similar their outlooks were not, which was appreciated by both men. Watson Sr. had been a relatively uneducated and unsophisticated young man, who had learned everything he knew by observing and imitating the salesmen and others with whom and under whom he had worked. He then applied what surely was a native genius to the problems and possibilities that came his way. The son, as has been seen, had seen much of life and the world, and while he had no experience with the kind of early pioneering his father had known, was more open to new ideas. Not the least of these was due to his direct exposure to electronics while in the Air Force and a knowledge of computers gleaned from readings and conversations with scientists. He was intrigued by the ideas presented by Norbert Weiner in his 1948 book *Cybernetics: Or Control and Communication in the Animal and Machine* and devoured all he could find on the new science of automation. Thus, Tom Watson was as equipped as his father had been in his day to capitalize on opportunities.

Such was the situation when he became president of IBM in 1952.

The Watson Blitzkrieg

There are two contradictory legends regarding the origins of IBM's commitment to computers as something more than an experimental research tool. The first has it that at the outbreak of the Korean War in 1950, Watson Sr. telegrammed President Harry S. Truman asking what his firm could do to assist the war effort, and the second is that not until Tom Jr. arrived did the firm make the move. Neither is correct; IBM entered the field prior to the outbreak of war, and it was done by the elder Watson. Though the SSEC never went into production, and was instead displayed at the firm's Manhattan headquarters as a demonstration of technical wizardry, in 1949 Watson Sr. authorized the development of a scientific computer, and work was accelerated once the war began. Tom inherited and expanded the project for what initially was called the Defense Calculator, but was later renamed the 701, and which was described to potential customers as a "Electronic Data

Processing Machine," a term devised by an IBM engineer, James Birkenstock. With the 701 IBM initiated its assault on RemRand, which resulted in a rapid business success comparable in its field to the blitzkrieg that destroyed the effectiveness of France's Maginot Line in 1940. For in 1950, it appeared RemRand was impregnable in computers.

While superior to the 600 series calculators, the 701 was not as flexible or powerful as the Univac I that preceded it. It too was powered by arrays of vacuum tubes, had miles of spaghetti-like wire, and utilized a tape drive.

Tom Watson announced that IBM soon would make available the 701 and was prepared to take orders. Univac was outraged, charging it was a "phantom" that would not be marketed until and unless IBM had sufficient orders to make it profitable. This was not so; the machine had been demonstrated and Watson committed the firm to its delivery. IBM received some orders, prompting Watson to order production of nineteen machines, making the 701 the first computer to be produced on an assembly line rather than on a custom basis, thus realizing important economies. The initial machine was delivered in early 1953, by which time additional orders had arrived. A few months later, IBM was shipping 701s at the rate of one per day, and designing programs to enable them to perform business tasks, such as preparing payrolls, as well as the scientific purposes for which they had been originally intended. Following the firm's traditional policy, the 701 was leased, initially at $15,000 per month.

A few words are in order regarding the sales effort. As indicated, IBM was famous (some would say notorious) for the power of its sales force. Here was an army of zealous young men who were doing quite well with calculators, raking in commissions and rising rapidly. Now they were being asked to lease computers, not only a relatively unknown product, but one which, if placed, could mean fewer calculator leases. And what if the machine did not perform as promised? After all, it was an untested technology. IBM's sales managers took pains to win over the sales force prior to the initial foray with the 700 series. In the first place, bonuses and recognition would be provided for those who did well with computers. Also, the machines were to be leased under generous terms. The customers were to be made to understand that placements would be relatively risk-free; those early contracts provided generous terms, with pledges of removal and replacement unless entirely satisfied.

Finally, the salesmen were informed that top management, from Tom Watson on down, were committed to computers. A salesman who did well with calculators would be appreciated but clearly considered part of the past.

The future at IBM belonged to the computer, which had the only sales force among the old business machine companies that truly believed this.

Watson now took his second important step: that spring he announced the creation of the 650, a smaller, less expensive system, stating it would be "adaptable to both commercial and scientific applications." On the basis of a customer survey, the firm projected placements on the order of 200 machines at $3,500 per month—quite a leap in so short a time—though there were some in the company who feared the 650 might cannibalize sales from the 701, and so destroy a most promising product. But Watson went ahead anyway, making the first 650 delivery in early 1954.

The 650 far exceeded even the most sanguine expectations. Customers used them for payrolls, industrial design, inventory control, college admissions, and a wide variety of tasks, obliging IBM to add software staff at a geometric rate. Well over three hundred 650s had been placed by the summer of 1956, and IBM had orders for an additional 920. Before its run was over, more than 1,800 had been produced, making the 650 comparable to the Ford Model T in cars and aviation's Douglas DC-3, which is to say it was a breakout product, one which legitimatized the industry.

For a while, it seemed RemRand and IBM each would concentrate on a different segment of the market, the former dominating large machines, the latter the smaller ones, and that they would have a relationship not unlike that of IBM and Digital Equipment two decades later. Then, in late 1954, IBM announced the 702, a large general purpose machine (some newspapers referred to it as a "giant brain") that was first delivered to Monsanto Chemical the following year. By then, IBM had two other machines on the way—the 704 to replace the 701, and the 705, which appeared to some an improved version of the 702—so fast were the technology and market developing.

That Tom Watson had a carefully conceived strategy and was implementing it with considerable skill became evident only in retrospect. A detailed discussion of the IBM culture and approach will be made later, but at this point it should be noted that IBM rarely has led the way in product introduction. Which isn't to say that the firm lags technologically, but rather that it will hold back and let others perform the pioneering work, after which it will come in and grab the marbles. The reason has nothing to do with innate conservatism, lack of imagination, an unwillingness to take sales from other areas, or any of a dozen other factors that might be mentioned. Rather, IBM won't enter a new area until convinced large-scale economies are possible. Thus, it will hold back, conduct the research and obtain patents, let others do the pioneering in manufacturing and selling, and then step in, and as a result of image and service, take a giant share of the now rapidly expanding market. What happened with the first generation of computers in the 1950s would be repeated in large computers (pioneered by Control Data) and minis (where Digital Equipment took the lead) and most recently in micros, when the IBM PC entered the arena long after the trail had been blazed by Radio Shack, Apple, and dozens of others. By then the pattern had become quite familiar. IBM's entry into the micro field was said to have "legitimized" it in the eyes of observers, but in fact it did nothing of the sort. Rather, the advent of the PC—like that of the 700s almost three decades earlier—meant that the customers were there and waiting, economies of scale were possible, and IBM was ready to unleash its technology and marketing skills.

With all of this IBM is ever prepared to take calculated risks and engage in what economist Joseph Schumpeter called "creative destruction," the business equivalent of Chairman Mao's Cultural Revolution. On several occasions, IBM has scrapped old, successful, and profitable enterprises to take off into relatively uncharted territory. The corporation does take risks with new technologies and marketing programs. Failures often have been of the sort that might have crippled smaller and less resilient firms; its successes have constantly renewed the enterprise.

Students of the industry tend to stress the factors behind IBM's successes, an admittedly important subject that will be analyzed in some detail. In so doing, however, they generally overlook two equally important factors: one of which is the reason IBM's rivals failed to make more headway than they did, and the other is how the relative few who did manage to carve out niches for themselves succeeded in the face of Big Blue's awesome power. So before examining the reasons for IBM's victories, we should know what sort of competition it faced in those early years.

II

THE ALSO-RANS

The Rem-Rand Flaw

In the mid-1930s, a radio tale called "The Chicken Heart" terrorized a generation of young boys and girls. It concerned a scientist who took the heart of a chicken and placed it in some secret solution, upon which the heart started to grow in an uncontrollable fashion. Concerned, the scientist called upon the police and fire departments for help in killing it, but they used conventional methods when he recommended harsher action. At various stages other methods were used, to no avail; the heart simply expanded and became stronger all the while. At almost any stage but the last the heart might have been vanquished, but no one seemed to grasp the method. Toward the end it engulfed the world, consuming all in its path, impregnable and all powerful.

Several young people of that period grew up to enter the computer industry in the 1950s. Not a few of them might have thought of the chicken heart when watching the upward march of IBM to computer dominance. For what transpired in this period wasn't carved in stone. It need not have been IBM; the leading role in computers might have been seized and held by another firm, at varying stages such powerful entities as RemRand, Honeywell, RCA, and even American Telephone & Telegraph and General Electric.

Which is to suggest that while IBM may have merited its successes, some of them were made possible by flaws in its competitors. In the early days, this group was known as "the Seven Dwarfs" (with IBM the Snow White), and these were: Sperry Rand, Control Data, Honeywell, Burroughs, General

Electric, RCA, and National Cash Register. By the late 1970s the main competition was referred to by an acronym, "the BUNCH," and was composed of Burroughs, Univac, NCR, Control Data, and Honeywell.

These are the firms (with the exception of Control Data) that attempted to meet IBM head-on, across the board, akin to the way Ford and Chrysler at one time attempted to match General Motors model for model. Some had limited success, others failed, none realized their early ambitions. As will be seen, RCA and GE dropped out of the race. None of the dozens of others in various parts of the rapidly evolving industry really threatened IBM's preeminent position, but they could have, especially when it came to the introduction of the second generation machines, based on transistors, in the late 1950s, and the third generation of the mid-1960s, which involved the use of integrated circuits.

The first of IBM's competitors, of course, was RemRand, which, as has been seen, was so far ahead of IBM in the early 1950s that any thought of catching up seemed far-fetched. Then, in 1955, Jim Rand made a move that at the time seemed brilliant, but in retrospect was a major blunder: he merged RemRand with Sperry Corporation to form Sperry Rand, with Sperry's Harry Vickers named president and CEO; General Douglas MacArthur, who recently had become chairman at RemRand, took the same post at the newly formed company.

At the time, it seemed a fine marriage. Sperry had been a major supplier of gear to the armed forces during World War II, was involved in electronics research, and its Ford Instruments division had some experience with military computers. The Vickers division, a leader in hydraulics, had done some work in computer-directed machine tools. The mesh with RemRand seemed obvious: it would be a wedding of Sperry technology with RemRand products. In 1955, this appeared to augur well for the Univac division. And, indeed, such could have been the case, given managerial vision, a carefully worked out strategy, and the wise allocation of resources. None of which existed.

To begin with, Sperry Rand had an overflowing plate. In addition to the previously mentioned items, the firm produced electric razors, automatic packaging equipment, farm machinery, missiles, and photographic equipment, all of which were clamoring for attention and capital and were able to promise faster returns on investment than could computers. Then, too, in Harry Vickers the firm had a capable manager but one with little imagination. Moreover, Vickers was an individual who never was able to make up his mind about the firm's role in computers. As for General MacArthur, there is little evidence that he was chairman for any reason other than window dressing—entertaining military and political leaders capable of swinging contracts Sperry's way and impressing the stockholders.

While Watson forged ahead, Vickers diddled, unwilling to risk capital, unable to create an effective sales force, and seemingly incapable of mobilizing forces in the laboratory or marketplace. At the time and afterwards, credence was given to talk hatched on Wall Street that Univac's machines were every bit as good as IBM's, and that all the company needed was better salesmen, but those within the industry knew otherwise. Watson plowed funds earned from calculator rentals into computers, while Vickers held back. Occasionally, the Univac technicians would come up with machines that were capable of contesting IBM's, but then Vickers would refuse additional allocations for sales and manufacture.

Later on, when the two approaches were dissected in business schools, it was realized that by producing machines and then trying to market them Univac was really selling obsolete technology, while by holding back until the last minute and then manufacturing and placing, IBM could provide clients with what later would be known as "state of the art" devices. In the summer of 1955, there were more Univacs in service or on order than 700s. A year later, IBM had the edge in installations by a margin of 76-46, and had booked 193 additional orders against Univac's 65.

To cite a specific example, the Univac II was all but ready for presentation in 1956, at which time the firm might have taken orders, but the machine wasn't unveiled until the following year, by which time it looked dowdy when set beside the 704 and 705. Eckert, Mauchly, and Kenneth Olsen of Digital Equipment wanted to produce a small machine, which they felt would meet with a tremendous reception. Olsen in particular was enchanted with the idea of placing relatively inexpensive computers in virtually every large and medium-sized plant in the nation.

But RemRand held back, and the File Computer, which was meant to go against the 650 and which could have been marketed in 1954, didn't appear until 1956. Thus, the File, which would have been acceptable two years earlier, was a flop in 1956. A more striking example of the differing approaches came later in the decade when Univac was working on a solid state computer—one which was to use transistors rather than vacuum tubes—that was the pioneer in the second generation of the technology. The Solid State 80 was marketed in Europe in late 1957 but was withheld from the

American market in order to protect Univac's installed machines, with which it was not compatible. Those domestic clients who knew of the Solid State 80 all but pleaded for permission to make purchases, but were rebuffed. Then, in 1959, IBM announced it would take orders for its own second generation machine, the 1401, and so was able to cut deeply into Univac's customer base, as that firm's decline continued.

There was an interesting sidelight to this, which would become even more so later on. Needless to say, in those early days there was no thought about compatibility of hardware or software; indeed, all software was custom-designed, and while the mainframes of each line were quite similar, it was rare to find two of them exactly alike. More to the point, in that period, when many machines still utilized cards for input, the IBM version had rectangular holes, while the Univac's were round. Each hoped to push the other into oblivion, and, of course, IBM won.

Finally, Univac was an organizational shambles. Its three laboratories in St. Paul, Norwalk, and Philadelphia held virtually no communication with each other, and, in fact, individuals at each conspired against the rest in order to win recognition. Duplication of effort and a feeling that headquarters was indifferent to their efforts resulted in low morale, which in turn led to defections. In utter frustration and worn down by battles with his counterparts in Philadelphia, Bill Norris resigned in 1957, along with several of his ERA colleagues. This is only one of the many tales of defections of technicians from Univac, refugees who in the next decade would help staff many other computer firms. Univac began wooing IBMers with fat salaries and perks, hoping they would bring along some of the IBM magic, and this, too, was a concession of failure.

The magic could not be transplanted so easily. The classic case was that of Dause Bibby, an IBM vice president who arrived as Univac CEO in 1959 with a mandate to shape it up. Bibby was not provided with sufficient funds for both sales and engineering, however, so he put most of his chips in the area he knew best, which was sales. And this meant drawing funds from research. The result was a revived sales force that had little to offer clients. Bibby left, others came, but the result was always the same. IBM prospered, and Univac was number two in the industry, unable to turn a profit, alternately looked upon as Sperry Rand's most promising unit and its financial black hole, into which was sucked profits from other parts of the company. By the early 1960s, still the dawn of the computer age, Univac was a perennial also-ran on the way to becoming one of the sadder "might have beens" of American business history.

Burroughs: The Logical Competitor

Were computers business or scientific machines? In this period they were both, but the stress increasingly was on the former application. Thus, scientifically oriented firms attempted to learn the needs of the office, while traditional business machine companies "went electronic."

Of the latter, Burroughs and National Cash Register were by far the most important, with Burroughs better equipped by force of tradition, inclination, and resources to make the run for the money.

Detroit-based Burroughs had gotten its start with adding machines sold to the several auto companies in that city, graduated to billing and other devices, and by the late 1920s was operating on a global scale. By 1928, it had become the third largest factor in the industry with revenues of $32 million (behind RemRand and National Cash, but ahead of IBM), and its earnings of $8.3 million was tops in the industry.

In the late 1940s, Burroughs CEO John Coleman opted to go into the new field of electronic machines, and so was one of the first to make that important commitment. He set out to develop experimental computers. Out of this came the Unitized Digital Electronic Computer (UDEC) and, in 1954, a commercial machine, the E-101, really a modified accounting machine that could be perched on a desk and might be considered the grandparent of the mini. Alas, the market was not prepared for such devices, and the E-101 was a flop. Undeterred, the company continued its research, but more importantly, in 1956 purchased Electrodata, a promising young outfit (which two years before had been divested by Consolidated Engineering Corporation), for $20 million in stock, a large amount for such an operation in that period.

Electrodata had already produced its first computer, the Datatron, a scientific machine that had attracted a good deal of attention and was besting the IBM 650 in some markets. At the time of the Burroughs takeover, 24 Datatrons had been sold with another 19 on order, and Electrodata's highly regarded technical staff was fairly itching to go against IBM in the market for large mainframes. Augmented by the Burroughs scientists and financed by Burroughs funds, they turned out the B5000 in 1959, novel in that it was the first to use a true operating system, which is to say a master program to allocate space in the memory. In addition, it permitted multiprocessing and multiprogramming, and ran on ALGOL, which technicians considered one of the efficient languages of the period. But the B5000 had two major problems.

45

The first was that with all of this it was a slow machine. But even more of a problem was the fact that it was so advanced that few customers wanted it. Indeed, even the salesmen appeared to dislike the equipment. Traditionally Burroughs had done well at the banks, where its accounting machines had become fixtures, but its salesmen either had little faith in computers or were unwilling to urge clients to accept the new technology when the old seemed to work so well. Thus, Burroughs's initial foray into computers fared badly.

As the cliché goes, the B5000 was ahead of its time. But time passes and customers become more sophisticated, so by the mid-1960s the machine and some of its stablemates met with good receptions.

Why, then, didn't Burroughs have greater success than it did? The answer rests in two words: support and sales. In 1963, Burroughs posted sales of $387 million, profits of $8.5 million, on current assets of $275 million, this in a year when IBM's sales were $2.9 billion, earnings $364 million, and current assets $1.4 billion. IBM could afford to plunge where Burroughs could not. Moreover, IBM had a deeper commitment to computers, which accounted for a greater share of its revenues, than Burroughs. IBM's electronic-data-processing revenues that year came to $1.2 billion, and Burroughs, $42 million. With limited resources, Burroughs opted to concentrate its efforts on research, development, and production, rather than service and sales. Executive Vice President Ray Macdonald boosted R & D, but because of this had to slash the sales force from 400 to 125. There was little else he could do—or much more Burroughs could have anticipated in the way of success. As a future CEO at Univac would later remark, "It doesn't do much good to build a better mousetrap if the other guy selling mousetraps had five times as many salesmen."

National Cash Register and the Failure of Nerve

If Burroughs moved quickly but with insufficient power, National Cash Register was sluggish, aimless, and in the end, almost a nonstarter.

John Patterson had created a corporation which was the undisputed leader in its branch of the business machine industry. After all, he appeared at a time when cash registers were unknown, and by the time he died they were found in virtually every retail establishment. And those manufactured by The Cash had a larger share of the market than IBM ever would in mainframe computers.

In 1922, NCR had the assets, reputation, and sales force to enable it to remain a top firm in the industry. It even expanded into new lines by diversifying into accounting machines, and in John Barringer it had a general manager of vision and experience who, given half a chance, might have made NCR the top company in other fields as well. But there was a problem in the form of Frederick Patterson, the tortured son of the eccentric father. Every time Barringer tried to move ahead, Frederick would hold back, as though hoping for a visitation from the ghost of John Patterson, who would criticize any move he made. The result was a corporate paralysis toward the end of the decade, and by the early 1930s the firm was close to bankruptcy.

At this point Edward Deeds, one of the many men who had been dismissed by John Patterson, returned to take command. Deeds reinvigorated the firm, but the scars of the Frederick Patterson period remained during the war and immediate postwar years. NCR was the nation's third largest business machine firm in 1945 (behind IBM and RemRand) with revenues of $68.4 million, but earnings of $2.2 million, a shade less than Burroughs had on sales of $37.4 million. It was, to state it bluntly, a bloated whale of a firm that appeared to have little future, especially not in the capital-intensive computer field.

The outlook changed drastically and for the better in 1953, when Deeds purchased Computer Research Corporation (CRC) from Northrop Aviation, a move which did for NCR what the purchases of Eckert-Mauchly and ERA had done for RemRand and the purchase of Electrodata for Burroughs: namely, it provided an infusion of fresh people and ideas into a stodgy entity and pushed it into the computer age.

The similarities between CRC, ERA, and Electrodata are striking. All were peopled by young men who were entranced with electronics and knew little of business, who expected to sell their products to laboratories and other scientists, and who had little thought about their products' business applications. CRC, which cost NCR $1 million, had sold three machines the previous year, and had just completed work on the 102D, which hardly made a splash. But the new NCR was willing to take chances, which was all to the good. Chairman Stanley Allyn later recalled that "One of our first important decisions was whether to make our first computer a vacuum tube machine or to jump directly into the onrushing solid state technology of the mid-fifties. . . . We took the risk, and skipped completely the first generation vacuum tube era."

In 1957 NCR announced the 304, a solid state machine that, as it turned out, was manufactured in part by GE, because, in its own words, NCR "thought that General Electric was more experienced in the art at that time than NCR was, and that a joint relationship would be helpful and profitable to NCR." The 304, of which 33 were installed, was used for business purposes, and may be considered one of the first of the second generation machines to be introduced.

NCR's inability to turn out imaginative machines continued. In 1960, it coproduced with Control Data the 310, a vacuum-powered small unit, which was followed by the slightly larger 315, and then the 360, a general purpose mainframe geared for small business applications. The 315 and the 360 were quite successful, especially among established clients who recognized the cost-benefit ratios these had over calculators and IBM and Univac first generation machines. NCR obtained orders for 135 of them by 1962 and in all delivered 700 over the life of the machines.

Trouble was, both machines should have done better, given their obvious advantages. NCR's failure to press its advantage in the early 1960s gave IBM breathing space—and, as mentioned, Watson could await the development of the market prior to moving in with his second generation gear. Given a more aggressive sales effort, which NCR could have afforded, the firm might have gained a beachhead at banks and insurance companies with small- to medium-sized machines that IBM would have been hard put to overcome.

In part, the problem was due to a muddled structure and a lack of coordination. NCR had separate divisions for computers and accounting machines, and the latter force attempted to woo clients from computers, thus preserving their commissions. It was a repeat of the Burroughs story, for, like that firm, NCR had done well at the nation's banks with accounting machines, and the firm's sales force took badly to computers. Notwithstanding, NCR had revenues of $30.7 million from electronic data processing in 1973, out of a total of $240 million. It was less than Burroughs and Univac, but sufficient to encourage Allyn to remain in the race.

Other smaller companies in the business machine area—Friden, Underwood, Monroe, and Royal McBee, for example—lacked the technological and financial muscle to make the move to computers, or did so in a half-hearted fashion and remained in their niches. For example, Underwood purchased Electronic Computer Corp. in 1952 and that December introduced the ELCOM 100, a perfectly acceptable machine that, due to Underwood's limited assets (revenues that year came to $66 million, earnings to $3.7 million), could not be effectively promoted or serviced. Underwood lingered for a while and left the field in 1959. Smaller players had even less success. El-Tronics purchased the computer business of Alwac Corporation in 1958, made a stab at the market, and two years later filed for bankruptcy. Others came and went in short order. Royal McBee was one of these, having made the leap with a joint project with General Precision in 1956 and selling its share six years later, taking a loss of $6 million. Perhaps for those companies their departure was all to the good. NCR and Burroughs faced a sea of red ink for the first decade and beyond and were not able to justify their commitments to the area until quite recently.

Philco: The Forgotten Competitor

Manufacturers of electrical and electronic gear comprise the second large category of firms hoping to carve out a niche in the computer field, thus going east while IBM, RemRand, NCR, and Burroughs were headed west, which is to say they had to learn to serve a client base, while the business machine manufacturers were obliged to absorb new technologies. Whether in the early years any of the established firms in either group considered joint ventures or mergers with one another is unknown—perhaps they were put off by the one that did take place, RemRand's union with Sperry. In the end, however, two of the big players would leave the field in just that way, and another would drop out early in the contest.

That dropout would be Philco, an all-but-forgotten name today but a one-time leader in radio set manufacture. Philco developed considerable expertise in military electronics during World War II and in the early 1950s was a robust growth company with a third of a billion dollars in revenues. By mid-decade Philco was developing airborne computers for the Air Force, was involved in advanced work in computers, and was preparing to explore the possibilities of a solid state machine for the National Security Agency and scientific customers. This appeared as the TRANSAC S-2000, which in 1956 was portrayed as one of the first of the second generation of computers and, as the 210, was sold to a variety of industrial clients, some of whom—GE being one—seemed to prefer it to their already installed IBMs.

Philco's future seemed quite promising; while relatively small as such companies go, it had the proper blend of management, finances, and technology, and while lacking a sales force, it might have done very well in the scientific field. Philco was one of the four finalists when in 1962 the National Aeronautics and Space Administration asked for bids for a giant computer to be used in the Gemini program. But even then it was being sidetracked from computers into other promising and related areas by a parent unconcerned with such matters.

The parent was Ford Motor Company, which purchased Philco in December 1961, in the hope of using it to gain entry into the space and defense fields and eventually, perhaps, to use some of its technologies in autos as well. Where Philco might have gone on its own or with some partner wanting to concentrate on computers will of course never be known. But in 1963, operating on momentum gathered while independent, Philco's EDP revenues came to almost $74 million, less than Sperry Rand, but more than Burroughs and NCR. Two years later Philco was behind these two, and soon would leave the field completely.

General Electric: The Giant at Bay

General Electric was another matter entirely. For one thing, it was bigger—much bigger, in fact—than IBM; in 1952, for example, GE reported revenues of $2.6 billion against IBM's $333 million. Moreover, GE's technological prowess was well known and respected, and while it was involved in a wide variety of nonelectronic and noncomputing areas, it possessed the financial depth to make the plunge. Management was superlative. Image was no problem: its two initials were as respected and familiar as the three of IBM. Of course, GE lacked knowledge of the business machine area and the requisite sales force, but few thought this an insurmountable problem. In the late 1950s, IBM feared GE more than any other concern and believed it the one company that, if it made a concerned effort, could mount a serious challenge.

Long time CEO Philip Reed was enthusiastic about computers; as has been seen, GE was one of the early users of the machines and by 1958 it was IBM's most important industrial customer. In 1958, *Business Week* described GE as "the most computerized company in the world," with more than 80 computers installed, most from IBM, Univac, and NCR. But some were its own.

GE entered the field slowly, starting with military computers in the early 1950s and going on to produce the ERMA (Electronic Method of Accounting) in 1956. Designed and manufactured for the Bank of America at a cost of $60 million, ERMA was the largest commercial machine of its day, and GE sold 30 of them. As has been noted, the following year (1957), GE worked with NCR on that company's 304, but what might have evolved into a profitable relationship for both didn't go beyond that, primarily because GE preferred to go it alone. All the while, the firm was developing its own internal expertise with computers.

For all of this, Reed was reluctant to take the next step: develop a sales force and make the capital commitment for large-scale manufacturing. He was reluctant for three reasons. In the first place, he had come to the conclusion that the effective world-wide market for large and medium-sized computers was limited to government agencies and perhaps to 200-300 corporations. To be sure, a few thousand machines could be sold to others, but that was it. Already the field was crowded, with only IBM making profits, and even these were questionable given that firm's refusal to sell, only lease. Then too, Reed was coming to the belief that many firms that had installed computers did so more to appear "modern" than out of any real need for the machines. In the mid-1950s, management experts had started debating whether and when computers were truly cost effective, with a majority coming down on the negative side. Third, Reed believed the country might soon undergo a new depression, and in preparation for this, he cleared GE of much of its debt at a time when his budding computer operation was literally pleading for funding. When Reed stepped down in 1958, GE had a clean balance sheet—but its promising computer venture was going stale.

Reed's place was taken by Ralph Cordiner, who immediately announced "Operation Upturn," part of which involved computers, a field in which he was most interested. Along with executives at IBM and Univac, he had concluded that through use of the machines "the office of the future" would be drastically overhauled, and unlike Reed he believed computers would become profitable for GE. At the same time, however, Cordiner saw great promise in other areas of the corporation—television, jet engines, atomic generators, aerospace, etc.—and recognized that even a firm as powerful as GE would have to ration its funds. Finally, like Reed he believed a depression was coming, and Cordiner not only refused to increase the firm's debt, he actually reduced it during his tenure as CEO.

Notwithstanding, GE did develop some interesting machines in the late 1950s and early 1960s, perhaps the most important of which being the DATANET-30. Recognizing that one of the reasons computers weren't paying their way for their owners and leasers was that they weren't being used effectively, GE developed "networking," a pioneering effort in distributive data processing by which dozens of users could be hooked up to a single machine and wait on line to use it. Thus, GE hoped to sell its mainframes to what amounted to consortia of companies, none of which really needed or could afford one on its own, but which together might utilize them profitably. Networking alone might have provided GE with an important niche in the industry, for it was far ahead of IBM and the others in this field. In addition, the firm turned out several important series, the first of which was the GE 100s, which, as will be seen, were intended to be manufactured and marketed in Europe through Machines Bull and Olivetti, the thought being that IBM would be hard put to defeat such an international combination.

But Cordiner and his successor, Frederick Borch, couldn't stand the costs. In 1966, for example, a year during which the firm earned $355 million, losses on computers came to more than $100 million, and the following year it lost $60 million. "How long can General Electric stand the strain and keep up the pace?" asked *Forbes,* and then provided the answer: "As long as it chooses to do so."

Which was not much longer. The turning point came in 1969, when Borch established an internal task force to study the firm and come up with recommendations, this at a time when earnings were down due to a strike and the company's stock had declined sharply. In a negative mood, the authors of the report—none of whom came from the computer end of the firm—wrote of a lacklaster product line, lagging positions in mainframe development, and an installed base which was described as "already obsolete and vulnerable." They went on to say that funds utilized in computers might be more effectively deployed into nuclear energy and jet engines. The authors of the report estimated that given slightly less than $700 million over a five-year period, GE would be able to wrench the number two spot in the industry from Univac. But that unless this money was spent, the firm would falter, computers would never become profitable, and GE might as well leave the field. Which is what happened.

And an unfortunate development. As will be seen, by then GE was internationally involved with computers and had important and promising representation in Europe. It still was the company best situated to offer a challenge to IBM. But Borch wouldn't buy that price tag. Years later, both he and Cordiner would regret their decisions not to pour funds into computers, recognizing that the report was overly gloomy and that it generally ignored GE's assets while stressing liabilities. Cordiner put it this way: "General Electric's mistake was that it failed to realize the opportunity and therefore made an inadequate allocation of resources, both human and physical, to the business."

The realization came too late. In 1970, GE sold its computer operation to Honeywell for $234 million in notes and stock, making that company the second strongest entity in the industry, with about 10 percent of the market. John Weil, a GE executive involved with the computer projects who went to Honeywell, later said that the former firm's problems derived from being "relatively naive when it came to the discipline of manufacturing large electronic systems or designing them or bringing them to market." Or all three.

Honeywell: The Guarded Success

Honeywell's involvement with computers began in that by now familiar way: the purchase of a young, innovative, undercapitalized entity. Minneapolis Honeywell Regulator (as it was then known) was a leading manufacturer of automatic controls, and also turned out a variety of electronic gear, mostly for the military. Honeywell's leaders were interested in computers, perhaps because a complex industrial thermostat is in fact a form of computer in that the operator programs it to perform certain functions, which it then does automatically. In 1955, Honeywell entered into a joint venture with Raytheon to form Datamatic Corporation, which was to design, manufacture, and sell computer systems.

Thanks to the marriage of Honeywell's superb sales force with Raytheon's technology, which was equally impressive, Datamatic might have developed into that previously described "dream company." In the early stages of World War II, Raytheon, then a small Boston-based manufacturer of vacuum tubes and related products, obtained military contracts which enabled it to develop experience in electronics. Out of this, in 1947, came a Bureau of Standards contract to create what became RAYDAC (Raytheon Digital Automatic Computer), which was delivered four years later, by which time Raytheon was involved in designing RAYCOM, a computer that was to be aimed at civilian markets. But money ran out, which was one of the reasons Raytheon formed Datamatic with Honeywell.

In 1957, Datamatic sold its first computer, the D-1000, and that year, too, Raytheon sold its interest in the firm to Honeywell for $4 million, and Datamatic became a division of the new parent, who turned it over to Walter Finke, a lawyer who had educated himself in electronics and strongly believed in the future of computers. While aware of IBM's strengths and Honeywell's limited resources (its working capital in 1955 was $86 million, a quarter that of GE), Finke had developed a sound and plausible strategy. The computer industry was expanding and bound to get much larger, he thought, and IBM clearly would become its dominant force. How long would it be before the Justice Department investigated, and perhaps subjected IBM to an antitrust prosecution? What Finke had in mind was to meet IBM across the board with Honeywell machines, which on a price/performance basis would be less expensive. It would be rough going, and Finke couldn't afford too many errors, but with the Justice Department on his side he might win. "We figured IBM was too smart not to let us take 10 percent or so of the market," said Chuan Chu, then in Honeywell's technical department.

In 1958, Honeywell announced the 800, a medium-sized second generation machine, and others followed. But Finke's first truly important entry was the 200 series, announced in 1963, and frankly aimed at wooing customers away from IBM's recently announced second generation 1400s, for which there was a long waiting list. This approach, as will be seen, was informed by the RCA experience. Not only were the 200s less expensive than the 1400s and available sooner, but Honeywell offered an option known as the Liberator, which enabled its machines to run 1401 software, and do so faster. Honeywell boasted of the Liberator in a series of advertisements, and the sales force performed outstandingly. The 200s were an enormous success, with Honeywell selling $1.5 million worth of them in 1963 and $4.7 million the following year.

What exactly did this mean in terms of industry position? In those two years, IBM placed $27 million and $29 million in 1400s, so its position hardly was badly damaged. But IBM salesmen were reporting customer switches, which, as will be seen, prompted a reaction from Tom Watson.

Perhaps without realizing it (though the thought is difficult to accept) Honeywell had "invented" plug-compatibility, the key concept for the next decade, and one which requires some elucidation since it is so important. By utilizing the Liberator, the user of IBM's 1401 might turn in that machine, install a 200, and then run all of his programs on the Honeywell without a hitch. This was and is quite important, for hardware really is simply a device needed to run software. Thus, the owner of an IBM machine with a large library of "off-the-shelf" and special software would understandably be reluctant to get a new machine if it meant all of that software had to be discarded or substantially reworked. The Liberator changed all of this. It meant that a company might develop a machine that could run IBM software, offer it at a lower price or rental, and capture the market. Of course, this also implied that IBM would be followed; manufacturers of plug-compatible mainframes (PCMs) would never be able to pioneer. But profits could be made, an alluring concept at a time when of all the mainframe companies only IBM was operating in the black.

In this period and later, IBM developed software as a lure to obtain computer placements; software was not particularly rewarding financially, and at Armonk was seen as a "loss-leader" of sorts. The manufacturer of a plug-compatible machine didn't have to concern himself with the software side and so realized important economies, having obtained what amounted to a free ride from IBM. The full implications of plug-compatibility weren't recognized at the time, however, for in the early 1960s Honeywell and others still hoped to displace IBM in portions of the industry. When it became evident that IBM could not be displaced, plug-compatibility came to the fore, a tacit admission that to fail to follow the leader was extremely dangerous, if not completely foolhardy.

Honeywell's purchase of the GE computer operation in 1970 has to be seen against this backdrop. As it turned out the two units meshed well. "It was one of those rare situations where even three years later everybody is happy," said Clarence Spangle, who by then had succeeded Finke. Not only did Honeywell Information Systems (as it was to be renamed) thrive—electronic data processing revenues rose from $27 million in 1963 to $211 million in 1970—but the company was profitable.

Honeywell hardly represented a threat to IBM's domination, yet it had shown how to manage in that difficult environment. The requirements included intelligent and foresighted management, a commitment of capital, a good sales force, fine service, and an ability to demonstrate that your machines are sufficiently like the standard to be acceptable. Even so, Honeywell could not garner more than 10 percent of the market, or attract sufficient bright, aggressive personnel to go much beyond that. CEO James Binger hinted at this in a 1970 speech: "We are not technologically limited, we are not capital limited, we are not basically market limited. We may at some point be people limited to some extent."

Honeywell demonstrated how to live with IBM. RCA showed what happens to firms that develop a similar strategy but are unable to carry it off; and RCA also showed what happens to firms IBM considers rambunctious and offensive.

RCA: The Perils of Hubris

Except for GE, RCA appeared to be the electronics complex best positioned to challenge IBM. A $694 million company in 1952, it owned one of the nation's two major radio networks, was expanding rapidly into television programming, was the nation's largest manufacturer of color TV sets, and in RCA Laboratories had one of the world's premier research facilities. The corporation was headed by an aging but still vital David Sarnoff, whose reputation in his field was more luminous even than Watson Sr.'s in office machines. Moreover, he was grooming his oldest son, Robert, for the succession, just as Tom Watson, Sr., had groomed Tom Jr. to take over at IBM.

We have seen how RCA was involved with computers right from the beginning but in a limited fashion, and this involvement continued into the early 1950s, with all its customers being either governmental or in scientific research. By 1954, Sarnoff claimed to be in third place in the industry, behind IBM and Univac, and implied that he expected to pass Univac shortly. Two years later, with great fanfare, RCA unveiled its BIZMAC, developed for the Army and carrying a price tag of $4 million. At which point the personal dimension became important.

In the early 1950s John Burns, a management consultant for Booz, Allen & Hamilton, who was retained by IBM, had become a Watson Jr. confidant. Earlier, Burns had been retained by RCA. There was no secret in any of this; both firms knew of Burns's clientele, and the practice was acceptable. This acceptance might change if RCA invaded IBM's turf; however, in 1956 that didn't seem likely.

But there were some disturbing signs. For example, why did RCA call its machine BIZMAC if it was to be sold to the government and not offered to commercial clients—an act which would pit it against IBM? If RCA were to enter commercial markets Burns would have to chose between his two clients, for he hardly could be privy to the secret plans of each. So Watson contacted David Sarnoff to ask if he had any plans to enter the commercial market and was assured that he didn't.

Then, a few months later, in March 1957, Sarnoff announced that Burns was to become president and chief operating officer at RCA, with several special assignments, one of which being a study of the firm's future in computers. Burns soon started to raid IBM for talent, especially in sales, and later Bob Sarnoff wooed and won L. Edward Donegan, a highly regarded IBM marketing executive, who brought on additional talent. By the late

1950s, RCA's computer operation looked like a gathering of IBM alumni, and Burns's strategy was hardly secret. He had set out to create an IBM lookalike—in personnel, technology, and all else—even as Watson Sr. had consciously imitated the best at John Patterson's National Cash Register. But there were differences. The nascent C-T-R wasn't taking on NCR, but rather was going into a different industry, and in those days the chips were much smaller.

IBM's reaction was what one might have expected from John Patterson under similar circumstances. Tom Watson was livid. He called in his sales chiefs and informed them that the loss of a placement to other companies might be accepted—grudgingly—but anyone who relinquished one to RCA would have some explaining to do. At about the same time, a story circulated in the industry to the effect that one had to be careful when talking with Booz Allen consultants, because they allegedly had a tendency of going over to the competition and using that information. The assumption was that the story originated at IBM's Armonk headquarters. Thus, the gauntlet was thrown, and accepted.

From the first, Burns attempted an early version of the strategy Honeywell was to use so successfully with the Liberator in 1963; in other words, the RCA computers would possess the same kinds of capabilities as their IBM counterparts but carry lower price tags. Burns was prepared to take losses along the way. After hiring as many IBM salesman as he could (another factor that incurred Watson's wrath), he instructed them to make as many price concessions as necessary in order to obtain placements.

When the BIZMAC performed badly, Burns rushed into development RCA's first solid state machines, the 501s, which were due out in 1958, and which, like BIZMAC, were aimed at the government market and were refitted for civilian sales; they did poorly. The company was able to gain a following through aggressive discounting, but the large 601 was a flop, the medium-sized 301 was balky, and as was the case at GE, RCA saw large profits from other areas—TV in particular—being drained by computers, with little hope for a change. (It will be seen that RCA's diversion into computers was a factor in enabling the Japanese to gain an important foothold in consumer electronics, and so the firm was a double loser.)

In 1963, RCA announced the 3301, to replace the 601 and hold the line until a new series could be created. As it turned out, the 3301 was a success, enabling the Computer Systems Division to break even in 1964, and giving heart to those who hoped to continue, especially since by then the computer was being "reinvented," due to the perfection of integrated circuits and the appearance of the initial third generation machines.

The pace of change within the industry can be appreciated when it is considered that in 1962, when several firms were still turning out vacuum tube models, and second generation transistorized computers were still considered marvels, scientists at IBM and the Seven Dwarfs were planning third generation machines, to be based on integrated circuits. Such devices would be less expensive, faster, and more trouble free. As will be seen, the IBM third generation entry was to be the 360 series, the announcement of which was made in 1962, with the hope that installations would occur within two years. As it turned out, the initial 360 was delivered in April 1965, by which time many of its details were known, and the rest of the industry was prepared to counterattack.

None so boldly as RCA. In 1964 the firm announced its Spectra series, which was compatible with the 360s, available (there was a long waiting list at IBM), and much lower in price. Indeed, under the terms of RCA's new Flexible Accrued Equity Plan (FAEP), a customer might lease a machine on a six-year basis at rates competitive with IBM and take ownership at the end of the period. There were cut rates on software and free service contracts to go along with this. "Being easy to switch to makes RCA the only logical alternative to IBM," the company advertised. "Giving you features IBM doesn't have makes us a better alternative."

All of which preceded Bob Sarnoff's regime at RCA. He moved into the presidency in 1966, became chief executive officer two years later, and in 1970 succeeded to the chairmanship. He arrived at a time when it appeared the flow of red ink had crested. There had been profits in 1964, when computer revenues came to more than $100 million, and orders doubled the following year, when profits improved. According to the company, deficits in the next two years were caused by an increase in the ratio of leases to outright sales due to the FAEP. Future losses were blamed on the need for heavy investment "for future growth." In 1969 RCA's computer revenues came to more than $200 million and the outlook was much improved. Donegan was on board as vice president for sales by then, and other former IBMers had also arrived and were expecting a push which would enable RCA's computer operation to pass Univac in a year or two, the unannounced goal being 15 percent of industry revenues. Tremendous growth and ambition, to be sure, but at a price: the operation was still unprofitable.

Sarnoff's position was akin to that faced by Fred Borch at GE, which is to say that while recognizing the appeal of computers he felt the operation could never show the kinds of profits others might. The impending IBM 370 series, rumored to be even more ambitious and far reaching than the 360s, left him aghast. RCA lacked the resources to meet that challenge; although there was brave talk of a New Technology System (NTS), little was done to implement it.

By 1970 Sarnoff knew IBM was too large, tough, and skillful to meet in a head-on confrontation. Perhaps, had he been in the position of Jim Binger at Honeywell he would have reacted differently; after all, Binger's main business was the manufacture of electronic controls and for him to give up on computers would mean to forswear a major part of the firm. But Sarnoff's vision of RCA was quite different. He gave a hint of this in the 1968 annual report by stating: "The word that best characterizes the modern RCA is diversity." In other words, he intended the company to become a conglomerate on the order of Harold Geneen's International Telephone & Telegraph rather than a business-machine-entertainment-electronics complex. During the next few years, RCA purchased such firms as Random House (publishing), Coronet Industries (carpets), Hertz (car rentals), and Banquet Foods (frozen foods), all of which required capital that was being drained by Computer Systems.

Psychologists might conclude that Bob Sarnoff was reacting against his father, attempting to make his own mark as a businessman rather than simply continue along a path set out by his illustrious parent. But businessmen would recognize that he had little choice but to act as he did. Sarnoff signaled the change in RCA's direction in 1971 by naming Alfred Conrad, an executive known to be critical of the computer business, as his president and chief operating officer. And the moment of truth came in April 1971, when Donegan projected a plan for the following year in which he estimated revenues of $261 million—and a loss of $37 million. This was followed by a revised loss estimate of $63 million. Moreover, additional losses of more than $100 million might be anticipated within the next two years, while Computer Systems might need an additional billion dollars in new capital by 1976.

By the spring of 1971, however, Sarnoff and Conrad were actively seeking a buyer, hardly a secret in the industry, and potential clients were cancelling orders, fearful of being stuck with an "orphan computer" impossible to service. In desperation, RCA slashed prices, but this only added to customer distrust. In effect, the division's value was eroding daily.

Gerald Probst, then head of Univac, knew of RCA's situation, and sensing a bargain, made an appointment in September to see Sarnoff. Two months later, in November 1971, the two firms announced the sale of RCA's Computer Systems to Sperry Rand for $70.5 million and 15 percent of the revenues from existing placements, which came to around $113 million.

It was a bargain, especially when compared to the previous year's purchase of GE's computer business by Honeywell. In return for less than the book value of the hardware, Univac obtained a customer base of some 500 companies and government agencies, 1,000 computers (the initial cost of which was more than $900 million), and a work force of 7,500, all of whom were interviewed and a third retained. "You could never go out in the open market and get so many people with that type of talent," said a pleased Univac executive. "It's like taking the Eastern Division of the National Football League and saying you can take the top ten guys from each team."

Just as GE's computer division invigorated Honeywell, so RCA's boosted Univac to a far stronger position than it otherwise might have enjoyed. A year later, Sperry Rand reported that it had retained 90 percent of the RCA customers, to whom they sold $130 million of new equipment. Later in the decade, when the old RCAs had to be replaced, Univac had a first crack at getting the business.

Industrial shakeouts in the early years of any industry hardly are new. After all, at one time there were more than 400 auto makers in the United States, and today there are four domestically based ones. That there would be a shakeout in computers was inevitable. But might one have anticipated that among the victims would be the likes of GE and RCA? Their failures were due to mismanagement, product failures, and misperceptions. More important, perhaps, was the strategy mentioned at the beginning of this chapter, which all the old line companies, whether in business machines or electronics, followed: namely, attempting to meet IBM across the board rather than aiming at weak spots and seeking targets of opportunity.

Later on, in retrospect, others would come to this realization. We have noted that a key IBM hallmark is its willingness to hold back on product introductions until the market is established. Thus, a newcomer could establish a beachhead, dig in, and await the IBM onslaught, which—if the product line, sales force, and balance sheet were in good shape—could be turned back. These firms might then witness an IBM withdrawal, but they had to know that "The Armonk Monster" would return; for if its blitzkrieg fails, IBM will switch tactics and try to grind the newcomer down.

There is nothing wrong with this or even remotely underhanded, but the survivors came to realize that the grinding down approach, too, could be met. In our time, Apple is doing so in micros; during the 1970s, it was done by Digital Equipment; and before these two, it was Control Data. The failures include a long line of leasing companies and manufacturers of peripheral equipment that either couldn't or wouldn't react effectively.

Yet IBM's domination wasn't preordained, for another of the old-line, major American corporations could have swept all before it—IBM included—because its financial assets and scientific expertise were greater even than IBM's, and its sales force larger, if not as aggressive. The company was none other than American Telephone & Telegraph, which by some lights might have been considered the world's leading computer company of the late 1940s and early 1950s.

Ma Bell: The Shackled Giant

AT&T's role in the emerging computer industry begins not with the researches of the 1930s, or even World War II, but rather an agreement entered into in the year prior to the outbreak of the first World War.

Largely due to complaints from independent telephone companies, the outgoing William Howard Taft administration signalled that it was considering antitrust action against AT&T, a firm that at the time had assets of close to $1 billion. Knowing of President-elect Woodrow Wilson's anti-big-business statements during the late campaign, AT&T President Theodore Vail sent his representative, N. C. Kingsbury, to meet with Attorney General George Wickersham to see if a deal could be cut. And one was. Under the terms of the so-called "Kingsbury Commitment" AT&T agreed to restrict acquisitions of independent telephone companies, divest itself of Western Union stock in its portfolio, and most important, remain out of related areas. For the next half century, AT&T attempted to maintain a low profile, as it remained fearful of antitrust action.

Yet it remained a leader in communications technology, mostly through its manufacturing division, Western Electric, and Bell Laboratories, which was spun off as a separate entity in 1924. Together and individually these two developed basic inventions in radio, television, motion picture, and other advanced areas, but all the while had to license their discoveries to others, and sell off interests when they became promising—and visible. At one time or another, AT&T might have become a dominant force in several emerging communications industries, but to preserve its position in telephones, left the field to the likes of RCA, GE, and IBM. Even so, it was hit by a Justice Department antitrust action in 1949 and had to defend itself against those who wanted to break up the system.

With all of this, the company did experiment with computers, and in 1940 had developed one of them for use in switching. AT&T provided several computers to the military during World War II, and was consulted by virtually every researcher in the field, Eckert and Mauchly included. Moreover, no American firm, IBM included, was better equipped to lead the way in the second generation; this is hardly debatable, since in 1947 two Bell scientists, William Shockley and Walter Brattain, invented the transistor, which was to be the heart of the new machine. AT&T also manufactured the first transistors, and every one of the two dozen or so firms that were doing so in 1956—the year Shockley received the Nobel Prize for his accomplishments—were Bell licensees. But due to its agreements with the federal government, AT&T wasn't free to capitalize upon the transistor, and for this reason, among others, Shockley left the firm to organize his own company, Shockley Semiconductor Laboratories in Palo Alto, and so became one of the godfathers of what came to be known as Silicon Valley.

Nonetheless, AT&T was always interested in computers, knowing they could have important uses in telephonics, and, of course, it had the financial muscle and the research facilities necessary for the task. And it had the will. In the mid-1950s, Mauchly believed AT&T had a stronger patent position in computers than any other firm, not excluding IBM. Were it not for antitrust considerations, AT&T would have been the first important manufacturer and vendor of computers. Alone of all the American firms it could have manufactured for inventory rather than individual clients, for it was, even then, the leading non-federal-government user of the machines, and in fact might have profitably produced them for internal use alone.

As it happened, in 1956 AT&T agreed to a settlement of the antitrust action, under the terms of which it was specifically enjoined from manufacturing, for sale or lease, "any equipment which is of the type not sold or leased or intended to be sold or leased to Companies of the Bell System...." There was only one exception: AT&T could develop and sell gear to the federal government.

This 1956 consent decree effectively barred AT&T from the development of computers for sale to others. Thus, IBM's most powerful potential competitor was locked out of the industry by the Justice Department. This is something IBM might have considered during the years when it argued it was being hounded unfairly by the Justice Department. Had the Anti-Trust Division not acted against AT&T in 1949, it might not have had to do so against IBM two decades later, for rather than enjoying what was claimed to be a quasi-monopoly, IBM might have been a strong second to AT&T, and the industry's structure might have been entirely different.

In spite of the settlement, research proceeded at Western Electric and Bell Labs, but most of it was telecommunications-related. Through its Teletype subsidiary, AT&T was able to vend a variety of products to others in the industry, but, of course, this was a minor part of its business. In 1963, for example, AT&T's total revenues were $9.6 billion. That year it sold $97 million worth of computer products to manufacturers, but none to the public. Thus, electronic-data-processing revenues came to little more than 1 percent of its business. Yet this was enough to make AT&T the industry's third largest factor (but not producer, of course), behind IBM and Sperry Rand.

It was a picture of what might have been. And for those prescient enough to look down the road to the 1980s, what might yet become.

III

MAKING OUT IN A
WATSONIZED WORLD

The Shark: Control Data's Strategy

As has been seen, along with Engineering Research Associates, RemRand had acquired its flamboyant, quirky leader, William Norris. A farm boy from Nebraska, Norris had graduated in 1934 from the state university, where he majored in electrical engineering. Unable to find a job during the Great Depression he returned to the farm. Later in the decade, Norris landed his first industrial position at Westinghouse, and then, in the Navy during World War II, he became involved with cryptography and computers. As has been seen, Norris founded ERA after the war, a firm which quietly dominated the field for a while before becoming part of RemRand. Chafing at being under the home office, Norris planned his departure in 1957, at which time he organized Control Data Corporation.

It was a good time to make the move. A bull market was taking shape on Wall Street, and interest had turned to high technology issues. The investing public had become aware of computers and was eager to obtain shares in firms which produced them. Norris was able to capitalize CDC at $600,000, of which he contributed $70,000, and with this he was on his way.

According to its prospectus, Control Data's original aim was to perform "primarily consulting business and research for the Government, the plan being that out of the research and development work, and possibly the consulting work for business, would come ideas for products which we could later put on the market." A modest ambition, perhaps, but also one that might be realized without disturbing IBM or any of the other behemoths. Not then or later did Norris harbor any ambition to challenge any company across the line, but rather he wanted to carve for himself a special niche and then defend it with all of his resources against large firms (to which his specialty would be only a sideline) and smaller ones lacking his resources. Or, as the saying goes, he aimed at becoming a big fish in a little pond.

Most apropos, because Norris later would compare the industry to the sea, in which IBM was a giant shark and most companies were akin to pilot fish, who swim in and out of the shark's jaws, taking the leavings, always afraid of being swallowed. As Norris saw it, one had to be either a pilot fish or a shark, and he intended CDC to be a shark, though in another part of the ocean, away from IBM. Which is the reason the CDC organization for star salesmen is known as the Shark Club.

Into CDC came a dozen or so former ERA engineers and scientists who, like Norris, had been unhappy at Sperry Rand. The most important of these was Seymour Cray, a retiring, not overly articulate individual who seemed possessed of a sole passion: to construct the biggest and most powerful computer in the world and then go on to design others still bigger and more powerful. Cray seemed to have little interest in business, nor did he appear to have a very clear idea of whether or not his giant machines could be sold or leased. All that seemed to matter to him was size and scope. Cray was to become CDC's chief designer and, next to Norris, the most important reason for the company taking the direction it did and having its success.

Another of CDC's advantages derived from this large-scale orientation. The kind of machines Cray was to design and Norris construct had no clear business applications, and so the new firm wouldn't have to pit itself against IBM and others in that market. Nor would Norris have to hire a large sales force. Since the only customers for large machines were government agencies and laboratories, where the purchase decisions were made by practitioners, Norris could send out a CDC technician to explain just what the machines were capable of doing. Nor would CDC have to create software or even offer technical support—all of which were within the capabilities of the customer. The support organizations and infrastructure other companies required to combat IBM might safely be ignored, at least as long as CDC hewed to this line.

Even prior to the stock sale, Cray set out to design what was to become the 1604, which was the first large solid state machine, and Norris was ready for orders in April 1958. A Navy purchase followed, along with other military orders. As expected, the 1604 sold to government and scientific users, while commercial clients continued to prefer the IBM 704s.

The 1604's arrival preceded by a few weeks that of the IBM 7070 and 7090, Watson's first transistorized machines, which became so popular that rentals from them *alone* in 1963 were better than half again as great as the total for all systems rentals by the other American manufacturers. This enormous success appears to have blinded IBM to the nature of the CDC challenge, or indeed even to recognize it as such. There were no signs Norris intended to enter IBM's traditional markets, the firm did not look like the other dwarfs, and while it was growing rapidly, it hardly was in the same league as Honeywell or GE, much less IBM. So there was no response at that time. The 1604 quickly became a standard in its special category and, along with variants, remained the company's most important product well into the 1960s. Earnings from it enabled Norris to begin work on the next series, the 3600, which was announced in May 1962, and which finally stirred IBM into action. The 3600s were followed soon after by news of the 6600, a large machine clearly superior to the 7000s against which they were to compete and much lower in price. By then it had become evident that not only had CDC arrived, but in the field of large computers it would be a formidable competitor.

Norris appreciated the reason for his success. "We picked out a particular niche in the market—the scientific and engineering part of the market—and then met the needs of the particular part very proficiently and much more so than any computer then available. . . . Our business took off like a rocket to the moon as our large computers made rapid and significant penetration in the education, aerospace, and large government laboratories markets."

The figures bore him out. For 1959, CDC reported revenues of $6.8 million and earnings of $300,000. In 1963, these figures were $67.1 million and $3.1 million respectively. The corporation would pass the $100 million figure the following year, by which time it was the third largest factor in the industry, with a 5.4 percent market share. Revenues would surpass $200 million in 1967 and come close to doubling the next year. It clearly was the industry's greatest success story of the decade (always excluding IBM).

MARKET SHARE IN THE COMPUTER INDUSTRY 1965

Rank	Company	Share	Gross Revenues*
1.	IBM**	65.3	$2,487,300,000
2.	Sperry Rand	12.1	1,279,800,000
3.	Control Data	5.4	98,000,000
4.	Honeywell	3.8	700,400,000
5.	Burroughs	3.5	456,700,000
6.	General Electric	3.4	6,231,600,000
7.	RCA	2.9	2,042,000,000
8.	NCR	2.9	736,800,000
9.	Philco	0.7	not reported

SOURCE: *Honeywell vs. Sperry Rand, p. 157; Moody's Handbook of Common Stocks, 166 ed.*

Digital Equipment: The Olsen Variant

At almost the same time Bill Norris was founding CDC in Minneapolis, Kenneth Olsen was searching for funds to start his computer firm, to be known as Digital Equipment Corporation. By the late 1970s, it was known as DEC, and so joined IBM as one of the few in the industry recognizable by its initials. And for good reason: in this period DEC was able to boast that it actually was placing more computers into the hands of customers than was the industry giant.

Olsen was the other side of the coin insofar as the personalities of founders in this industry were concerned. Quite a few were very individualistic and demanding, intent on stamping their personalities on the firm and eager to test their mettle against the IBM megalith—Norris pretty well fit that mold. Then there was the withdrawn, introspective sort, who pondered problems, sought unexplored markets, and weren't all that eager for conflict, though they were willing to accept it when necessary—this describes Ken Olsen. Perhaps it was no accident that, while Norris decided to build and sell computers that were

---

*These figures refer to the gross revenues for each company, not only computers and related products and services. In 1965 this category accounted for a small fraction of GE's total revenues and all of those for Control Data. The other firms fall in between these two.

**Excluding IBM World Trade

larger and more powerful than any in the IBM stable, Olsen opted to produce cost-effective machines smaller than any turned out by IBM.

Thus the two men struck at the two extremes: IBM seemed to believe that the markets for both giants and minis were limited, the former because all that power was not needed by many clients, the latter because small companies and professionals either did not need computers or would obtain services through time sharing. In both cases IBM was wrong and came in too late to dislodge its rivals. Then, too, both CDC and DEC intended to concentrate initially upon scientific customers rather than businessmen. Neither company had much interest in being acquired by another firm, and in time both became incubators for entrepreneurs who went on to found their own companies. Interestingly enough, Seymour Cray left to organize Cray Research when Norris balked at creating even larger machines, and a team of researchers at DEC, feeling the path to the top was closed to them and having some ideas regarding smaller units that were rejected, went off on their own to create Data General.

Control Data's successes were manifest, but DEC's were even more so, since they directly affected far more individuals. Until the advent of the micros and IBM's entry into that area, DEC was able to claim more unit sales than any computer manufacturer in the world. Now it is content with the number-two position in the industry in terms of units in operation. Finally, while the CDC *élan* would be watered down in time to the point that it might be compared with others of the BUNCH, DEC remains an entrepreneurial, adventuresome operation, and not a few industry analysts believe the Japanese will have more trouble competing with it than even with the mighty IBM itself. As though to underline this, DEC mounted a major campaign in the Japanese market in the early 1980s, with some success.

The company began with Olsen and Harlan Anderson, both researchers at the Massachusetts Institute of Technology's Lincoln Laboratories, where they worked on large computer projects. In their work, the two men became convinced of the need for much smaller machines. They weren't the first to entertain the thought. For example, a group of technicians at Bendix, which included Max Palevsky (more on whom later), was trying without success to convince management there was a crying gap in the market. And there were others at a number of companies with the same ambition. But Olsen and Anderson were the first to make the grade. The two men rented some space in an old, ramshackle woolen mill in nearby Maynard, Massachusetts; hired three employees; and set out to manufacture their first product: printed circuit boards for others. The idea was that profits from these circuit boards would be used to fund work on the initial small computer.

For a while it seemed nothing was going right, and within months DEC was close to illiquidity, with Olsen spending more time seeking funding than working on his computer. Then he ran into Georges Doriot, a retired general who taught some courses at Harvard Business School while running one of the nation's first venture capital businesses, American Research & Development. Olsen impressed Doriot, who agreed that for an infusion of $70,000, AR&D would receive 60 percent of DEC's stock, with Olsen and Anderson remaining in command and Doriot acting as an advisor. And his advice in those early months was to stick with components for a while, at least until the capital was expanded, and they did so for the next three years.

Meanwhile, Olsen honed his strategy to a fine edge. He would concentrate on manufacturing a machine simple enough to be employed by technicians in a matter of days and mastered in weeks. Initially, these would be produced on order, but Olsen hoped to mass manufacture for inventory in time. All the while, there would be improvements combined with price reductions. After the beachhead with scientific laboratories had been secured, DEC would start marketing the machines to factories, to be used in process controls, then on to the offices. Where CDC targeted the most sophisticated scientific applications and IBM thought in terms of automating large corporations, DEC wanted to sell its machines to companies and researchers who previously hadn't thought of using them.

The need for capital would be less than at IBM or CDC, since DEC machines were simpler to put together, would benefit from economies of scale, and were sold rather than leased (when a customer opted for rental, DEC would put him in touch with a finance company). And since improvements were constantly being made, the firm would present its potential rivals with a moving target and offer clients computers incorporating the latest technologies. Finally, DEC intended to employ technicians as salesmen, believing they would relate best to the kinds of clients to whom DEC's machines would appeal. Olsen intended to remain in the mini field and avoid confrontation with the established mainframe manufacturers.

What he did not seem to realize at the time, however, was that the nature of the technology was such as to make clashes inevitable. Then, as now, there would be more bang for a buck with each succeeding model, which is to say that the power of DEC computers and those of other producers was rising more rapidly than the price was declining.

DEC's first machine, the PDP (Programmed Data Processor) 1, was marketed in 1960 and sold for between $125,000 and $243,000, depending upon the peripheral equipment desired. It was followed by the PDP 4 two years later and the PDP 5 in 1963, by which time orders were coming in so rapidly that the firm had to borrow $300,000 from AR&D to expand.

Olsen was soon planning to move to more powerful machines, a decision which was more the result of a desire to keep up with customer needs than a desire to enter the ranks of the large mainframe manufacturers. The PDP 6, introduced in 1964, could cost as much as $750,000, and competed in power with IBMs more than twice its price. And the PDP 8 was four times as fast and sold at two-thirds the price of the 5 that it replaced. A well-received unit, the PDP 8 constituted DEC's most ambitious entry in the office market, and the PDP 10, the first of which were sold in 1967, competed head-on with some of the IBM 360s.

By then, DEC occupied most of the old woolen mill, employed over 1,000 people, and had sold some 800 machines. Three years later, DEC was manufacturing its machines in the United Kingdom, Puerto Rico, and Canada as well as in Maynard, had a workforce of 5,800, revenues of $142.6 million, and earnings of $14.4 million. The firm now had more computers installed than any other firm except IBM and Sperry Rand.

The tale of what happened to that original $70,000 investment may serve to cap this part of the DEC saga. By the time AR&D sold and distributed its holdings, the worth came to more than $400 million.

Max Palevsky and SDS

Selling small computers to scientific customers made sense, and soon DEC had many competitors—Perkin Elmer, Hewlett Packard, Varian Associates, Bunker Ramo, Packard Bell, Monroe, and Raytheon, among others. Most concentrated on the low end of the spectrum. Entry was easy, requiring relatively little capital for start-up manufacturing. Manufacturing the machines wasn't the problem; rather it was placements. Once the small units were accepted by scientists and researchers, the firms would attempt to expand out of that base, and it was then they usually came across the hard reality of life in the business computer field. DEC overcame this reality, of course, as did Hewlett Packard and a few others. Several had the good sense—some would call it the lack of daring—to cash in their chips early by selling out to older firms eager to enter the rapidly growing field.

Seldom did these purchases of small entrepreneurial firms by large management-oriented operations work out well. A case in point is that of Scientific Data Systems (SDS), organized four years after CDC and DEC, which at one time appeared more promising than either.

As is the case with virtually all of these firms, there was a unique, brilliant scientist/technician at the heart of SDS.

One of the legendary figures of the early period, Max Palevsky was a second-generation American, who attended the University of Chicago, where he majored in philosophy and mathematics, hoping to continue on to a doctorate and become a college instructor. While scholarly, he also was a restive soul, who, when he considered a cloistered academic existence at a time when technology was popping, abandoned graduate work for a position at Bendix, where he joined that group that was attempting to win support for small computers. Frustrated, he left Bendix in 1957 for a job at Packard Bell, which promised him the requisite support, and where he turned out a computer for the young space program, one that was also sold with some success in the scientific market. When it became clear Packard Bell couldn't finance his activities, Palevsky left, by that time believing the only way he could do what he wanted was to organize his own company.

It was 1961, a time when Silicon Valley was being born and venture capitalists were all the rage. Palevsky came upon Arthur Rock, who later would prove to be one of the more astute of the breed. Together with some associates, Palevsky raised $100,000, while Rock and his group added $900,000, and with this capital Scientific Data Systems came into being.

Palevsky intended to concentrate upon two markets: the one for small-to-medium-sized scientific computers and the other for "real time" applications, which in computerese meant units to monitor industrial functions or help guide missiles as they sped on their way. Both markets meant placements with knowledgeable users who would not need much in the way of software or support, and both could be sold by technicians—which is to say, SDS would be modeled after Control Data and DEC, not IBM or Honeywell.

The first of the company's machines, the SDS 910, which holds claim to being the first second-generation scientific unit, was shipped early the following year (1962). This was made possible by the fact that Palevsky purchased

72

components, often off the shelf, from suppliers, and fabricated rather than manufactured the unit. The SDS 910 was a success, and others followed, many of a pathbreaking variety, and usually sold at highly competitive prices. By mid-decade SDS was considered in the same league as DEC when insiders talked of promising young firms.

And, like DEC, SDS found itself moving upward in the product line to compete with IBM. In 1965, Palevsky initiated work on the Sigma series, meant to compete with the 360s. The Sigma 7 and 2 came out the next year, and were followed soon after by others in the group. Like so many SDS products, it was cobbled together from parts purchased from others, was priced 10-15 percent under comparable IBM products, and was much faster—the firm claimed it had a 26-65 percent advantage in cost/performance. Initially targeted at scientific users, to whom IBM's vaunted reputation counted for little, the Sigmas were being placed with commercial users by 1967.

Taken as a whole, by then SDS was competing with IBM across almost as wide a spectrum as did Honeywell, and a wider spectrum than DEC and CDC. It had gone from nothing in 1961 to a $113 million company (in assets) eight years later, with a workforce of more than 4,000; SDS was, by some calculations, the eighth or ninth largest factor in the industry, and certainly the fastest moving of the lot.

It was then that Palevsky sold the company to Xerox for $920 million in stock, which was four times what Honeywell had paid for GE's computer division and approximately eight times what RCA received from Sperry Rand for its highly touted operations. Of course, there were differences. GE and RCA were holding distress sales; in 1969 SDS appeared not only a promising operation, but combined with Xerox—itself highly regarded insofar as management, technology, and sales forces were concerned—it was a potential powerhouse, a more vigorous version of Honeywell, perhaps the firm to finally give IBM a run for its money.

One can understand why Xerox wanted SDS and was willing to pay that price. But why did Palevsky sell? The argument that he wanted to cash in his chips is appealing, but this wasn't in character. There is another, more plausible explanation. Some of his associates argue that even as early as 1967 he had started losing interest in the business, for it was then he started getting involved with the motion picture industry, and later on with the peace movement, and in 1968 with Robert Kennedy's bid for the Democratic presidential nomination. It might have been that the Kennedy assassination crippled his spirit. But there is yet another explanation that might be considered.

In common with many of the entrepreneur-founders, Palevsky was most comfortable in the laboratory, working with small groups; he was uncomfortable and felt out of place in the board room. Taking SDS from nothing to $100 million per year was an achievement, but to go from $100 million to a billion, and in the process compete squarely with IBM, was another matter entirely, and Palevsky might have shrunk from the prospect. Then, too, competition with non-IBM manufacturers was heating up. Hewlett Packard and DEC were also eager for a place in the constellation, and Palevsky must have been troubled by them. He said he would stay on with the company, but in fact he started to ease out before the merger with Xerox was completed.

Old Wine in New Bottles Doesn't Go: Xerox Data Systems

Thus far, we have seen how some great companies failed to make their way in the data processing industry, how others weren't able to make an important dent in IBM's market position, and the way start-up operations became important players by concentrating on special segments of the market prior to spreading out into other areas. Now we will explore the method by which one of the most promising high technology companies of modern times, Xerox, became involved in what arguably was the greatest managerial fiasco in the industry's short history.

During the 1950s several firms were being touted as "the IBM of the future," but during the next decade the palm was bestowed upon Xerox alone. Revenues and earnings rose from under $28 million and $1.6 million in 1958 to over $700 million and $97 million ten years later. Xerox's 914 and 813 copiers were more a standard in their fields than any IBM product ever had been or would be in computers, and the copier market was growing more rapidly than that for data processing equipment.

Toward the end of the decade, rumors were heard that Xerox was considering a venture into computers, while several major firms were thinking about turning out copiers, among them Polaroid, Eastman Kodak—and IBM. That a battle in the office equipment area was coming between IBM and Xerox was accepted as a fact of life at both companies.

As usual, IBM refused to comment on plans, but Xerox President Peter McColough told a reporter that "A lot of computer peripheral gear is going to depend on graphics, putting images on paper," going on to note that "Xerox and IBM are two big companies exclusively in the information business. IBM owns the manipulative data processing part, and we own the part that puts things on paper. But the lines of separation are getting blurred, and it will be harder and harder to distinguish them. Sometime in the 1970s, we intend to say to any big customer, 'We can handle all your information needs.'" Thus, Xerox's takeover of SDS, followed by the purchase of Diablo Systems for $29 million. A manufacturer of peripheral equipment, Diablo would seem a good complement to SDS, which still purchased many of its parts from vendors. There was talk of additional acquisitions—of almost anything that would make the new Xerox Data Systems as thriving a concern as its parent.

At the time of the acquisition, Palevsky told reporters that if all went well, Xerox Data Systems would be firmly entrenched in the mainframe area within five years. McColough disagreed, thinking it could be done much earlier. He quickly discovered that slugging it out with Honeywell, DEC, and Univac—not to mention IBM—was quite a different game from the situation in copiers, where as yet there weren't any major competitors. The situation was complicated by an economic recession in 1970-1971 that impacted upon the business machine market. But the more serious difficulties were in wedding the two corporate cultures.

The SDS salesmen were freewheelers, accustomed to offering discounts in order to make placements, while their Xerox counterparts, having the market to themselves, often functioned more as order-takers. Xerox insisted on an end to discounting, which resulted in a fall-off in sales and profits, and this in turn led to dismissals, demoralization, and more red ink. There followed problems in manufacturing, resulting in customer disaffection. "Morale in the field is terrible because of the delivery schedules," said marketing vice president Donald McKee in 1973, "and made worse because commitments are missed with no notification from Manufacturing." Reorganizations and a shakeup followed, to no avail.

Xerox Data Systems had become a cash drain on the parent. In its last year as an independent, SDS had earned $10 million; in the next three years, as Xerox Data Systems, it lost more than $100 million.

By 1974, it had become evident that Xerox Data Systems was in trouble. At one time McColough had hoped to open a crack in the market and drive right through it. Perhaps this might have been done a decade earlier, but not when the IBM 360s and 370s virtually wrapped up the ballgame in mainframes.

Which isn't to say that the Xerox machines were in any way inferior; indeed, from customer reports it would appear that satisfaction was quite widespread and loyalty strong. Nor was there any erosion of sales, which were still quite strong. It simply was a case of the inability of *any* company to strike a blow against IBM at the heart of its business by that time—which is to suggest that by the early 1970s "the chicken heart" had grown to impregnable size and strength.

In July 1975, McColough announced that Xerox Data Systems was leaving the mainframe business, conceding that the SDS acquisition had been a mistake. This didn't mean Xerox no longer was concerned with the design, manufacture, and sale of data processing equipment; in fact it went on to acquire other small companies in that area—Daconics, Versatec, Shugart, Century, and WUI, among others—and its revenues expanded significantly. Xerox was active in networking and a wide variety of other fields that brought it into conflict with IBM, and it had its share of victories. For example, in the following decade the firm would have signal successes with its electronic typewriters, to the point of capturing leadership in this area from IBM itself.

Nor was this the last of the challenges to the industry leader; even while Xerox Data Systems was foundering, Amdahl Corporation seemed to have found a means whereby IBM might be bested. But as CDC and DEC had shown, this could be accomplished only by an indirect approach, one made on the periphery.

IBM had its weak spots, and clever businessmen were able to seek them out, and some of them did quite well for themselves—until the inevitable, shattering counterattack came out of Armonk.

One of those weak areas was leasing; in the 1960s scores of companies entered the leasing business, and their stocks became stars of the bull market. But not for long. Here, as in so many other areas, IBM watched, waited, and then launched a savage counterattack that wiped out a subindustry in a matter of a few years. Only the nimble—those that recognized the hiatus as a pause before the storm rather than succumbing to the hubris of believing they really had bested the Armonk Giant—were able to come out of the experience with some prosperity and dignity.

On the Periphery: Saul Steinberg and the Leasco Saga

Before going into both the rise and fall of leasing one needs to have a background in the legal imbroglio that made the entire subindustry possible.

In 1952, IBM was engaged in another of its skirmishes with the Justice Department. This time the government challenged the company's refusal to sell its equipment. Four years of discovery and probing followed, at the end of which Watson accepted a consent decree that gave the government much of what it wanted. Specifically, IBM agreed to sell machines, and to do so without a requirement that the client accept IBM service for it. This meant a customer could purchase an IBM mainframe without software and the traditional service—thus opening the way for the three new subindustries: leasing, software creation, and servicing, of which the first was the most important.

The first of the subindustries appeared soon after the consent decree was accepted, although some leasing companies had been around since the early 1950s, when they purchased used, often obsolete, office equipment, and then resold or leased it at rock-bottom rates. Most of these companies are now gone, but at the time they seemed quite aggressive, astute, and even powerful. Among the leaders were Leasco Data Processing, Levin-Townsend, Management Assistance, Randolph, University Computing, Boothe, Diebold, Greyhound, Bankers, and Data Processing Financial & General. There were almost a hundred of them in the field in 1966; four years later the number had grown to over 250.

IBM eyed them warily and with mixed feelings. The success of the 360 program was in part due to purchases by the leasing companies. In the first nine months of 1966 alone the lessors took delivery on $75 million worth, and in this period they owned more than a third of them. That year, partly so as to recover costs on their huge development program by encouraging purchases, IBM raised its leasing charges by 3 percent and simultaneously lowered the purchase prices of its machines. This set off a buying spree among the leasing companies; by 1969 lessors had $2.5 billion of gear, and as a group they were considered the firm's leading customer, and indeed in the aggregate were larger than any other competitor.

Still, what IBM gained in terms of sales it lost in leases, and clearly this could not be permitted to continue any longer than necessary. That a reaction was coming should have appeared likely, if not evident, but few in the subindustry seemed to have given the matter sufficient thought.

The business was really quite simple. The leasing company would arrange for a line of credit and use it to purchase IBM mainframes, which would be offered at competitive rates to customers who then could go to IBM for software and services or obtain them from other vendors. Typically, a firm might lease out an IBM machine for 10 percent less than the manufacturer would and still show a 30 percent profit, this due to low overhead but also to another factor: the nature of IBM accounting.

Typically, IBM would depreciate its machines rapidly, even more so than might have been realistic. This was a conservative method of keeping books, one which showed losses in the early years and then, if the machines were kept on lease after they were fully depreciated, almost pure profit. The leasing companies depreciated their gear over a much longer period, and so showed higher profits on their placements. But this depreciation policy placed the leasing companies at risk.

For a while, however, it seemed an almost foolproof method of participating in the data processing industry, both against IBM and as a quasi-partner. Leasing appeared particularly enticing in the period after the introduction of the 360 series, which at the time appeared to stabilize the industry on a plateau. The leasing companies' problems weren't anything like those faced by Honeywell or Univac. After all, the lessors were placing IBM machines, the very same ones that might have been obtained from the manufacturer, but they were placing them at a lower cost.

There were several flaws in the arrangement, which worried some of the more astute practitioners but seemed to have been given short shrift by others. Suppose IBM decided to slash its leasing charges; might not the client cancel his contract and come back to Armonk? Not if the contract were carefully written, which was one of the more important matters facing the lessors. A more serious consideration was the matter of obsolescence. What would happen, for example, when IBM introduced its next generation of mainframes? This did not seem too serious a problem at the time, when the thinking was that IBM would rest on its laurels for a while, recouping costs and raking in the profits. Thus, a lessor might write attractive long-term contracts that would undercut IBM and still realize fine profits.

Still, that long depreciation period was worrisome, since after a while the customer might return the machine, which would then have to be placed at a lower rate since it was older and perhaps obsolete. This was a major chink in their armor, one duly noted in Armonk. It was upon this rock—depreciation—that the leasing operations were erected. As will be seen, it was to prove sandstone rather than granite.

One of the more interesting of the leasing operations, due to the sophistication of its founder, was Leasco Data Processing. Saul Steinberg was unusual not because he knew how to seize the main chance, but rather because he also realized when the time had arrived to leave.

Steinberg was a soft-featured, rather undistinguished, but also precocious student at the Wharton School of Finance in the late 1950s, when one of his professors suggested he write a paper on the many problems IBM would face in the computer industry. "I was the kind of student who was prepared to believe anything bad, so I accepted the assignment," he later recalled. As it turned out, Steinberg came to an opposite conclusion. "IBM was an incredible, fantastic, brilliantly conceived company with a very rosy future," he said, but also one with some interesting quirks. Steinberg spotted the depreciation methods utilized and instinctively realized that this was an opening for an aggressive merchandiser. Steinberg never did write the paper, but his realization remained with him.

Steinberg pondered the matter while working for his father, the proprietor of Ideal Rubber Products (which manufactured kitchen accessories like dishracks). He realized that though a leasing company might report terrific profits, everything hinged on being able to keep those machines out there for a long period. Steinberg thought it highly unlikely this would occur—but while the game was being played, the balance sheets and profit and loss statements would make pleasant reading for investors and speculators alike.

In 1961, with $25,000 in borrowed funds and at the age of 20, Steinberg founded Ideal Leasing Company (He also borrowed the name from his father's business) and prepared to challenge IBM.

Steinberg pounded the pavements seeking customers, the first of which was signed on after three months. Others followed. In 1962, he incorporated Ideal and two years later, by which time revenues came to $8 million and earnings $255,000, Steinberg decided to sell his first issue of common stock. The next year the renamed Leasco made the same revenues, but earnings rose to $750,000. Reported earnings doubled in 1965 and did so again the following year. Leasco was a success—at least as far as Wall Street was concerned—as the stock rose from 5 to 80 in this span and then just kept on climbing; by 1969 it was over 110.

Those investors who believed Leasco could keep it up and purchased shares had their capital gains, but Steinberg never forgot his initial study of IBM's power. He knew the situation could not last and took steps to make certain Leasco would be around after the contest was over.

Steinberg did this by using his inflated stock (called "Chinese money" by the conglomerateurs of the period) to purchase other assets for his company. Into Leasco came Carter Auto Transport & Service, Documation, and Fox Computer Services. But the big move took place in 1968, when he took over Reliance Insurance—which had revenues of over $350 million a year, and which was ten times Leasco's size—through a tender offer of Leasco convertible debentures. Nor was this the end of Steinberg's ambitions; he next attempted to purchase Pergamon Press, and failed. Then he went after the $9 billion Chemical Bank, again with Leasco stock, and again he failed. Nonetheless, Steinberg came out of the binge as head of a major insurance firm—with a leasing company on the side.

Thus he was well positioned when the counterattack began. It started to roll in 1968, when IBM brought out the last of the 360s. Two years later, IBM introduced the first of its new generation, the 370s, which shuffled the deck once again. The firm simultaneously lowered leasing charges and boosted purchase prices, thus reversing the policy initiated two years earlier. These actions led to a sharp decline in direct sales and leases of 360s, as customers lined up for their improved, more cost-efficient 370s, returning the 360s to the leasing companies. Those companies that tried purchasing and leasing 370s had to go against the tough new IBM rates. The combination was disastrous for them.

Vainly did the lessors fight back. They initially attempted to match reduction with reduction, but only wound up in a bath of red ink. Moreover, due to the introduction of the new series, the old 360s dropped sharply in price, in most cases far below what the lessors were carrying them for on their books. Massive writedowns were required, causing earnings to vanish, stock to decline, and companies to face illiquidity. And to further complicate the situation, IBM offered generous trade-ins on the 360s—but only to its own customers, certainly not to those who had obtained their machines from the leasing companies.

It was a lesson few users would forget.

Some of the lessors went under, others merged in their struggles to survive, and a few attempted to fight IBM by purchasing and then leasing plug–compatible machines (more on this later). But the most effective means of striking back was not on the business front but rather in the courts. During the 1960s and 1970s, IBM was embroiled in a constant war on the antitrust battleground, the ramifications of which offer insight into what once appeared a fruitful way for rivals to gain advantage, but which no longer is so. But before turning to the courtroom struggles and their significance, it is necessary to understand the principles that guide IBM—to uncover the reality behind the reputation.

IV

IBM: THE MYSTIQUE

Images

Redoubtable ITT Chairman Harold Geneen was cruising through one of his factories when he paused at a workbench, picked up an electronic device, and asked how much it listed for. When told the price was $90, he put it down, shook his head, and said, "If the initials on that gizmo were IBM instead of ITT we could get $200."

The IBM salesmen who were gathered for breakfast at a regional convention looked at one another warily, and finally one asked, "Any of you guys get a note under your door last night?" It turned out all did. The message was from a rival computer company, inviting them, one and all, to come over for a chat regarding a switch in employment.

At an elegant restaurant, two businessmen were swapping stories over martinis. "Did you hear the one about the fellow who, on his wedding night, discovered that his twice previously married bride was a virgin?" began one of them. "He asked how that could be, and she replied that her first husband was elderly and died of excitement before he could consummate the marriage. The second was an IBM salesman, and all he would do was sit on the bed and tell her how wonderful it was going to be."

The Japanese management professor was addressing a group of visiting Detroit auto executives in a seminar room at the University of Tokyo. "Americans come here regularly to discover our so-called secrets, but there really aren't any," he intoned. "Simply put, after the war we decided to emulate the best in the country that conquered us, which meant learning America's management skills. So we sent our people to the United States to study your methods—especially those at IBM. The secrets of our success can be unearthed as easily at Armonk as at Toyota City."

Yet another tale regarding IBM: When Chairman Frank Cary stepped down as CEO everyone moved up a notch and the company hired a new office boy.

No corporation has been the subject of more anecdotes and jokes than IBM, and like the ones above, each offers hints as to the corporation's reputation and mystique. Simply stated, IBM—or Big Blue, the Armonk Monster, and the several other names by which it is known—is generally conceded to be among the best managed and smoothest operating firms in the world, one in which everything goes off without a hitch and where the sales personnel and scientists are clear-eyed, firm of jaw, trim of figure, and awesomely intelligent and well-informed.

It is also perceived as a juggernaut capable of crushing any rival, the quintessential transnational, whose employees seem more loyal to the firm than to their governments (during one Arab-Israeli War, trainees from Israel and its Arab neighbors attended IBM seminars without a hitch), and a firm more deeply rich in talent than the 1927 Yankees.

While much of this is exaggerated (even the IBM annual report contains pictures of overweight, balding, and bearded men with some—*pace* Tom Watson, Sr.—in sports shirts, alongside women who clearly are middle-aged and less than glamorous), there is an important kernel of truth to the image. IBM *is* a highly efficient, powerful, well-managed and dedicated entity. The Japanese *do* study it carefully and approach its turf cautiously. By virtually any measure, IBM is the most successful American corporation in all of the nation's history. It inspires sentiments of awe, reverence, fear, hate, distrust, and skepticism. Competitors, from small electronics firms to AT&T, have hired away top executives in the hope of emulating Big Blue. Yet with all of this attention there is little understanding of what it was and is that makes IBM tick, the key to its operations and continuing prosperity.

Board meetings take on the appearance of Presidential Cabinet reunions: Defense Secretary Harold Brown, Transportation Secretary William Coleman, HEW Secretary Patricia Harris, HUD Secretary Carla Hills, Attorney General Nicholas Katzenbach, and Secretary of State Cyrus Vance all served on the IBM board, as does William Scranton, former Governor of Pennsylvania and former Ambassador to the United Nations. When Nancy Teeters stepped down as the first woman governor of the Federal Reserve Board in

1984, it came as no surprise when she joined IBM as director of its economics department.

IBM's successes are the result of historical forces hatched and incubated under Watson Sr., brought to fruition by Tom Jr., who led the corporation from 1952 until 1971, and hewed to by Tom Jr.'s successors: T. Vincent Learson, Frank Cary, John Opel, and John Akers. There have been five organizing principles which have guided the corporation from the time it was a manufacturer and purveyor of census machines, cheese slicers and time clocks, to now, when it is generally conceded to be the world's premier manufacturing-service-research corporation.

The IBM Spirit

The most obvious principle guiding IBM is that of *élan,* which is to say that early on Watson Sr. recognized the need to inculcate dedication and zeal in his employees. As he put it, "You cannot be a success in any business without believing that it is the greatest business in the world," adding that "You have to put your heart in the business and the business in your heart."

Watson pioneered in what a later generation would call "humane management." At a time when most factories were dreary places, and, in general, management tried to squeeze every bit of work out of laborers, who, in turn, felt little loyalty to their firms, Watson set out to make IBM a pleasant place to be. In the 1930s, when managements had their choice of workers in a period of double-digit unemployment, Watson abolished the post of foreman in his plants, and he replaced foremen with managers, who were instructed to treat workers with respect, to listen to ideas relating to productivity, and to encourage innovation. Workers on a line would gather together to share ideas and initiate changes. Three decades later, when American management philosophers discovered "quality circles" in Japanese factories, they rushed to encourage others to accept the concept. But it had been invented not in Japan, but at IBM, as were so many other concepts that only now are becoming popular. For example, Watson developed the principle of continuous learning, bringing teachers into the company to assist workers in improving their lot. Today IBM spends more than a billion dollars annually in training and retraining. This too is not a technique borrowed from the Japanese, but rather is home-grown.

By so acting, Watson sought to enlist the entire family of his employees in laboring for the corporate good, and he provided workers with free insurance and benefits packages long before they were demanded by unions. Watson pioneered in paying assembly-line workers weekly salaries rather than hourly wages. During World War II, the wives of IBMers in the armed services received a minimum of $25 a week up to a maximum of $1,000 a year, based upon their husband's prewar salary.

One final bit of IBM legend: In the 1930s a group of executives about to be promoted into middle management were invited, with their spouses, to a week at an elegant country club, where the men spent most of their time in conferences and the wives played tennis, went to fashion shows, and were waited on with great care and attention. After the week was over, there was the usual farewell talk to the new managers by Watson Sr., while his wife, Jeannette, spoke to the women. "Have you enjoyed yourselves?" she asked, knowing, of course, they had. "Well, if you want to live this way," she announced, "your husbands will have to exceed their quotas."

The entire affair had been for the benefit of the wives, not the newly minted managers—each of whom now had a company booster awaiting him each night asking how things went. Apocryphal? Perhaps. But to the IBMers of the time the story rang true.

A number of executives and scientists leave IBM each year to start their own enterprises, to take top posts elsewhere in the industry and in other fields, or quite simply because they can't take the strain. Few are fired; at IBM below-par performance usually results in a person being frozen in place or shifted to one of the corporation's several "Siberias," divisions generally recognized within IBM as such, where they might serve a term and then return to other posts later on, or perhaps try to find a better position in another firm.

In speaking with those who've left IBM—for any reason—one is struck by the admiration for Big Blue that remains. A manager admitted to "withdrawal symptoms" and a nagging belief that his new employer could never match IBM in sophistication. A salesman was shocked to learn that some of his old clients thought him foolish to "take a step down" when actually his responsibilities and salary had doubled. Many talk of missing the challenge, though quite a few did not call it that, referring instead to the "constant pressure." One of those salesmen, Ross Perot, who left IBM in order to found Automatic Data Processing, said being at the Armonk Monster was comparable to serving a hitch in the Marines. Which is to say, you know the demands are severe, but you also realize you are operating at the top of your form, convinced you are better than anyone else.

This can be explained by one of the more unusual and seldom-noted facts regarding IBM: It is one of the rare large American industrial corporations founded more than a half century ago that has, for the most part, expanded internally and not through acquisition. In the early 1920s, Watson took over such small firms as Ticketograph, Peirce Accounting Machine, and Electromatic Typewriter, but there would be only a few minor buyouts thereafter. Not until 1984, when it purchased Rolm, did IBM attempt to enter the acquisitions game. IBM's tradition of internal expansion enabled the firm to maintain the corporate identity in all of its divisions. And even though Rolm had revenues of more than half a billion dollars, this was dwarfed by IBM's better than $44 billion, and Rolm's workforce of 7,000 was quite small compared with IBM's close to 400,000. This homogeneous culture is another reason for the company's sublime self-confidence and belief that it can perform most tasks better than others.

IBM will purchase large interests in firms when this is called for; in addition to the Rolm buyout it has a substantial interest in Intel (semiconductors and related devices) and MCI (telecommunications). There are arrangements to sell equipment turned out by others under the IBM logo, such as is taking place with Epson in printers and several Japanese copier manufacturers. The PC is cobbled together of parts purchased from a wide variety of suppliers, while the PCjr was even being manufactured at a plant owned and operated by Teledyne.

None of these developments seems to have disturbed the IBM *élan*. Rolm CEO M. Kenneth Oshman revealed that IBM purchased his firm with some reluctance. As will be seen, IBM initially took an equity position in the firm the previous year with the hope of coordinating efforts and little more. Soon the two companies were stepping on each other's toes. "We found ourselves paying less attention to the market and more to what IBM wanted Rolm to do and what Rolm wanted IBM to do," said Oshman, which led him to approach Armonk with the takeover recommendation, one which wouldn't have been made had he thought his independence would have been threatened. As Oshman put it, "Paul Rizzo [IBM's vice president and chief of development] assured me that we wouldn't have 10,000 IBM folks" descend upon Rolm.

The promise was kept; each firm went its own way, with Armonk limiting its control to fiscal matters. This was done as much for its own sake as for Rolm's. IBM has no intention of altering what it considers a winning combination at Rolm—or of watering down its own—with a closer merger.

The Slant Toward Sales

An orientation toward *sales* is the second principle. Go through Control Data and Digital Equipment, and some of the newer firms like Cray, and you'll come out realizing that these are established and run by scientists and technicians who turn out machines and software much admired by their scientific clients. As has been seen, the CDC established by Bill Norris considered this a virtue, in somewhat the same fashion as discount houses of the 1950s boasted of their plain pipe racks, which kept costs down. Later on, however, when CDC started selling medium-sized and small computers to business users, Norris beefed up his sales force and consciously imitated IBM's methods.

Digital Equipment, which in the beginning concentrated on small machines to be sold to sophisticated customers, was noted more for the amount of computing it offered for a dollar than sales and service. Then, when DEC entered the micro field with its office and home machines, potential buyers discovered what others long knew: many DECs were superior to their IBM counterparts, but the sales force was ragged and service poor. Those interested in DEC Rainbows often railed against the treatment they received from the company, and often wound up with IBM PCs. A call to an IBM salesman or office will bring rapid action, if not always desired results.

Until quite recently, IBM was considered a salesman-oriented firm. Each of the corporation's CEOs began in sales. Even now, young men and women entering the corporation with management or finance in mind know that at one time or another they should put in some time in sales if they hope to wind up in the executive suite. In the past, a superior performance in sales had been more likely to be rewarded with promotions and perks than one in any other area. In recent years, scientists and financial people have gained more prominence, but the salesperson still rules at IBM. John Akers, who took over as CEO in early 1985, started in sales, and so did his predecessors—John Opel, Frank Cary, T. Vincent Learson, and Tom Watson, Jr.

The sales orientation, of course, began with Watson Sr., who, as noted, in the 1930s admitted that "collecting salesmen is my hobby," and later on said that if he had it all to do over, he would rather have been sales manager than CEO of IBM. As with so many other Watson beliefs, his feeling for sales originated in his experiences rather than in any deep philosophical reflection.

Watson had started out as a traveling salesman for a variety of products, at a time when that breed was considered not quite respectable. Older Americans may still recall jokes about traveling salesmen that portrayed them as boozing, wenching, unscrupulous individuals out to cheat customers; and the "drummer" was always identifiable by his flashy clothes. Watson would have none of this. His salesmen would be impeccably and conservatively dressed, and altogether respectable and sober. "I want my IBM salesmen to be people to whom their wives and children can look up to," he told Peter Drucker in 1939. "I don't want their mothers to feel that they have to apologize for them or have to dissimulate when they are being asked what their son is doing."

At the time, Drucker assumed Watson was thinking of his own mother when he spoke. And he might have added that he saw something of himself in the newly arrived salesmen. Nothing pleased Watson more in the early days than presenting flip-card presentations and "chalk talks" to his sales force. Watson stressed the importance of sincerity, integrity, and loyalty. In addition to being well groomed his salesmen had to be in good physical shape, always alert, and well-informed. One should consider this when observing the squadrons of Japanese executives in *their* dark suits and white shirts. They are right out of the IBM book.

And, as already indicated, the IBM salesman was sober; rumor has it that Watson Sr. became revolted by intoxication because his father or an uncle drank heavily. Prior to World War I, the central Computing-Tabulating-Recording installation in Endicott was close by the Endicott Johnson Shoe Company, well-known for its progressive labor relations and headed by a management that regularly organized picnics for the workers at which the liquor flowed freely. The E-J people would deliberately direct their buggies— beer casks strapped to the sides—by the CTR facility and sing a song, the key line being, "While You're Thinking, We'll be Drinking."

IBMers had songs of their own, and the company songbook was given to all new employees, who were made to understand that conclaves would open with a song or two, like this early one, to the tune of "On the Trail of the Lonesome Pine," which hailed one of C-T-R's founders.

> Herman Hollorith is a man of honor,
> What he has done is beyond compare.
> To the wide world he has been the donor
> Of an invention very rare.
> His praises we all gladly sing,
> His results make him outclass a king.
> Facts from factors he has made a business,
> May the years good things to him bring.

Another celebrated the virtues of Harvard Professor Theodore Brown, who regularly journeyed to the firm's Endicott, New York, facilities to offer instruction in statistics:

> Theodore H. Brown, Professor so well-known,
> At our schools in Endicott his seeds are sown
> In the minds of students of the IBM,
> Helping them develop into greater men.

And of course there were ditties in honor of the CEO.

> Our voices swell in admiration;
> Of T. J. Watson proudly sing;
> He'll ever be our inspiration;
> To him our voices loudly ring.

> Mr. Watson is the man we're working for
> He's leader of the CTR,
> He's the fairest, squarest man we know;
> Sincere and true.
> He has shown us how to play the game
> And how to make the dough.

Which, after all, was what it was all about. Successful IBMers had healthy paychecks to go along with that *esprit*. It must have seemed the best of all possible worlds in that period. The sentiment continues to the present.

A good deal of this—the omnipresence of the bold, black word "Think" on the walls and desks, the songbook, the attitude toward liquor, and even the IBM uniform—consisting of a Brooks Brothers black pin-stripe suit, white shirt, and subdued tie—was phased out gradually when Watson Jr. took over. The stern image and reality changed, and it did even more so under Learson, Cary, Opel, and now Akers. The uniform remains pretty much the same for sales personnel, but the scientists' and technicians' clothes can reflect any life style they choose. Moreover, IBM has pioneered in the hiring and promotion of minorities, beginning when this was not popular or even accepted. And this, too, was a reform introduced by Tom Jr.

The High Tech Firm

Tom had become interested in electronics while in the Air Force and gently nudged IBM into a position of technological leadership. This isn't to suggest the elder Watson held back on research and development, but rather that more often than not he heeded the prompting of his salesmen, who reported the need on the part of customers for new equipment. Watson Sr. was willing to experiment for its own sake, but always with an eye toward the future products discussed by his beloved salesmen. In contrast, Watson Jr. often developed prototypes for which there was not any present need and on more than one occasion went up blind alleys. This *devotion to high technology* is the third of the organizing principles.

Nothing riles top IBMers more than charges that while the company has a superb service and sales operation it lags behind technologically. Armonk is quick to point out the many technological breakthroughs it has made and the fact that IBM spends more on research and development than the rest of the industry combined. Yet, surprisingly, the allegation persists in the face of recent events regarding the Japanese challenge in the field of information processing.

American industries from textiles to steel to autos to copiers have been savaged by the Japanese. But not computers, despite regular predictions that the Japanese are coming.

We shall see how IBM has been able to keep the likes of Hitachi and Fujitsu at bay, while IBM Japan, with estimated 1984 revenues well in excess of $2.3 billion and profits of approximately $270 million, was then the second-largest data processing firm in the home islands, and would be first were it not for aggressive intervention by the government, which provides the local industry with the kind of assistance that is outlawed in the United States.

Indeed, not only hasn't Big Blue been favored by government, but as will shortly be explored, it has been subjected to more antitrust actions than any other firm, the most recent ending two years ago, when litigation begun in the closing days of the Johnson Administration ended with IBM's total vindication. The removal of this threat has liberated the people at Armonk. Always a tough competitor, IBM now is a positive terror in the marketplace. While under the antitrust cloud, the firm almost feared victories, knowing they would revive charges of unfair competition. This fear is now gone. IBM will compete more vigorously than before, since victories no longer will be considered a reason for antitrust action. And few doubt this will lead to future impressive victories and technological breakthroughs quickly translated into new products. As CEO John Opel put it, "We intend to be the product leaders, to stay in the forefront of the industry in technology, reliability, quality, and value across the entire product line." This is another way of saying that IBM will do all in its power to dominate every aspect of the information processing industry.

Thus, IBM combines superb salesmanship with advanced technology. But this presents a paradox. If this is so, how can one explain why Big Blue's introduction of new products often lags behind others in the industries it dominates?

The Evolving Role of Service

The answer is the fourth of the organizing principles that guide IBM. Other manufacturers are equally concerned with *service,* but at IBM it is almost a fetish. Hand-holding used to be the norm during the Watson Sr. and Jr. eras, but this is changing. Sophisticated users of large computers don't need it as much as earlier, while buyers of PCs don't require the services of half a dozen technicians and trainers. In its place is a renewed dedication to quality control and concentration on cost/benefit ratios.

In 1984, IBM put it clearly and bluntly: the firm intends to be "the low-cost producer, the low-cost seller, the low-cost servicer, the low-cost administrator." During the 1950s and 1960s, IBM won customers by standing prepared to perform any amount of hand-holding the client needed or wanted. This is still the case today, but hot lines, well-written manuals, and trouble-free hardware and software fill much of this need.

Still, IBM clings to and tries to perpetuate itself as the firm that cares for customers around the clock, no matter what the cost. One of the firm's early computer clients tells of the time when at a cocktail party he mentioned, casually, that something was wrong with his 700, and he planned to get in touch with the company about it. The next morning he found an IBM technical team at his door prepared to do any amount of debugging needed. "How did you know?" the amazed executive asked? He never did find out, and to this day is half-convinced IBM has extrasensory perception.

Orientation Toward Risk

In spite of their huge R & D commitment, few credit the firm with a willingness to innovate and experiment, and in the past it has permitted others to do so while waiting on the sidelines. Yet IBM stands prepared to abandon highly profitable products if and when a better technology comes along, thus engaging in what Joseph Schumpeter so vividly described as "creative destruction." "Our competition is getting stiffer all the time," wrote Tom Watson in 1961. "We need constantly to spend large sums in research and development of new products which will not produce revenue for some years to come. Without funds for this vital expense, competition would eventually surpass us." At its Armonk headquarters is the functional equivalent of an in-house graduate school of business, and other centers are to be found elsewhere on the globe. The firm is quite free with research grants to large universities, which is one reason why it is usually among the top three firms in obtaining patents.

When asked for examples of the firm's willingness to accept risks, top executives invariably point to the 360 campaign, indicating that it is a classic example of IBM's commitment to the need to regularly throw the dice, accepting the possibility of defeat as a price to bear. After coming up with the successful 600 and 700 series in the early 1950s, IBM wagered its computer future on machines designed to be a hundred times faster than the top-of-the-line 704.

This gamble was the beginning of a messy affair that opened in 1954 when the Atomic Energy Commission's Livermore Laboratory asked for bids on a giant machine. IBM entered the race but lost to Univac, whose LARC (Livermore Advanced Research Computer) turned out to be a dud. In the process IBM gained experience, and when the AEC's Los Alamos Laboratory went to the market for another large machine, IBM was there with a refurbished design and won the contract with a bid of $3.5 million. Out of this came the STRETCH (not an acronym this time, but rather as in "stretching the state of computer development art"). IBM set out to develop what was intended to be its initial second generation machine. STRETCH would require research, development, and production charges of from $25 million to $40 million, depending upon which of several sources are to be accepted, substantial for the period though not deemed unusual since IBM expected to market STRETCH to commercial clients and so recoup the expenses.

The machine was a marketing failure. IBM had expected to sell versions for $13.5 million a copy, and when no one seemed interested, the price was slashed to $8 million. Eventually eight systems were taken, and by the end of the decade, it was considered a fiasco. "Our greatest mistake in STRETCH," said Watson, "is that we walked up to the plate and pointed to the left field stands. When we swung, it was not a homer but a hard drive to the outfield."

Yet IBM did gain valuable experience on the project, both in terms of technology and how to organize management of so large a project. Indeed, several years later Watson concluded that "A better fifty million we never spent, but it took us seven or eight years to find that out."

The reason was the drive on the part of others to supercomputers—what STRETCH was supposed to be—which caught IBM unaware.

Risk: The 360

In August 1963, Bill Norris announced the 6600, sending reverberations through IBM. Emmanuel Piore, IBM's chief scientist, long had been troubled by the rise of CDC, and he warned T. Vincent Learson, then in charge of engineering, manufacture, and sales, of the growing nexus between scientific and commercial computers.

> There are a number of scientific institutions in the world that require very large installations to make progress on their problems. These institutions are easily identified; they work very closely together; they all have the point of view that their current installations will be too small for, or lack the power to solve, their future problems. These future problems also can be identified. Thus when these institutions obtain a computer complex, they are always projecting what will come next that is more powerful. These same scientific institutions set the tone for industrial users requiring a large amount of scientific computation.

That was Piore's way of saying that IBM no longer could afford to ignore the market for giant computers. It also meant that the demand for them had reached that critical mass, that the highly successful 700s and their successors, the 7000s, would have to be superseded by new models, and (inferentially, at least) that the greatest threat in the future might be from Control Data, not Univac, GE, RCA, or the other familiar large, well-established, giants. When he heard of the 6600, Tom Watson became livid; on August 28 he sent the following memo to Learson and other section heads:

> Last week CDC had a press conference during which they officially announced their 6600 system. I understand that in the laboratory developing this system there are only 34 people, "including the janitor." Of these, 14 are engineers and 4 are programmers, and only one person has a Ph.D., a relatively junior programmer. To the outsider, the laboratory appeared to be cost conscious, hard working, and highly motivated. Contrasting this modest effort with our

own vast development activities, I fail to understand why we have lost our industry leadership position by letting someone else offer the world's most powerful computer. At Jenny Lake [the location of a forthcoming management conference] I think top priority should be given to a discussion as to what we are doing wrong and how we should go about changing it immediately.

Nor was CDC's the only challenge. At the same time, GE was talking about its new series, which would cost about the same as the 1401 but be 40 percent faster, and in December that company announced the 400 and 600 series, designed to meet IBM almost across the board. The RCA 3301, to be offered soon after, was 50 percent more powerful than the 7010 and slightly lower than it in price. Then there were the Philco 212, the Univac 1107, and the CDC 3600, all of which were taking sales from IBM.

Fortress Armonk was under siege as never before, from several quarters simultaneously, and while no one seriously doubted IBM would remain the industry's leader, there was some question as to just how much market share it could retain.

IBM's response wasn't hastily prepared or improvised. In 1962, it had organized a group known as the SPREAD Committee to consider a New Product Line (NPL) to be erected on third generation technology, to replace the 7000 series. Now, with the seven dwarfs nipping at its heels, IBM came up with a barrage. As Watson Jr. recalled:

Finally we awoke and began to act. We took one of our most competent operating executives with a reputation for fearlessness [T. Vincent Learson] and put him in charge of all phases of the development of an IBM large-scale electronic computer. He and we were successful. How did we come from behind? First, we had enough cash to carry loads of engineering, research and production, which were heavy. Second, we had a sales force which enabled us to tailor our machine very closely to the market. Finally, and most important— we had good company morale. All concerned realized that this was a mutual challenge to us as an industry leader. We had to respond with all that we had to win, and we did.

On April 7, 1964 (a key date in computer history), Watson Jr. announced the System 360 program, an ambitious attempt to create an entire series of computers. These machines were truly revolutionary in design and purpose. Based upon the then-new microchip technology, they all but removed the former differentiation that existed between the so-called "business" and "scientific" computers, thus, as the designation indicated, the 360 covered all points on the compass.

The 360s would employ new software, meaning that they would make obsolete overnight the much-vaunted 7000s and highly successful 1400 series that they were to replace, causing no little distress on the part of the much-prized customer base. Within the industry the 360 series was known as "IBM's $5 billion gamble." Bob Evans, one of the managers of the project, told a reporter, "We call this project, 'You bet your company.'"

As it turned out, the 360s were a huge success, ushering in a new family of computers and erasing the traumas associated with the STRETCH failure. Before 360, IBM had shipped some 11,000 computers; toward the end of the series run, the total came to 35,000. In 1966, Learson wrote: "Observers have characterized the 360 decision as perhaps the biggest in its impact on a company ever made in American industry—far bigger even than Boeing's decision to go into jets, bigger than Ford's decision to build several million Mustangs," and indicated his agreement, concluding, "IBM has certainly not been the same since, and never will be again." Learson was referring to corporate direction, but he might also have been alluding to the penchant to accept risks, and if so, it was there earlier, as witness the STRETCH episode.

More than any other move, the 360s provided the corporation with new credibility in the area of technology and enhanced IBM's reputation in marketing. The 360s also signaled IBM's willingness to move boldly to assure leadership. IBM's next generation of CEOs—Learson, Cary, and Opel—were said to have won their battle stars during this campaign, which finally annealed Watson Jr.'s reputation for business acumen.

The Succession

Frank Cary took command in 1973, after a two-year Learson interregnum, and he was to be CEO for eight years. A tough, scholarly individual, with a steely glance and a reputation for impatience with excuses, Cary authorized the development of the next generation of giant computers, but more important, perhaps, he led the way into new fields.

There were several miscalculations, too, which was one of the prices of taking risks. A joint venture with MCA in DiscoVision failed, and in late 1983 IBM abandoned its daring venture into Josephson Junctions, a radically new semiconductor, which if successful might have made most others obsolete.

The financial loss on this venture is estimated to have been $220 million. This loss followed one of the firm's rare management errors. In 1977, at a time when the corporation had cash items and equivalents of almost $6 billion, it earmarked $1 billion for the repurchase of its own shares; this decision was based on a miscalculation of future capital requirements. Two years later, IBM was obliged to return to the capital markets to float that much in debt, while the price of its common shares had fallen. This has to be considered the corporation's most serious financial blunder. Both Cary and IBM survived.

On the other hand, it was Cary who initiated the massive facilities expansion program that provided the backdrop for today's major leaps forward, gave the go-ahead for the PC, and made the big move into telecommunications as a partner with Aetna Life & Casualty and Comsat, thus positioning IBM for the forthcoming clash with the new AT&T. Like Watson Jr., he proved willing to abandon successful technologies when at their peaks and enter new fields with major investments.

The move into personal computers, arguably IBM's most important new venture since the 360 period, was expected to add some $2 billion in revenues to the corporation's bottom line in 1985. The initial decisions were made by Cary, but Opel carried on afterwards. Under Cary's aegis, IBM welcomed independent software writers, making them partners in the new venture. Within a year the PC software rivaled that of Apple, until then the industry leader in this department, and today the PC is setting the industry standard. Under Cary, IBM has become a more open, accessible corporation. The signal has been given, though not many have accepted it: the drawbridge is down at Armonk, and IBM is ready to talk, up to a certain point, that is, but the point is far more advanced than it had been until the dawning of the Opel era.

For example, a journalist wishing information in prior regimes might have been given short shrift; nowadays he will receive a hearing, if nothing more. Independent vendors know IBM has established a process whereby they can submit software for consideration. IBMers wanting to go off on their own realize that to do so today doesn't necessarily mean cutting the umbilical; Big Blue hopes to retain relationships with such individuals, to the point of giving them preferential treatment. The firm that once rejected joint ventures now eagerly seeks them out. We shall see in future chapters how Cary was willing to alter the image in even more drastic fashion, to the point where sandaled, bearded young men in what another generation would have called "hippie attire" occupy positions of no little importance in the IBM universe.

Under Cary there were equally startling alterations in marketing. In the past, IBM catered to managers and ignored the general public. A decade ago a student wanting to purchase an IBM Selectric would have had difficulty contacting a salesman, for at that time Armonk was geared to service business clients and perhaps the occasional small-town dentist or doctor, but certainly not to a high-school sophomore wanting a typewriter with which to bang out term papers. Now, the PC is available to just such individuals.

At one time, Big Blue's symbol was that aforementioned eager salesman; today the PC ads feature a Charlie Chaplin double. If this isn't creative destruction nothing is.

Who or what can stop IBM? As we have seen, six of the seven dwarfs failed in their frontal assaults, and the seventh—Control Data—succeeded by utilizing an oblique approach. Later on we will see how IBM managed to thwart these firms and their European counterparts, and then go on to discuss reasons the Japanese information processing industry probably won't duplicate the triumphs of that country's automobile and consumer electronic exporters. But here will be explored the techniques IBM employed and is still using against one of its more formidable American challenges, namely the brigades of antitrust attorneys arrayed against it by rivals and the Justice Department.

V

IBM: THE POLITIQUE

The Antitrust Battlefield

Imagine if you will a lively fly, buzzing around the room, alighting in one place for a while, only to take off soon after. You want to get rid of it, but alas, the only weapon at hand is a howitzer operated by a three-man crew, and none of them are truly adept. So no sooner does the gun get into place than the fly is off to some other location, and the piece must be re-aimed. Occasionally it is fired, often missing, but sometime smashing the insect. But even when it kills the fly, the operation often causes more damage than benefits received.

Such is one view of antitrust in the United States. The howitzer is antitrust doctrine, and the crew the Justice Department's Anti-Trust Division, a goodly number of whose lawyers appear to be displaying themselves to the corporate clients they are prosecuting, believing perhaps that a good showing in court may lead to an offer from a Wall Street firm. Some, to be sure, are skillful and intelligent, and believe in their work. But others are not deemed sufficiently sharp or bright for such bids, and these are the ones who often have to spar with some of the most clever, most experienced, and, of course, most expensive attorneys in the land.

Go to any of the nation's best law schools and speak with those who are in the top 10 percent. Ask where they hope to wind up, and most will indicate a yearning for a career in lower Manhattan, defending important corporate clients in their antitrust actions. These actions can last for a decade and more, and victory in one of these contests often results in a partnership and the customary perks. Then speak with the professors and ask their opinion of the "dark and murky ground of antitrust law," as it sometimes is characterized. There are those who will argue effectively that more harm than good has been done the country by close to a century of litigation, that the United States would have been better off had some of the major cases resulting in penalties to corporations been lost rather than won.

Other countries, including Japan, have antitrust laws on their books, but in none has the government so often acted to penalize success, or considered bigness an evil in itself. Nor is there any other country where disgruntled competitors can so easily bring actions against industry leaders. The United States is one of the few nations where major corporations are troubled by being *too* dominant in their field.

That the United States has more lawyers per capita than anywhere else is almost a cliché. At times it appears that a goodly percentage of them are employed either defending or attacking IBM. During one particularly tempestuous period a *New Yorker* cartoon showed two men looking out a picture window at a long line of black limousines. "Someone important must have died," one said, and the other replied, "No, it's just the IBM lawyers going out to lunch."

Cravath, Swaine & Moore is an old, distinguished law firm, whose origins go back to 1819; William Seward, Secretary of State under Abraham Lincoln and the man who purchased Alaska from the Russians, was an early partner. By virtue of defending IBM against the Anti-Trust Division and against several of Big Blue's competitors who brought private actions, Tom Barr is one of its most valued partners today. His chief contact at IBM is Nicholas deB. Katzenbach, a senior vice-president and the firm's general counsel. Prior to coming to IBM Katzenbach had an even more prominent employer; he was Lyndon Johnson's first attorney general. Johnson's second attorney general, Ramsey Clark, filed one of the more important antitrust actions against IBM, just prior to leaving office.

Barr had been defending IBM for a decade when the government case began, so it hardly was a new experience. Nor was it unusual for the corporation, which rarely has been free of litigation initiated either from government or competitors. While able to thwart all of those that contested its industry domination in the marketplace, IBM often was obliged to meet them in the courts as well. And always, there was the specter of the Justice Department, readying that antitrust ax whenever it seemed IBM was becoming a trifle too successful. Yet the firm has proven at least as rough a competitor in the courts as anywhere else. It has lost only one case that went through the appeals procedures, and that prior to World War II. But it has settled several key contests through consent decrees and out-of-court arrangements.

The courtroom, of course, is a tricky theater of operations, and, in common with most powerful firms, IBM much prefers to settle product decisions through market forces. As will be seen, however, it now appears that both domestic and foreign competitors will no longer find so ready an ally in the Justice Department and the courts as previously had been the case.

Watson Sr. and the Law: Background

Even so, it can be argued that without antitrust IBM might have fallen by the wayside, and indeed might never have existed. As has been noted, Watson Sr. was a defendant in an antitrust action while an executive under John Patterson at NCR, one begun in 1910, and in 1913 he and his codefendants were found guilty. The decision was reversed two years later, by which time Watson had been fired and was working at C-T-R. Throughout the appeal process he insisted upon his innocence, writing to one friend, "I do not feel humiliated. My conscience is clear." The thought would be paraphrased by all of his successors.

IBM was not troubled by antitrust actions during its first two decades for two obvious reasons: it was not the dominant force in the data processing industry, and there was no recognizable industry as such. Rather, IBM was considered a subspecies of a category known as "industrial machinery," into which it and the likes of Underwood Elliot Fisher, which was about the same size, were cast. But in 1933, the Justice Department filed an antitrust action against the firm, charging that IBM's practice of leasing and refusing to sell its equipment and obliging users to purchase its cards rather than those of competitors constituted a violation of trade.

The practice of leasing, which would serve IBM so well in the computer age, had its origins in the nature of the census machines it marketed, and indeed in the federal government's attitude toward these machines in the late nineteenth century. The census, of course, occurred every ten years, and the government saw no reason to purchase machines that would sit idle several years at a clip. So Hollorith arranged for their leases and did the same with commercial clients. Watson merely continued the practice.

As for the cards, Hollorith's major competitor, Powers, had entered into an agreement whereby he was permitted to produce the same kind of cards utilized in the 1890 census. After RemRand acquired Powers, the contract was renegotiated, with IBM to produce cards for Powers's machines. Since there were no others in the field, IBM became the sole card supplier. The government recognized this, and so named RemRand as a co-conspirator in the case. But Jim Rand agreed to accept the court's finding, and RemRand was effectively severed from the case, so IBM was the sole defendant.

As it turned out, the government decided to stress the matter of card sales rather than leasing in its presentation, and in 1936 it won a hollow victory: thenceforth IBM could not oblige customers to purchase cards. A meaningless decision, for then, as before, no other company wanted to enter the field, given the low prices IBM had established for its cards. And so ended IBM's first encounter with the Anti-Trust Division.

The next clash occurred in 1952, when once again IBM was charged with monopolizing the tabulator market as well as that for cards, and the Anti-Trust Division demanded it sell as well as lease its machines. Watson Sr. was irate, charging that a vindictive Harry Truman had initiated the case to punish him for supporting Dwight Eisenhower in the election that year. With some justification, he noted that in almost all of its product areas IBM had rivals, and that it was dominant in only several narrow categories of tabulators. Even so, it hadn't the kind of clout in tabulators that Underwood enjoyed in office typewriters, a much larger and more important category. Why single out IBM, he asked, and ignore Underwood?

While sharing his father's feelings, Tom Watson, Jr., thought the relatively unimportant. It was one of those instances in which the howitzer was being aimed at the fly. Tabulators? Punch cards? Didn't the government realize that these were technologies that soon would be obsolete? In his view, forcing IBM to share the tabulator market was akin to obliging a local horseshoe manufacturer to accept competition when autos were replacing the horse and buggy.

Leasing was another matter. IBM's lease terms were so attractive that clients preferred leasing to outright purchase, and, in any event, were accustomed to the practice. Moreover they associated IBM's by-now traditionally excellent service with the fact that the manufacturer, not the user, owned the machines. And if customers turned out to prefer purchase to leasing, it might not be all that bad, since Watson Jr. realized IBM's financial resources would be strained by the switch to computers, and the cash could come in handy. Finally, why make a fuss about it? Users of telephones didn't reflect that they couldn't purchase them, but in effect were really "leasing" the instruments from the local telephone company. Watson Jr. clearly believed the issues involved not worth the company's bother. For these reasons he urged his father to agree to a consent decree under which IBM would admit no wrongdoing but would accept terms.

Watson Sr. still smarted from the 1910 experience, and he was at first adamantly opposed. Eventually he weakened, especially when IBM's lawyers observed that with a settlement the firm would at last know just what the ground rules for competition would be in the coming electronic age—for a while, that is. Almost with tears in his eyes he gave in, and when Tom Watson went to the courthouse in 1956 to sign the decree he found waiting for him there a typically terse note from his father:

> 100 percent
> Confidence
> Appreciation
> Admiration
>
>   Love
>   Dad

The experience sharpened IBM's awareness both of governmental power and the possibilities of losing in the courts what it might win in the market-place. "After that 1956 consent decree we had serious thoughts about how to run IBM," Watson Jr. told a writer a quarter of a century later. "We had a team of lawyers lecture on antitrust law and what we couldn't do, and we had signoffs on that. I think it's sad that the government is not more specific in laws governing business." There was little he could do about it, however, but to stand prepared to meet government and private suits with batteries of attorneys. A sign of the times during the next few years was a running joke in Armonk: while Watson Sr. had stressed sales and his son technology, the next chairman would have to be someone from the Supreme Court, lured to IBM in its age of litigation.

Bill Norris Lays Down the Law

IBM's first important antitrust encounter was with Control Data, and the trouble begain in the late 1960s, when both firms were marketing their large machines to a variety of commercial clients, and their salesmen literally bumped into one another coming and going at customers' corporate offices. By then Bill Norris had become convinced that during the immediate future the industry would be selling and leasing huge, complex systems to users who would need a great deal of support, and he was busily transforming his original technically based operation into one that could provide these services. What he was doing, in effect, was creating his own version of IBM's Service Bureau.

Under terms of the 1956 consent decree, IBM would sell its machines to the wholly owned Service Bureau Corporation that, as the name indicated, then offered a wide variety of services to clients. Service Bureau wasn't a particularly exciting place. In fact, it was known at the time as IBM's Siberia, the place to which executives who didn't measure up were sent as an admonition to perform better; assignment there was an indication that the employee's career was in jeopardy, and once transferred, the IBMer often prepared his résumé in anticipation of having to move on. With all of this, however, it was a well run and successful operation.

In order to compete with the Service Bureau, Norris opened data centers where clients could sign on for whatever their computing needs happened to be. These installations, the first of which was opened in 1963, utilized a variety of machines tied together through a system of telephone lines known as CYBERNET. In 1968, Control Data acquired C-E-I-R and Pacific Technical Analysts, both involved with customer services. There were more than a score of other acquisitions, most of technical firms whose products could be used in the CDC machines.

In 1973, Norris conceded that he was taking advantage of the high price/earnings multiple afforded his company during the bull market to exchange paper for assets. "Our high P/E ratio stock, or Chinese money as we often termed it, was used to acquire companies with complementary technology, products, services, and markets."

All with an eye toward matching IBM in as many areas as possible. Or, if possible, to surpass it. For example, Norris recognized the allure of leasing, and in 1966 worked out a deal with Steinberg whereby Leasco would purchase and lease CDC equipment. But this was only a prelude to the major move, which came two years later, when CDC took over the $3.5 billion Commercial Credit for almost three-quarters of a billion dollars in stock; it did this so as to better finance computer leasing. Now Control Data's customers could arrange their leases through an operation as prestigious as IBM's.

Yet with all of this IBM not only maintained its lead but actually improved upon it. Indeed, CDC's revenues leveled off in 1966, a year during which there were several top-level resignations, technical problems with the 6600s, and Norris seemed to have lost control over costs. The following year was even worse, as the company went from earnings of $7.9 million to a loss of close to $2 million, and the price of the common stock was halved.

What was particularly galling was the fact that in 1964 IBM had announced a new machine, the 360/90, which was to be matched against the 6600 and offer more power for the dollar. This forced Norris to cut prices and offer augmented machines of his own, upon which IBM would lower prices and boost power. The trouble was that at the time the 90s existed only on paper, and for a while there was doubt such a machine ever would be created and marketed. But the mere hint that IBM was readying a new offering sufficed to warn customers away from rival machines, especially after the initial 360 introductions.

Eventually fifteen of the 90s were manufactured, and even then four were used internally at IBM. But in 1965, when Norris asked his lawyers to investigate the possibility of a private antitrust suit against IBM, he believed that IBM was, as Norris later claimed, selling "paper machines and phantom computers which were not yet in production, and as to which it had no reasonable basis for believing that production or delivery could be accomplished within the time periods specified" in order to steal customers from his 6600.

CDC approached the Justice Department's Anti-Trust Division with some of Norris's ideas and evidence, but was put off. Although the government was monitoring IBM, a distressed, distraught, and angered Norris decided to go ahead on his own, and in December 1968 filed a private antitrust suit alleging violations of the 1956 consent decree, suggesting inferentially that the Justice Department had been lax in its oversight. In addition, CDC charged IBM with encouraging its salesmen to use unfair tactics "by imposing unreasonable quotas and severe penalties for the loss of orders, customers, or prospects." For which it asked treble damages and "the dissolution . . . or divestiture" of assets by IBM to prevent future abuses.

Thus began a sixteen-year government battle that will be studied in the law schools for years. It was the legal equivalent of the 360 campaign in that it provided IBM with another benchmark, and it ended with IBM's industry position solidified.

IBM denied all allegations, adding they would be refuted in a "vigorous and complete" fashion. Everyone involved with the matter realized this was an important case, for the entire industry was watching. If Control Data were repulsed few would dare to take on IBM in the courts, since the costs would be prohibitive. But should Norris obtain any kind of victory many other firms would line up, like sharks tearing at the side of a wounded whale once they've tasted blood.

They didn't have long to wait. Ramsey Clark, who succeeded Katzenbach as attorney general, filed his complaint on January 17, 1969, indicating the Justice Department would seek a breakup of the firm. Norris was beside himself with glee, remarking that had he known this was coming CDC would have been content to remain on the sidelines. As it was, he was looking forward to the two-front battle.

As might have been predicted, Ramsey Clark's action prompted a slew of private suits, from the likes of Greyhound Computer, Telex, Data Processing Financial & General, Memorex, and so on. Some, like the Justice Department and CDC cases, were of consequence, but most were by way of annoyances. In essence, these firms were getting on line, hoping that one of the majors would breach IBM's defenses, and then they could obtain what amounted to a free ride in parallel actions or, at the very least, wind up with a substantial out-of-court settlement.

As with so many such matters, a good deal depended upon the skills of the rival attorneys and their teams and the proclivities of the judge hearing the case. CDC couldn't match Cravath in terms of reputation, but it did put together a respectable team headed by Oppenheimer, Hodgson, Brown, Wolff & Leach, a leading St. Paul, Minnesota, partnership led by John Robertson. Most important, the case was to be heard in the federal district court in Minnesota by Judge Phillip Neville, who happened to be a friend of Robertson's. Recognizing this, Tom Barr attempted to seek a change of venue, which Neville denied.

As was customary, IBM and CDC exchanged huge amounts of documents during the discovery phase, and teams of lawyers and paralegals pored over them, seeking evidence of wrongdoing. CDC went through 25 to 40 million documents, while the IBM team perused 120 million CDC documents. Each made copies of the other's papers and constructed indexes; later on, a bystander remarked that he wasn't sure who would lose the case, but Xerox surely would be one of the major winners, since so much copying was required.

Within the paper mountain poured on it, the CDC team claimed to have found evidence to substantiate its claims. More significant, however, was

104

what the Cravath staff uncovered in the CDC papers: nothing less than a plan to create an international consortium with the United Kingdom's International Computers and France's Compagnie Internationale pour l'Informatique to undercut IBM, and then fix prices and allocate market share. This discovery in hand, IBM filed a countersuit charging CDC with conspiring to monopolize the large computer industry and in addition misusing Commer cial Credit's assets.

CDC might have been permitted to claim that the documents IBM had uncovered were of a privileged nature and so couldn't be used in the case, but Robertson realized IBM would appeal and more than likely win. So he was amenable to an out-of-court settlement, which was arrived at in January 1973.

Under the terms of the settlement, IBM agreed to sell CDC its Service Bureau Corporation for what amounted to net asset value. As has been noted, this was no great loss; it meant that IBM would have to find some other way to provide customers with services and another Siberia for underperforming executives. IBM also would pay CDC $101 million, $15 million of which specifically was earmarked for CDC's legal expenses. It would appear, from this, that IBM had settled in the firm belief it was losing the case. But then it was learned that under the terms of the agreement CDC would destroy the data base constructed from the IBM documents. And so it was done, as Cravath's lawyers watched.

The Telex Scare

The Justice Department was furious. It had been counting on using that base in its own case and now had been foiled. Immediately, the government filed a motion either to have IBM reconstruct the base at its own cost or pay $4 million for a new one, but was rebuffed. It mattered little to IBM if the motion had been accepted, since at that time it wanted a delay, and it obtained one. In addition, the government's case was far more important than the CDC matter, and Barr was happy to have CDC behind him so he could switch to the main arena. So the apparent defeat in *CDC vs. IBM* was, in reality, a victory for the defendant.

IBM did experience a defeat—and a surprising one at that—in the Telex case. An Oklahoma-based manufacturer of hearing aids and audiometers that had expanded into tape recorders, Telex had been one of the first firms to recognize that a market existed for peripheral equipment and components that could be used with IBM mainframes. This recognition was the initial stage in what will be seen as the plug-compatible challenge, part of the most successful attack upon Fortress Armonk. The firm's major product was tape drives, which were compatible with those of the 360s and lower in price. In order to counter Telex's product, IBM developed the SMASH program, which involved slashing prices and developing an aggressive new sales program. The Telex case was filed in January 1972, before SMASH had swung into action. The company charged IBM with unfair practices and asked damages of $239 million, which if trebled, under law, would come to $717 million, and soon after asked but was denied a restraining order for SMASH.

Telex had at least a couple of things going for it. In the first place, the case was to be tried in Tulsa, and so the company was on its own turf. Then, too, the Telex attorney, Floyd Walker, was a local whose folksy manner masked a shrewd litigator. Telex was risking relatively little on legal fees, too, should it lose, for in accordance with quite common practice Walker had agreed to take the case for a small retainer and a share of the damages should the decision go his way.

Finally, by associating himself with the CDC litigation, Walker was able to use the index created by that company and not only save himself time but a great deal of money. It was in the files, for example, that he learned of the SMASH campaign, which led to an amended complaint in January 1973, after the CDC-IBM agreement. Sensing the tide was going his way, Walker now asked for $416 million in damages.

It was then Telex had its first setback. Walker moved to have the case separated from that of CDC, but before anything could be done the index was destroyed and with it the evidence he needed. As did the government, Walker demanded the index be reconstructed, but Federal Judge A. Sherman Christianson rejected this, noting that by failing to pay for a portion of the original costs Telex had indicated a belief that the index was of inconsequential importance.

Tom Barr now attacked. In going through the Telex documents in the discovery phase, he had learned of thefts of IBM secrets, a practice, which as will be seen, wasn't all that unusual on the part of IBM's competitors. Telex had sought out IBM employees, hired them, and then attempted to pick their brains for information on new products. Indeed, several Telex documents indicated that this was company policy, a vital part of its activities. Armed with this evidence, Barr countersued; this was shortly after IBM had won a directed verdict in a similar action brought against it by Greyhound Computer. Barr asked for a directed verdict this time, too, but the judge denied it, and the trial began in April, 1973. The decision was handed down five months later.

Christianson's verdict satisfied no one, but clearly represented a major blow against IBM. He found both companies guilty. In his view, IBM had violated Section 2 of the Clayton Act by attempting to "destroy its plug-compatible-peripheral competition by predatory pricing actions and by market strategy bearing no relationship to technological skill, industry, appropriate foresight, or customer benefit." For this he awarded Telex damages of $352 million. Christianson found that Telex, indeed, had conspired to steal IBM secrets. IBM was to be paid slightly less than $22 million, and, in addition, Telex was to refrain from using certain information and IBM manuals that were in its possession.

To say that Armonk was stunned would be a vast understatement. Telex had won the largest settlement in American legal history, and around Tulsa it was thought Walker's share would come to upward of $60 million. There would be appeals, of course, but the blow was devastating. On Wall Street, IBM common fell 37 points in the next two days, while Telex shares nearly tripled in price.

The Telex decision set off the inevitable flood of similar actions. Lester Kilpatrick of California Computer told a reporter, "I think almost any company in the computer industry has got to be thinking about bringing suit against IBM, even the big mainframe companies," and soon after filed his $350 million action. In addition to Greyhound, others had entered the lists prior to the Christianson award; Data Processing Financial & General, Memorex, Itel, and Advanced Memory Systems had sued in minor actions, to no avail. Now they talked of renewing their cases. Memorex filed for $3 billion; Marshall Industries asked for $108 million; Itel and Potter scouted for law firms and joined the chorus. Applied Data Research, Programmatics, California Computer Products, Forro Precision, Symbolic Control, Hudson General, Saunders Associates—all lined up in what was a terrific season for antitrust attorneys. Considering the Telex decision, who could blame them? Kilpatrick was refreshingly frank when, in replying to a reporter's question as to CalComp's major asset, he said: "It's our lawsuit against IBM."

The situation wasn't as bad as Armonk and Wall Street believed it to be. For one thing, there was the size of the award, almost certain to be lowered on appeal. Then there was Christianson's post-trial actions. On receiving additional information from IBM, he lowered the fine by $100 million and modified injunctions against the company. Did this mean he was uncertain about culpability? And where did he get those numbers? Then came news out of the appeals case, which seemed to be going IBM's way, but few anticipated by just how far.

In January 1975, a three-judge panel on the Tenth Circuit reversed Christianson's opinion, finding that "when evaluated under the Sherman Act and when set in the context of the prevailing court opinions [IBM's actions] do not constitute a violation of law." But Telex's actions were another matter: the Court awarded IBM $17.5 million in damages plus another $1 million punitive award, indicating gross culpability.

Telex didn't have that kind of money—its balance sheet showed less than $1 million in cash and liquid assets—so it had no recourse other than to appeal to the Supreme Court or to obtain some kind of settlement from IBM. The firm did both; an appeal was filed and discussions with IBM commenced. In the end, both companies agreed to drop their claims, and Telex was off the hook. And fortunately so, for soon after the Supreme Court indicated it would have refused to hear the Telex appeal.

Now the others fell into line; most simply dropped their cases. Soon all that remained was the government's action, which toward the end of the decade was turning into a fiasco.

The United States vs. IBM

The case was tried before David Edelstein, chief judge of the Federal Court for the Southern District of New York, in Manhattan. To begin with, Edelstein appeared irate over the destruction of the Control Data papers and seemed to form an instant dislike for Barr, who at times appeared to be lecturing the judge on points of law. On one occasion the government introduced as a witness a former industry official who had been sued by the SEC for fraud, who testified that IBM had engaged in predatory pricing. When Barr attempted to raise the fraud issue in his cross examination the government's attorney protested such matters were irrelevant, and surprisingly, Edelstein upheld the objection. Then Barr tried to introduce as evidence an article from *The Wall Street Journal,* of which he had a photocopy. Another objection, and Edelstein ordered Barr to produce the original, which he did after a hurried search. On other occasions, Barr and other IBM attorneys felt that Edelstein bullied them, and there were times when the judge would leave the bench while depositions were being taken, as the lawyers droned on.

Witness after witness—including several of those who testified for the government—complained about Edelstein's conduct, and all the while Barr held back, letting what he felt to be abuses pile up. Then he let go, filing a motion in 1979 to have Edelstein disqualified on the basis of "personal, extrajudicial bias and prejudice against IBM and in favor of plaintiff," observing among other things that he had interrupted IBM witnesses no fewer than 1,200 times, and while sustaining government objections 60 percent of the time did so for Cravath attorneys less than 3 percent.

Edelstein seemed furious, and as expected denied the motion, upon which Barr took the matter to the Court of Appeals, which also denied it. But Edelstein's conduct now seemed to Barr and his colleagues to become even more antagonistic than they had previously felt it to be. Some observers felt that by June 1981, when both sides rested their cases, it appeared that the Supreme Court would have little choice but to find for IBM on appeal.

This seemed to be the government's point of view as well. Its case was looking worse all the time. The industry had evolved rapidly since 1969; the 360s and 370s, which had dominated the markets, had been consigned to the scrap heaps. New developments abounded; fully two-thirds of the corporate witnesses charging that IBM had acted to restrain entry hadn't existed when Ramsey Clark filed his charges, thus giving the lie to the allegation. When the case opened such important players as Amdahl and Apple hadn't come into existence, and the Japanese Challenge wasn't a factor in industry planning. The case began when Lyndon Johnson was in the White House and continued through the Nixon, Ford, and Carter years as one of the longer litigations in antitrust history. To return to the analogy, the fly had buzzed around and then out of the house, and still the gunners struggled to line it up in their sights.

In 1981, President Reagan named William Baxter to head the Anti-Trust Division, knowing he had little stomach for the case. Almost at once negotiations to settle it commenced. The case was dropped in January of the following year, with the government conceding that its case was "without merit." It seemed quite evident that IBM was now freed from constraints and could be expected to promote itself more vigorously in the information processing arena than ever before. As for the domestic competition, little was expected from the BUNCH, and the plug-compatible assault was in the process of being thrown back.

But two other challenges were on the horizon. The first was the settlement—within days—of the long American Telephone & Telegraph antitrust case, under terms that would break up the giant, leaving a "new

AT&T" free to compete with IBM in data processing and distribution. The other was from "Japan Inc.," which by the early 1980s had given unmistakable signs of its intention to become a factor not only in the American market, but to contest IBM throughout the world.

The irony of all of this went unrecognized. Europe, the continent on which the Industrial Revolution began, wasn't to be a major player in this most recent round. The reason for this was obvious and, to the Japanese at least, should have been more than a trifle disturbing. In the early 1980s, IBM World Trade was the largest factor in the European information processing industry.

AND ABROAD

VI

IBM CONQUERS EUROPE

Dividing the Empire

It might have been a scene out of Shakespeare or some other classical dramatist. The old monarch, weary and knowing the end is near, calls in his two sons and divides the empire between them, the elder taking the central core, the younger the provinces.

That such a scene took place in medieval Europe is quite likely, but this one was played out on Manhattan Island in late 1949, when Watson Sr. bestowed IBM upon Watson Jr., with the understanding that he would conduct business in the United States, while Arthur K. Watson, more commonly known as Dick, was given the rest of the globe under the rubric of IBM World Trade.

That isn't to suggest the empire was separated into two autonomous units; both were under the control of the IBM board, of which Tom would be chairman while Dick was given a variety of titles—president of World Trade in 1954 and its chairman in 1963, vice chairman of the parent three years later, to name three—but none so exalted. Still, he did have a measure of autonomy, and this was what the old man had in mind. Watson Sr. knew that while his sons got along well enough with one another, Dick needed independence if he was ever to come out from under Tom's shadow.

It was at the same time Dick's good fortune and misfortune to have Tom as a brother. The problem was that Tom was so picture-book perfect, the kind of individual difficult to match. Tom was strikingly handsome; Dick was darker,

113

slighter, and quite ordinary in appearance. Tom had been a golden boy in his youth, enamored with flying and yachting, caring little about academic matters, and yet he was on his way to becoming a superlative businessman. Dick was something of a grind at college, where he showed talents in foreign languages and became conversant in Spanish, French, German, and Russian. But he also was a heavy drinker, whose moods shifted abruptly from high humor to despair.

Had Tom not gone into business he might have wound up a pilot; Dick's interests were in writing and similar solitary activities. Where Tom had friends, Dick attracted cronies. And so it went.

Both served in the Army during World War II; Tom ending up as a lieutenant colonel in the Air Corps, Dick a major in Ordnance, serving much of the time in a dusty Manila depot. Yet he liked the Army and would have remained in the service had not his father urged him to return home to complete his education. This he did, graduating from Yale in 1947, upon which there was the expected entry into the IBM training program.

Dick performed well enough—but nowhere near as well as Tom. Always he was the second son, who, for example, had to abandon thoughts of a honeymoon in order to accompany his parents to Europe on a plant tour during which he acted as interpreter. Later on Dick, who was a Republican, became the U.S. ambassador to France, leaving the post under a cloud due to inebriation; Tom, a Democrat, served as U.S. ambassador to the U.S.S.R., and did so in an outstanding fashion, after which he became something of an elder statesman. Dick died young, in a fall at his home; the rumors were that he had been drinking at the time.

Yet with all of Dick's problems, World Trade grew faster than domestic IBM and in time was at least as important if not more so. Though there always were those who claimed Dick deserved little credit for this showing, saying that it resulted from superb direction from home, an excellent staff, and the ineptness of the foreign competition. And in the end, Dick's departure from IBM was quiet, and today he is one of the firm's forgotten men. During the first half of his life he was subordinate his father; during the second Dick played second fiddle to Tom.

The World Trade that Dick inherited had nine factories turning out machines and twice as many for cards, with offices or representatives in more than fifty countries. With all of this, revenues came to a mere $6.3 million—out of a total for the corporation of $119 million. In part this was due to the fact that rebuilding was the order of the day in 1949, and like so many other

American firms IBM was still busy picking up the pieces and trying to put things together again.

The world market hadn't been important prior to World War II, even though entry into it predated the origins of C-T-R. The old International Time did business in Europe at the turn of the century, while Computing Scale had a facility in Canada in 1902. Herman Hollorith's census machines had been used by a variety of European and Asian governments, and in 1908 he granted the independent British Tabulating Machinery Company (BTM) a nonexclusive license to manufacture his devices throughout the Empire except for Canada.

During the interwar period, IBM erected plants in Germany, France, and the United Kingdom and established agencies in Latin America and parts of Asia. One of these was in Japan; in 1935 "Watson Business Machines," as IBM was then known, not only fabricated machines in Japan from kits but also owned a factory there from which cards for the entire Asian market were produced and marketed. There were agencies in the Dutch East Indies ("Watson Java") and Australia as well. Still, revenues were minor, peaking at $1.6 million in 1935, with cards accounting for the bulk of this.

The foreign affiliates were far more independent than those of the vast majority of American concerns. "[They] must be run by natives of their own country and not by expatriates," Watson Sr. had insisted upon before World War II. "They must be accepted as members of their own society. And they must be able to attract the best people their own country produces. Yet they have to have the same objectives, the same values, the same vision of the world as the parent company. And this means that their management people and their professional people share a common view of the company, of the products, and of their own direction and purpose." These objectives were set in place and implemented during the interwar period.

As was the case with other American firms, IBM's assets on the European continent and in Japan were seized during World War II, but they continued to operate, turning out cards and parts for the Axis powers, while the major plants in the United Kingdom expanded, to the point where the BTM Hammersmith facility rivaled those in Poughkeepsie in size and importance. By 1945, international revenues reached $2 million (out of a corporate total of $142 million), most of which came out of the U.K. Thus, IBM was deemed a minor European player, this at a time when Powers (Hollorith's old nemesis) was almost a household name there and British Tabulating a major force.

The BTM Blunder

Consider the Watson view as of 1949. World Trade was in place with Dick about to come on board. Foreign revenues had more than tripled during the preceding four years, with most of the money coming from the British Commonwealth. The London facility not only was booming but its research and development in many areas, including computers, were superb, often in advance of such work being done in the United States. Given this situation, Watson Sr. moved to renegotiate the 1908 agreement with BTM.

The deal sounded attractive enough. Watson offered BTM *gratis* a nonexclusive license on all existing IBM products in addition to selected ones then in the process of being developed, in return for which the old arrangement would be abrogated and IBM would have the right to sell or lease products through its own organization. Watson proposed to establish a new entity, IBM United Kingdom Ltd., which interestingly enough wasn't to be fully owned. So as to convince the British that it was a native rather than American-dominated firm, they would be permitted to purchase shares, which Watson expected would be listed on the London Exchange and traded there.

What this meant was that a Commonwealth customer wanting an IBM machine then in service would have the choice of buying or leasing it from IBM U.K. or BTM, this arrangement to last until the newer products came to market. By accepting, BTM would be able to forego the relatively small licensing fees it then was remitting to the United States. Rejection would mean that the British firm would retain the right to manufacture, sell, and lease all present and future IBM hardware and software throughout the Commonwealth and be privy to all research and development as well.

Had BTM taken this latter path, it might be the second-largest business machine company in the world today—after IBM. But in what must be considered one of the worst blunders in business history, BTM accepted Watson's offer.

Why? The answer seems clear enough. BTM's board looked at IBM and saw a relatively small factor in the market, whose punches, sorters, and tabulators were interesting enough, but hardly unique. Besides, no matter how many shares of IBM U.K. were owned locally, the firm would still be considered under the control of Yankees. Why would any patriotic British, South African, Australian, or any other Commonwealth firm lease a machine from IBM when it could have the same one at the same price from good, old, familiar BTM?

IBM U.K. was the centerpiece of the overseas operations when, on January 1, 1950, IBM transferred all of its foreign assets to IBM World Trade in exchange for 100 percent of its stock. At the time, the U.K. operation existed mostly on paper; anyone wanting a machine in early 1950 went to BTM, which had been handling them for more than four decades. How could IBM crack that market?

The answer would become familiar to many foreigners during the next quarter of a century. In the first place, IBM U.K. wasn't to be an American company; rather, it was to be staffed by Britons, in keeping with the interwar IBM practice, when the French operations were headed by Baron Christian de Waldner; Valentim Boucas, a native of Rio de Janiero, ran the Brazilian shop; and these men had counterparts throughout Europe and Latin America. Having IBM U.K. listed on the London Exchange also helped; many customers took machines not knowing they were turned out by an American company, so complete was the identification.

IBM erected factories, but until they were ready imported some machines from the United States. Gradually, the rental base expanded, as the British IBMers, imbued with the Watson *élan* and offering more attractive rates than their BTM counterparts, obtained placements. In place of the somewhat lackadaisical servicing to which BTM customers had become accustomed, was the highly efficient IBM brand so common in the United States. Then, in the early 1950s, as computers replaced calculators, IBM completely stole the march on BTM. By 1959, when IBM bought out the minority interest, making IBM U.K. a wholly owned World Trade subsidiary, the victory was complete. That year IBM U.K. was the leading business machine company in that country.

Notwithstanding all of this, the United Kingdom had several formidable and respected computer companies, such as Elliott Automation and International Computers & Tabulators, many of whose basic patents helped create the industry; indeed, during the 1960s and 1970s, the United Kingdom was a net exporter of computer technology second only to the United States. Moreover, the Americans were effectively barred from a major market by what was known as "the 25 percent rule," meaning that government agencies had to purchase British-made machines if they were less than 25 percent more expensive than their American counterparts.

The trouble was that while the domestic industry was formidable in the aggregate, no single firm possessed the clout to go against IBM. Still, the British firms did well in the domestic market during the second generation phase, and together accounted for a majority of placements in every year of the 1960s.

In part this was due to several mergers that narrowed the field considerably but resulted in larger and stronger companies. By 1967, the major player was International Computers and Tabulators (the new name for BTM after a 1959 merger with Powers-Samas Accounting Machine and the subsequent acquisition of EMI's business machine operations and that of Ferranti). ICT had approximately 40 percent of the market—about the same as IBM U.K.—and after 1966 its computer business turned profits, in large part due to government aid and favoritism. In fact, it was the major European computer exporter, sending a third of its products overseas, mostly to the continent.

Another factor in the U.K. market was English Electric, a licensee for RCA (which hoped to use it to gain entry into that market). English Electric, too, had several important mergers, with such as Lyons Electronic Office (LEO), and Marconi, and Elliott Automation. While hardly as large and vital as BTM, the company was the third largest domestic concern.

In 1968 ICT, English Electric, and Plessey (a components manufacturer) came together to form International Computers Ltd. (ICL), which in terms of placements and resources was second to IBM on a worldwide basis. ICL had able sales and service departments, several of the most advanced laboratories in the industry, and in the System 4 a series that could meet their IBM counterparts on a cost basis. For a while it did quite well; in 1969 ICL installed 409 machines against World Trade's 156. At the time, it appeared that the U.K. had come up with a formula to challenge the leader. This formula was a combination of a unified national effort supported by contracts from government agencies, with additional funding available if and when needed.

Britons rejoiced at what they took to be a sign of technological success—but industry observers noted that while IBM U.K.'s profits and margins were expanding, ICL was becoming a consistent money loser. The firm was a government-subsidized attempt to remain a player in this major new industry. As such, it was a technological success, but a business failure. ICL soon developed problems with several of its new products and this, combined with a strong pound sterling, which harmed exports, led to a decline. By 1981, at which time ICL required a $200 million government loan, it fell behind IBM in its national market. This was followed by an infusion of new managerial talent, including some from the United States, and licensing and related arrangements with other computer manufacturers. ICL returned to profitability, but not to its leading role. By then, it was evident that the British bid had failed.

International Marriages

At that, the Britons did better than any other European nation. Even after the continent had recovered from the war it failed to make a deep impression in the market. It wasn't that Europe lacked business machine companies of its own, nor were IBM's successes preordained. Rather, the Europeans not only failed to invade the United States but couldn't even prevent World Trade from seizing their domestic markets.

The European firms, which included France's Machines Bull, Germany's Siemens and AEG, Philips of the Netherlands, and the United Kingdom's International Computers Ltd. among others, all possessed excellent research facilities, but came late to the game with limited products, inadequate sales and service facilities, and most important, none had the financial muscle to last it out against IBM. Finally, in those pre-Common Market years each guarded its frontiers jealously against potential competitors. Had the French, Germans, British, and Dutch united to create a consortium, they might have been able to withstand World Trade—which, after all, was a kind of consortium of its own. As it was they failed to do so and, by the 1970s, when the political climate had changed and something of this sort might have been done, it was too late.

How might the individual nations have preserved their markets at that time? Through tariffs and quotas? Hardly likely since IBM's factories in all western European countries provided the machines that were sold there. The IBM computer sold in Stuttgart was manufactured by IBM Deutschland, located in that city, and the story was the same in other countries. Might IBM have been stopped by massive government aid to national companies? Perhaps so, but would it have been worth the cost? Moreover, if IBM could offer a better machine at a lower price, were not the users being penalized unduly? And might not there be repercussions if IBM could convince Washington it was being discriminated against? A better way out might have been to find common ground with others who were suffering from IBM's market domination—namely, the Seven Dwarfs.

All of IBM's American competitors had international ambitions but lacked the wherewithal to realize them. Moreover, none had IBM's experience in selling abroad or the sales and service organizations required to make such a push. But given national partners that had the blessings of their governments, they might have overcome IBM's long lead and apparently infinite resources.

Consider the case of Machines Bull, a company that offered a wide line of products, but usually not devices as advanced in design as their IBM counterparts. Bull had the strong backing of President Charles de Gaulle, anxious for a showcase for French technology. Its Gamma series, introduced in 1960, were second generation machines that came to market a year after IBM had placed its initial 7000s, and at a time when the 1401 had been announced and orders for it were being taken.

Recognizing its lag, Bull entered into a cross-licensing agreement with RCA, under which Bull personnel would be trained in the United States and RCA would be permitted to sell its machines in France without having to go through the bother of obtaining special import licenses. Thus Bull gained exposure to RCA technology, then considered among the most advanced in the industry, while the American firm congratulated itself on gaining admission to the continental market without having to develop factories and train personnel in France.

For a while everything seemed to be working out well. Disregarding costs, the French government placed large orders for Gammas and pressured corporations in that country to do the same. De Gaulle had his own version of the Japanese Ministry of International Trade and Industry policies; he subsidized the industry, established a marketing agency to seek placements through Europe, attempted to sell Gammas behind the Iron Curtain, and made a stab at the Latin American market. Industry talk in 1962 had it that Bull soon would offer its machines in the United States as well.

It was only then that World Trade responded. Prices of the 7000 and 1400 series were slashed, forcing Bull to do the same, after which further price cutting was conducted. Due to economies of scale IBM could afford to do so. Not Bull, which was a relatively small company. Revenues for the French company expanded, but each placement resulted in a loss, so that in 1963 the firm posted a $25 million deficit, which was a prelude to effective bankruptcy the following year, and in 1965 IBM France established new sales and profit records.

In 1966, de Gaulle had set into motion a scheme known as *Plan Calcul,* under which was created what he termed an "all-French" Compagnie Internationale pour l'Informatique et les Techniques Electroniques de Controle (Cii), a loosely organized holding company to engage in the creation of large computers that would be used in France's military effort and space program.

Into Cii went virtually all of the nation's computer companies; the idea was to have a unified effort similar to that of the U.K. with ICL. Naturally, it was hoped that Cii would also provide computers for civilian business as well, computers which perhaps would have export capabilities.

General Electric found this situation intriguing. It will be recalled that the company entertained high hopes for its GE 100 series and was seeking overseas partners to join in manufacture and marketing. The strategy had the virtue of being both simple and direct: by uniting with like-minded Europeans, GE might create almost overnight a patchwork but viable version of World Trade.

Why didn't the firm go it alone? Alone of all the would-be challengers General Electric possessed both the financial resources and the technological expertise to offer stiff competition to IBM, though these were spread over a far wider range of products. It realized, however, that given the nature of the industry and the accelerated growth anticipated over the next decade or so, to begin at scratch would be to lose precious time.

GE started out with a cross-licensing and technology-sharing agreement with Cii. Having this foothold in France, it was simple enough to approach Bull, which was a member of the group, with an offer of cooperation and then loans. After more than $100 million had been poured into Bull, the two firms formed a subsidiary, Bull-General Electric, which became the *de facto* inheritor of the Bull business, for which in 1964 GE paid $43 million. Now GE's European computer sales force was united with Bull's, and with de Gaulle's blessings, GE computers were imported into France under favorable tariff arrangements.

In this fashion, Bull was reborn. Placements grew to the point where Bull-GE had approximately one-third of the French market, placing it second to World Trade. Despite this, the binational firm continued to lose money, while World Trade's profits expanded annually. In 1967, GE paid an additional $30 million to obtain additional equity, which boosted its share of the binational company to two-thirds. The red ink continued.

A similar situation developed in Italy whose largest and best-known computer company, Olivetti, was undergoing troubles similar to those that had plagued Bull. A wide-ranging business machine company rather than one specializing in computers, Olivetti had a reputation for excellent styling and ingenious computer designs but, sad to say, one marred by poor product performance, late deliveries, and indifferent sales and service. The firm was best known for its typewriters, and in the 1950s it sallied forth to the United

States to take over the moribund Underwood operation, whose manuals had fallen before competition from IBM's electrics. Olivetti electrified the line, primarily by manufacturing its Italian models in the American plant and selling them as Underwoods. The company enjoyed some success in this venture, and while never challenging IBM's leadership, bid fair to replace Remington as the runner-up in the field.

Around this time, Olivetti made its foray into computers, coming out with the Elia line in 1961. It was the Bull story all over again. The machines sold well enough in Italy due to government intervention, but they were in third slot in Europe, behind World Trade and Univac, with Bull a close fourth. After two years of diverting much-needed funds from typewriters, Olivetti threw in the sponge, and like Bull, found an eager suitor in GE, which purchased the computer business for $20 million.

Following the French pattern, General Electric formed Olivetti-GE, which soon surpassed Univac and took a distant second behind World Trade. It, too, was a money-loser, however. Still, GE had hopes. By 1965 it was producing machines in France and Italy as well as the United States, and the international entity seemed to be shaping up. Attempts to obtain similar arrangements with Philips in the Netherlands and Saab in Sweden failed, however, (Philips had a tie-in with RCA and Saab with Honeywell) and GE had to find smaller, less prestigious partners elsewhere in Europe. For example, there was a partial ownership of De La Rue Bull Machines, Bull's operation in the U.K., and a 10 percent ownership of Germany's Allgemeine Elektrizitäts-Gesellschaft (AEG).

General Electric's "confederation strategy" was strikingly unlike IBM World Trade's more unitary approach, with GE hoping its strategy would provide the strengths of diversity and appeal to national pride. Such wasn't the case. Coordination was poor, there were overlaps and gaps in product lines, and despite bursts of strength at Bull-GE the experiment failed, ending when GE left the business. As for Olivetti, it sought other partners and found one in Philips and—eventually, in the mid-1980s—with AT&T, which as will be seen was preparing to become a major player in the game.

But back to the 1960s. Toward the end of that decade, at a time when IBM Domestic had around 70 percent of its market, World Trade subsidiaries accounted for 75 percent of France's large computers, 80 percent of Italy's, half of those in the U.K., 40 percent of Japanese placements (by value, however, 60 percent), and, most intriguingly, 73 percent of all large German mainframes carried the IBM logo.

The German Puzzle

The Germans, who had so much success with automobiles and machine tools, might have been considered a likely challenger to IBM. The country had several strong electronics companies, a respected scientific community, and by the early 1960s sufficient capital to enter the field. Yet most of the German firms held back.

Siemens was the exception. One of Germany's largest corporations, it committed $150 million to computers in the early 1960s, but even so had less than 10 percent of that country's placements at mid-decade. Siemens then acquired a majority interest in Zuse, a smallish German company engaged in sophisticated work in process control computers, hoping to supplement and invigorate its own efforts. Siemens was the largest domestic company, but it was far behind IBM Deutschland at the end of the decade. In 1983, a year during which IBM shipped 700 large systems bringing in revenues of $3.5 billion, which was 55 percent of the market, Siemens's comparable figures were 112 systems, and $392 million in revenues, which amounted to 9 percent of European placements, with most of these in Germany. This was enough to make Siemens the largest continental computer manufacturer, but it was hardly a standing one might have expected of the top German firm a decade or so earlier. Yet Siemens was a puzzling company. Generally known as one of Germany's most astute exporters, Siemens didn't try to send its machines to the United States at a time when due to Volkswagen that country's wares were deemed high quality and well-priced.

AEG was another German giant, with even more experience in the international arena, and it, too, might have made an important move into computers; as it was, the AEG commitment, through its Telefunken subsidiary, was smaller than Siemens. As indicated, it worked with RCA and was partially owned by GE; assistance from these firms did it little good.

Only a handful of newcomers, the best known and most successful being Nixdorf, entered the industry, and that firm didn't really get going until the 1970s. The firm began in a fashion familiar to those who witnessed the explosion of new companies in the United States. In 1952, Heinz Nixdorf, an engineer, had a chance to produce a calculator for a large German electric utility when several of the bigger companies showed no interest. With $6,000 in funds, he started work in an abandoned factory cellar. The machine was delivered, the payment made, and Nixdorf was on his way, beginning with components and working his way up to computers.

While doing fairly well in small machines, Nixdorf failed to capitalize upon its investment in Amdahl, which as will be seen pioneered in plug-compatibles, and didn't enter the American market in any important way until 1977, when it purchased Massachusetts-based Entrex Inc., which became Nixdorf Computer and started seeking placements. With some success; by 1980 its American revenues came to $100 million. Still, Nixdorf's worldwide revenues were less than $1 billion, and the firm couldn't be considered an important factor in the field. Not that the firm isn't making the effort today, especially in small computers, in which category it is the leader in the German market—but in third place behind IBM and Olivetti in the European market as a whole. Like the others, Heinz Nixdorf views Big Blue as the target to be brought down. But how to do it?

For a while it appeared that several smaller firms might carve out niches in the market. Triumph-Adler and Kienzle rose only to decline. Diehl, a small firm specializing in minicomputers, made a splash before fading. There were others whose records were pretty much the same.

Why didn't the Germans mount a major offensive in computers? In the light of the experiences of the other European countries one is tempted to say that they might have been shrewd enough to recognize the difficulties in going against IBM, but there may be more to it than that.

In the first place, the Germans lack the kind of central planning and implementation agency found in Japan and even in France, and the U.K. when Labour governments rule. Thus, there was no state entity to put together a firm like ICL. Then too, Siemens and AEG were organized more along the lines of GE than IBM, which is to say they had interests in a wide variety of products, and their leaders recognized that to make the commitment to computers would mean to starve many worthwhile operations.

Beyond all of this, however, is the way the Germans tend to view IBM. To them it isn't really a foreign company. The German-led IBM Deutschland has managed more than any other subsidiary to take on the coloration and tone of its host nation. "They still call us 'Eye Tee Tee,'" complained one of the firm's Stuttgart neighbors, "but when they refer to Big Blue, it's always 'Ee Bay Em,' the German pronunciation." Which is to suggest that Germany didn't need a representative company in this industry; it already had IBM Deutschland, which in the 1960s was the clear leader in that country, with Univac and Bull-GE tied for second place. More to the point, bright young German engineers and scientists were at least as likely to seek employment at IBM Deutschland as with Siemens, so that the American-controlled company was siphoning off some of the best domestic talent, leaving an insufficient amount for the German companies.

Not much was left in Europe for the other American firms. Honeywell had an arrangement with Saab to use Saab's salesforce to market Honeywell's American-manufactured computers in Scandinavia, and later on Honeywell inherited GE's arrangement with Bull. Burroughs generally went it alone, as did NCR, both having a measure of success with banks and insurance companies but not much elsewhere. In time, Digital Equipment did quite well with its smaller machines. But all these companies suffered by virtue of having machines that were incompatible with the IBMs. Most looked longingly at Amdahl, which for a few years appeared to have uncovered the secret of competing with and besting Armonk.

VII

EUROPE AND JAPAN VS. IBM

Amdahl: The Trojan Horse

Within the industry, Gene Amdahl is known as one of the half dozen most original thinkers in the area of computer design. He arrived at IBM in 1952, just as that firm was wetting its feet in the commercial end of the business, and rose swiftly in the scientific hierarchy, to the point where he was entrusted with the design of the 360s and was named director of the company's Advanced Computing Systems Laboratory in Menlo Park, California. Amdahl was there in 1970, designing a supercomputer whose architecture was unlike that of any other IBM machine and which he hoped would become the basis of the company's next series, the fourth generation.

Amdahl's design made the rounds at Armonk, but in the end was rejected as being economically unfeasible. Besides, the 360s were still selling well, and there seemed no reason to disturb the market so soon. Irate and frustrated, Amdahl resigned, but not before arranging for a new place of employment, one where his ideas would never again be rejected and his word would be law. In this world there is only one such place—a company you control. Thus was born the idea of Amdahl Corporation.

Amdahl knew IBM's technology as well as anyone within the firm, and in addition he had a keen sense of how it operated. More to the point, he had given considerable thought to just how IBM might be bested, namely through plug compatibility. Honeywell, which a dozen years earlier had come out with its Liberator, enabling customers to run IBM software on its machines, showed the way, and as has been observed, their idea became a key concept during the late 1960s. Amdahl hoped to refine it by presenting machines that not only were IBM compatible but were technologically superior. For example, in those years the giant computers required expensive plumbing to prevent overheating; Amdahl's machines would be air-cooled. Moreover, they would be faster, more flexible, and substantially less expensive. What he hoped to do was akin to offering what might be compared to a Cadillac without the nameplate but with more modern technology and for several thousand dollars less. Many customers would reject this, preferring the name on the car, but others would find it a bargain. Or at least, this was what Amdahl was banking on.

While he had expertise and a viable plan, Amdahl lacked capital. This came from three sources: Heizer Corporation, a Chicago-based venture capital firm; Nixdorf Computer, the German manufacturer of small machines—and Fujitsu.

Especially Fujitsu. Just as Amdahl was searching for funds in the late 1960s, so Fujitsu wanted American technology. In common with all the other Japanese computer companies, Fujitsu had been monitoring IBM for years, and, knowing of Amdahl's reputation, was eager to work with him. This hardly was a new occurrence; earlier on the Japanese had cultivated former IBMers, hoping to pump them for information. Now Fujitsu had the chance to do the same with one of the top men in the field. But this was not the only path open to the Japanese in their quest for American technology. Knowing little of real value could be obtained from IBM, they opted to try to work deals with the BUNCH.

The European Dilemma

During the 1970s, all of the BUNCH companies had manufacturing as well as sales facilities in Europe, but taken as a group they weren't as large and dominating as World Trade. By then, too, there no longer was talk of a European computer industry capable of challenging IBM. Indeed, no continental rival could compare with the likes of Univac or NCR, while the smaller, more aggressive American firms swept all before them.

All the while, the combinations continued. In 1972 Cii, Philips, and Siemens came together in a collaborative venture known as Unidata, in the hope that in time the three could unite to form a solid continental front against

World Trade. This venture didn't work out; the firms were unable to cooperate effectively to develop what was to have been its major project: large-scale mainframes. In 1975, Cii withdrew to enter into a different alliance, one with Honeywell-Bull, with the new Cii-Honeywell-Bull receiving the same kind of support from the French government that ICL had from the United Kingdom. The next step was "understandings" with Olivetti in the early 1980s. By then, however, such talk counted for little in terms of truly challenging World Trade. ICL continued to lead the pack in its market, though not for long, and only as a result of regular government capital infusions.

Siemens took another tack: cooperation with the Japanese, who were seeking a lever with which to enter the European market, which was second only to the United States as a target for Japan's information processing gear, and one which might be easier to crack.

The first sign of this cooperation with Japan came in the early 1960s, when France attempted to purchase an American supercomputer for its atomic energy program. Bargaining was proceeding with IBM and Control Data when the State Department indicated it wouldn't grant an export license for the machine. Reverberations were felt throughout France (it was one of the reasons de Gaulle established Cii) and the rest of Europe, resulting in domestic programs and also in consideration of consortia with the Japanese. During the next decade, Fujitsu and Hitachi erected some plants in the U.K. and on the continent, while several European firms imported Japanese machines, slapped on their own nameplates, and marketed them as domestically manufactured (this was one of the unnoticed developments of the decade).

In 1978, Fujitsu president Taiyu Kobashi announced an agreement with Siemens to market his firm's large mainframes throughout the Common Market. The Fujitsu machines in question were 370-compatibles, which weren't much different from Amdahls. That the agreement really represented a united effort on the part of Siemens/Fujitsu/Amdahl was obvious—a three nation union to combat World Trade in Europe. But like Unidata and other impressive creations it wasn't all that effective. IBM Deutschland reigned supreme at the end of the decade, with some 60 percent of the German market in hand—as opposed to slightly more than half of that for all of the Common Market. Together with Amdahl and Fujitsu, Siemens had around a quarter of the German placements, but was a poor fifth for the Common Market as a whole, behind IBM, Honeywell, ICL, and Univac.

ICL soon went the same way as Siemens. In 1981 it had become clear that the British entry couldn't halt, much less throw back, IBM in the Common Market, so ICL, too, took the PCM plunge and with the same company: Fujitsu.

In 1983, Fujitsu agreed to sell its FACOM VP-200, advertised as the fastest in production, through ICL and Siemens. In announcing the decision the Japanese stated: "The Fujitsu-ICL-Siemens alliance is aimed at challenging the dominant European position held by Cray," not IBM, indicating the consortium would concentrate on supercomputers and not the entire line. Similarly, Hitachi's arrangement to sell its computers through NASCO, Olivetti, and Germany's BASF was advertised as an attempt on the part of the Japanese firm to expand its market while the Europeans wanted to "fill out their product lines." No one seriously doubted, however, that these were salvos in the developing battle between the Japanese and IBM for the European market.

But the transcontinental consortia didn't work out well. In 1984, ICL became the object of a takeover bid by Standard Telephones & Cables, a large British manufacturer of a wide variety of electronic telecommunications gear, much of which was purchased by the government. STC used to be controlled by International Telephone & Telegraph, and at the time ITT still owned 35 percent of its shares. There was a hue and cry regarding "an American takeover," which signified little. At mid-decade it had become clear that ICL needed a partner, and if it wouldn't be an American, it might have to be a Japanese.

So STC's $552 million bid was accepted. The new entity would have combined revenues of better than $2.6 billion, and was immediately hailed by one British newspaper as "a telecommunications giant, one capable of taking on either IBM or AT&T." But anyone who knew the ICL history and that of others who tried to contest IBM on its own turf knew better.

Nonetheless an intriguing contest was shaping up in Europe. Several of the national companies were uniting with the Japanese to combat IBM, this at a time when Fujitsu, Hitachi, et al. were vending their plug-compatible machines (PCMs) in the United States under American nameplates. In this way, some Europeans sought independence from Big Blue—by flying into the arms of the Japanese. The Japanese connection might yet turn out to be the method whereby the rest of the world tries to meet IBM's competition, though some Europeans gag at the thought.

And what of World Trade? To return to the beginning of the tale, the firm was a huge success in the 1950s and 1960s, growing far more rapidly than the domestic company. In 1956 Domestic posted revenues of $734 million, which ten years later had risen to $2.9 billion; in this same period World Trade's revenues went from $133 million to $1.1 billion, and reported profits of $144 million against Domestic's $333 million. It didn't take much imagination to realize that within less than a decade World Trade would be as large as, if not larger than, the American business. It appeared that what the Japanese were doing with cameras and consumer electronics IBM was achieving in data processing equipment. By then, too, the Japanese were carefully monitoring World Trade, attempting to unravel its secrets, and observing how IBM went about restructuring as needs developed and how IBM integrated World Trade's work with that of Domestic.

Antitrust European Style

There might be yet another way to counter World Trade. For a while the Europeans seemed to entertain the same notions held a decade earlier by Control Data and other American companies, namely that what they couldn't win from IBM in the field, namely market share, might be obtained in the courts. Heinz Nixdorf speaks for most European and Japanese manufacturers in saying, "IBM is a sacred cow that should have been slaughtered years ago." In words sounding for all the world like those of Ramsey Clark and his antitrusters a decade and a half ago, Nixdorf observes, "IBM has 70 percent of the market; . . . that Companies like Amdahl cannot survive [and] that is to the disadvantage of the United States." And of course to foreign companies that, seeking a way to counter the Armonk Giant, turned to antitrust.

During the late 1970s, the European Economic Community investigated IBM's marketing practices, and in 1980 brought an antitrust action against it. The key demand was that the firm provide rivals with technical data for the 370 series—data that would enable those rivals to compete more effectively in the market. Armonk complained that to do so would be tantamount to sharing valuable research information with others, providing them with secrets obtained at great cost. To this the Community responded that without such knowledge other companies might have to devote considerable time to unraveling designs, and so come to market with their plug-compatibles too late to obtain an important market niche. There was considerable merit in both cases.

The implications were important. IBM was arguing that its leadership position had been earned fairly and in accord with the rules, rules which the

EEC was attempting to change in order to reward those with less ability. On its part, the Community was saying, in effect, that IBM's technology had become the industry standard, and to withhold such information unjustly penalized every other manufacturer.

It was at the same time a serious challenge, a concession of IBM's commanding position, and the admission that it was the standard setter, and no confrontation in this area might be expected.

In August 1984, both parties announced a compromise. The EEC dropped most of its more drastic demands, and, in return, IBM agreed to provide some information on the 370s, the agreement to run until 1990. In its communiqué, the EEC stated: "The undertaking will have the effect of substantially improving the position of both users and competitors in the market for System/370 products," while IBM chairman Opel observed, "This undertaking satisfies the Commission's desires and puts the matter behind us without requiring us to make significant changes in how we do business."

Others observed that with the EEC challenge out of the way, for the first time in more than fifteen years—or since the CDC case—IBM was freed from significant antitrust challenges.

The question remained: would the EEC agreement help the Europeans? The answer was an almost unqualified "No." Rather, the settlement might enable some of them to get their plug compatibles to market a few months earlier than had previously been the case and at a somewhat lower cost. Indeed, at first blush it might have appeared that the settlement's major beneficiaries wouldn't be Siemens, ICL, or Cii-Honeywell-Bull, but Amdahl and NASCO, third and seventh respectively in the European market, with one of ten large system placements. Of course, these two were selling Fujitsu and Hitachi machines under their own nameplates, and the agreement meant that those Japanese firms might obtain information that the latter firm had attempted to purchase illegally only shortly before.

Was this really to be? Not necessarily. For one thing, any information the Europeans might obtain from IBM would serve to make them more rather than less independent of the Japanese. Then too, during the course of the case IBM took pains to make clear that its subsidiaries were national companies, manufacturing more than 90 percent of their products within the Common Market (from 13 plants and six research laboratories), implying that the Japanese were outsiders, sending their mainframes from the home islands. Thus was created the picture of an IBM employing more than 90,000 Europeans, paying over $1 billion a year in taxes, investing heavily ($1.2

billion in 1983), and in other ways being a "good guest," while the Japanese were merely out to seize market share at the expense of European labor. Furthermore, a section of the agreement provided for mutual exchanges of information, meaning that the Japanese would have to provide IBM with some of their secrets in return for whatever they got. Tamizo Kimura, a computer industry analyst with Yamaichi Securities, characterized this as a "two-edged sword," and together with others, concluded that IBM had given up virtually nothing under the terms of the settlement.

The International Nationalist

The evolution of World Trade during the past three and a half decades offers clues as to why IBM has remained so successful. Simply stated, over the years the corporation has demonstrated an uncanny knack for adjusting its structure to meet changing circumstances and strategies. In this, as in so many other areas, IBM is a master of the fine art of creative destruction. But the personal factor must be considered as well, and here too IBM demonstrated an ability to adjust to tensions and conflicts.

In order to understand World Trade's structure in its early years, one must go back to the fact that it was a wholly owned subsidiary of IBM, which in turn functioned as a holding company for the individual national entities. World Trade's headquarters remained in Manhattan for a decade after IBM's corporate offices relocated to suburban Armonk (a move made only after much grumbling). In part World Trade stayed in Manhattan to indicate independence, but more so because some World Trade people believed that the international company had to be situated in the world's premier city. Still, the operational work was conducted from a striking office building on Paris's place Vendôme; from this office were coordinated the efforts of the individual operating units.

World Trade's national companies were expected to be just that—national in every sense save ownership, reporting, and some aspects of manufacturing. Capital allocation was always a problem between Domestic and World Trade (should a new research facility be erected in California or Stuttgart?), but it was less so between World Trade and, say, IBM Deutschland, because the latter was expected to develop and retain relationships with German banks, which would provide much of its financing. The idea was to function as a national company and also avoid currency risks. As for the salesmen and technicians at IBM Deutschland, they would work out of an office or lab and report to a manager, who in turn would be responsible to Stuttgart, and who in turn kept in contact with Paris, and then up the ladder to World Trade in Armonk and the IBM management itself in the same building.

The national companies were given leeway in deciding product mix, pricing policies, and even how to proceed with research and development. There was gear developed and sold by IBM Deutschland and IBM France that was only available in their national markets because of the particular needs of customers—gear which might later be shared with other overseas units and even with Domestic. As a result a rivalry developed, and by the early 1960s World Trade executives were quietly but firmly insisting that their products and the quality of their research were if anything superior to that of Domestic in some areas. Thus, IBM enjoyed what GE had vainly hoped to obtain: the blessing of both diversity and unity.

There were problems, however. In time, personnel at the national companies had clashes with their counterparts at other nationals—disputes that bordered on the unpleasant. For example, IBM Deutschland's management and technical staff was quite close to their American counterparts. It was the largest of the national companies, with the best R & D, and was regularly providing other World Trade companies with specialized machines for testing in their markets. This to the occasional chagrin of Dick Watson, a confirmed Francophile who liked to surround himself with Frenchmen, the most noted being Jacques Maisonrouge, an engineer who came to IBM after the war and by 1957 was placed in charge of virtually all European operations. Maisonrouge and other French managers such as Jean Ghertman and Raymond Pailloux, were among the more important decision makers at World Trade's operational office in Paris, along with a Canadian, Jack Brent, and Luigi Castaldi of Italy, and the Germans occasionally found it necessary to take their case to Armonk when they felt slighted. It would be going too far to suggest that the rivalry was intense and harmful; the IBM *élan* transcended all, here as in so many other areas. Still, the tensions did exist.

And between Armonk and Paris. Consider how World Trade appeared from the offices of the top IBM executives in the United States. There was Dick Watson, nominally in charge of the fastest growing segment of the corporation, surrounded by all those Frenchmen, while the Germans were pleading to be allowed permission to sell their products not only in other parts of World Trade but in the American market itself! Might there be a danger of the child swallowing the parent, which is to say the tilt in the future might be more to World Trade than Domestic? When and if this came there would be no clear signal given, and certainly no one in either Armonk or Paris entertained notions of IBM becoming less of an American firm than it was. Still, there was the possibility that due to World Trade's performance Dick could come to be seen as Tom's heir, thus closing the door on the ambitions of others.

Of these, none was more ambitious than Vince Learson, whose competitive nature permitted him to employ the firm's expertise when it came to designing a yacht he hoped would defeat Tom's in trials. "Tom did his job well, and with grace," he later conceded when asked about the 360 program, going on to indicate this was just short of a put-down. "He knew his limitations and relied on others. Tom was more interested in personnel and morale and the management team and the organization. I was interested in product. I had no plan or strategic program—all I wanted was to do a job in a pretty decent way." Which he certainly did, in more ways than he might have meant. For during the 360 program some within the firm thought Learson did a job on Dick Watson, one Tom couldn't tolerate.

The 360 Cauldron

As has been noted, the 360 campaign established a benchmark for the firm, and may be considered the rebirth of the corporation and its true beginning as the industry's acknowledged leader. IBM's dominance might have been challenged prior to 360 but not afterward. But little noted except within the firm was the way the campaign altered power and personal relations.

The new family of computers not only was to replace existing IBM machines and software but it was to bring together the combined resources of Domestic and World Trade in a unique fashion. Prior to then, the two divisions had never combined their efforts on so important a project. Now unity was necessary if so vast a program was to succeed.

But there were problems that wouldn't have surfaced had the 360 project been initiated a few years earlier. As it was, World Trade was an emerging force in the early 1960s. In those years, IBM Deutschland had asked for and received permission to create and market its own small computers; this request was granted because Armonk couldn't believe there was much of a market for such machines. The line, known as the 3000s, were simple workhorses that might be purchased for less than $17,000; the 3000s were well received in Europe, leading to a sales effort in Latin America and Africa as well.

135

While Tom Watson, Learson, and others were discussing the vast 360 program, IBM Japan was converting facilities for construction of the 3000s, and Dick Watson petitioned to bring the machines to the American market. Thus, as IBM prepared to make the drastic 360 change, it seemed that World Trade was equally ready to challenge Domestic on its own turf. Or at least this is the way it appeared to some in Armonk, who were troubled by World Trade's growing independence.

According to at least two who were involved with the project, Tom and Learson differed as how best to deal with World Trade. In Tom's view, for World Trade to continue independent research and development would involve wasteful duplication of effort at a time when charges were skyrocketing. During the 1950s, the high point for annual capital expenditures was around a third of a billion dollars; in 1963 they came to $570 million, and two years later, when the 360 program was in full swing, $1.6 billion. There was little left for anything else.

Anticipating problems, Tom Watson called for a unification of R & D and marketing and, in general, a closer relationship between the two parts of the empire. Learson took a somewhat different view of the matter: as he saw it, Dick Watson was making a bid for leadership. One Watson was fine and two certainly acceptable, but a third would imply that a dynasty had been created, closing out opportunity to an entire generation—and to Learson in particular.

In many areas Tom and Learson agreed, as in that of organization in preparation for the 360 project. World Trade was brought closer to Domestic in the early and mid-1960s. Dick Watson's international team in Paris was broken up and sent to the national companies; the reason given that the talent was needed at home for the 360 effort. Dick was to spend more time at headquarters and less in Paris. He was awarded the title of senior vice-president, the same as Learson, and was assured that his position within the empire was secure. Maisonrouge's influence at World Trade expanded, and he was to serve as a coordinator for relations between the two branches.

Finally, at the time IBM had two major product divisions: General Products, which concentrated on medium-sized machines such as the 1400s, and Data Systems, charged with turning out the large units like the 7000s. Each was separately funded, with its own sales force. Rivalries had developed due to overlaps in product capabilities, which meant that General Products and Data Systems were vying with one another for placements, so that margins were reduced. Something had to be done about this, so Watson ordered Learson to bring the product divisions together for the 360 campaign, with the understanding that Learson was to be in charge of the coordinated effort, second in command only to Tom Watson himself. Learson's skill was matchless, disguised by his bluff, brutally frank approach, and Dick Watson was to find himself in a difficult if not impossible position.

World Trade's Undoing and Metamorphosis

Tom Watson now embarked on what until then was the firm's most ambitious building program. Six major installations, four at Domestic, one apiece in France and Germany, were erected.

For its time IBM's global strategy was breathtaking, and its construction program unprecedented in peacetime. In 1961 IBM valued its plant and properties at less than $2 billion; in 1967 the figure came to more than $6.6 billion.

Learson was in overall command of the project, with an implied mandate to share authority with Dick. Neither man seemed to care for or trust the other, and from the first they clashed repeatedly, with talk in Armonk that Dick had threatened to resign unless Learson was either demoted or fired. To this Learson responded by offering to give Dick even more responsibility than the latter had expected. Noting that his own forte was sales and service, while Dick had headed an enterprise also involved with manufacturing, Learson suggested that he retain primary responsibility for placements, and that Dick should assume more authority for manufacturing. The two areas would be coordinated, of course, but those who were were savvy clearly expected orders to outstrip the ability to turn out machines.

For a while everything seemed to be moving smoothly. The small 360/20 was designed and manufactured in Boeblingen, West Germany, and some in Vimercate, Italy; large numbers of the bigger 360/30, intended to replace the ubiquitous 1401, were turned out in Mainz, West Germany, and the flagship plant in Poughkeepsie, New York; and the 360/40 came from the Montpellier, France, and Horsely, U.K., installations. Peripheral equipment was manufactured in Stockholm, among other locations; memory systems came from Stuttgart, while later on a Brussels factory was to recondition machines for sales to developing countries. Integrated circuits came out of Sindelfingen, West Germany; Corbiel-Essones, France; and four domestic plants in New York and Vermont. Other factories throughout the world contributed as Learson and Dick Watson coordinated their efforts.

As Learson had anticipated, there were few problems in marketing the machines; given attractive lease arrangements, customers lined up for their models. But as has already been discussed, there were the inevitable snags in manufacture. We have seen how Tom Watson initially expected the machines to be in the market in 1964 and had to apologize for the delay of a year. Due to this delay, revenue flow didn't come up to anticipation and IBM was obliged to raise capital by selling equity—$371 million in 1964, all for the 360 project—and cut back on other areas of development, all of which contributed toward making Dick appear a blunderer, while Learson's star was on the ascendant. World Trade executives, angered at suggestions that they had somehow failed, observed that IBM Italy and IBM Deutschland shipped 360/20s before the American plants could do so, but this was of little help. By late 1965, Learson had assumed greater authority in the manufacturing end of the project, while Dick's role was diminished.

The following year Learson was named president of IBM, while Dick was relegated to the largely symbolic post of vice-chairman, with special responsibilities for World Trade, where Maisonrouge had become president and chief operating officer.

But a different World Trade was to emerge. Believing an important part of the difficulties with the 360 program had been organizational in nature and troubled that a unified World Trade might someday challenge Domestic if permitted to continue as it had, Tom Watson acted to alter the organization. In the process the national companies became somewhat more independent than they had been in the 360 campaign, thus making them more akin to the kind of operations his father had envisaged.

The Paris operational group was disbanded, with Brent returning to Canada and Castaldi to a top post in Italy, while natives, often prestigious ones at that, supplanted Americans at the few top posts U.S. citizens had held at national companies; for example, in 1967 George R. S. Baring, the third Earl of Cromer and former Governor of the Bank of England, became chairman of IBM U.K. Simultaneously, Americans from Armonk took important posts at World Trade headquarters. Gilbert Jones assumed Jack Brent's old post as vice-president with Charles Smith as his chief of staff; both men came out of Domestic.

As time passed, Dick came to feel increasingly out of place in Paris, and as noted, he left the firm in 1970 to become ambassador to France. Maisonrouge, who at one time might have succeeded him, was told the time wasn't ripe for a foreigner to head World Trade and was passed over in favor of Jones, who proceeded to restructure World Trade into three segments:

Europe/Middle East/Africa, Asia/Pacific, and Latin America (the last was short-lived and soon was merged into Asia/Pacific to form Americas/Far East). Maisonrouge was given command of Europe/Middle East/Africa, and a veteran Asian hand, Gordon Williamson, took over at Americas/Far East.

What came out of all this, by the 1970s, was a World Trade dominated by Americans from Domestic, who had close ties with Armonk, supervising two major divisions, each of which was composed of national units staffed almost completely by natives of the countries in which they operated. The cooperation initiated by the 360 program and its successor, the 370, continued. That cooperation has been led firmly by World Trade's hierarchy and entered into by the national units, whose leaders appreciated the need for colaboration even while they maintained considerable leeway in their local markets.

This cooperation continued into the 1980s, when additional decision-making powers were granted leaders of national companies. Moreover, to assuage those who still felt IBM was a foreign entity, the nationals entered into alliances with local firms. For example, IBM U.K. allied itself with British Telecom, and IBM Italy with STET, the government-controlled telephone company. World Trade was able to participate in the U.K.'s Alvey Project, that country's attempt to achieve some kind of parity with the Americans and Japanese, and has a role in Esprit, the Common Market's $3 billion cooperative research-and-development program in electronics and automation equipment, as well as computers.

Critics charged that IBM had entered these alliances in order to dictate standards to the Europeans, and that these alliances would enable it to continue dominating the field. This became a major issue in 1984, when the Thatcher government announced its intention of selling 51 percent of the stock of British Telecom for $4.43 billion. Soon thereafter the firm announced its intention to cooperate with IBM in creating a nationwide electronic data network (known as Jove), which would link together thousands of computers in that country and eventually perform for information the role that the national telephone company does for voice communications.

This set off a major debate, which raged throughout the summer and into autumn. *The Economist* warned of an American takeover of a vital British industry. "Believers in competition need to be thoroughly suspicious of a proposal by the world's (and Britain's) biggest computer company and Britain's near-monopoly telecommunications company to start holding hands." The upshot would be a de facto monopoly over a key technology—a monopoly that would stifle all competitors. "Their proposal runs too big a risk of interfering with the competitive free-for-all that is Britain's, and Europe's, only real hope of getting back into the technology game." Not surprisingly, Michael Watson of ICL agreed, arguing that "The Government is essentially talking about endorsing standards for a national infrastructure—one as important as highways or railroads—that can be set or changed by a company that is not a U.K. resident. We ought not allow it. We find it incompatible with building a U.K.-focused information technology business." But Alvey's program director, Brian Oakley, disagreed. "Technically, [IBM] is always interesting and surprisingly open. We've got a lot of reasons to like IBM." Oakley concluded that IBM's presence "was in Britain's interests." The fact remains that IBM's presence in such a venture would all but guarantee it a leading role in a vital part of the European market.

The government backed down in mid-October, when the Ministry for Trade and Industry blocked plans for Jove. IBM and British Telecom appealed, and at this time the network's future is in doubt. What is not in doubt, however, is the fact that IBM persists in attempts to take a major role on the European telecommunications scene.

And so it goes. Alberto Demacchi, Olivetti's director of marketing, called World Trade's policy of working with European companies "IBM's Trojan Horse," explaining, "It's a dangerous attempt by an American company to set communications standards for the Common Market"—this from a top executive of a company that recently had sold a quarter of its shares to AT&T! Rhetoric aside, the Europeans really had little choice; given the fact that IBM-compatibility was still the name of the game, it would have been foolhardy to proceed without Big Blue.

Notwithstanding IBM's continued domination of the European markets, its share did decline, due largely to the European-Japanese alliances, and the statistics may offer a clue as to what might be expected for the rest of the decade. In mid-1984 World Trade was accounting for 68 percent of new placements of large systems in Germany, and the figures for France and the U.K. were 65 percent and 63 percent respectively. The European-Japanese were doing better in medium-sized systems, taking almost three out of four in this category. IBM's small units, including microcomputers, accounted for less than 20 percent of Common Market sales, and only 7 percent in the U.K., which is the leading market in small units and microcomputers. Industry observers note that this low percentage in small units was due to the fact that the IBM PC was introduced later in Europe than in the United States due to problems of availability, and that the PCjr wasn't scheduled for introduction until 1985. That an IBM push was coming in medium-sized machines and especially micros wasn't in doubt, but as will be seen, this is one area in which competitors might hope for a measure of success. But how much?

Clearly, IBM is concentrating on the large mainframes, telecommunications, and standards under which information is shifted between units. This will be the key to future technology, and World Trade is a commanding presence there. And things are getting better, especially since the end of the EEC antitrust action. In the afterglow of the settlement, IBM Europe's chairman, Kaspar Cassani, reflected that it was becoming easier to compete in Europe: "The preferential treatment [to native firms] has been reduced dramatically. We have a much better situation today than we had four years ago." That is another way of saying that the Japanese have little hope of gaining much market share from Big Blue in the Common Market.

In the 1920s, Alfred Sloan of General Motors gained considerable fame by his structuring of that corporation. There were Cadillac, LaSalle, Oakland, Oldsmobile, Buick, Pontiac, and Chevrolet, each competing against rivals from other firms, but also with one another, while at the same time sharing components and services. In this way GM enjoyed the positive aspects of unity along with those of competition. Tom Watson performed a similar task for IBM in the 1960s, fashioning a global enterprise where the obvious benefits of nationalism were wedded to those of central strategic planning. Anyone attempting to understand, much less compete with IBM, should keep in mind the nexus between Domestic and World Trade, the two major divisions, and the national companies. It is an apparently seamless pyramid of power, with no chinks in the facade.

VIII

THE JAPANESE APPROACH:
THEORY AND BACKGROUND

Some Conventional Wisdom

You have heard similar stories. This one, which has the virtue of really having happened, is typical of the genre.

The time is autumn 1980, when Japanese products seemed successful throughout the western world, when Americans were seeking to keep Toyotas and Datsuns from their shores, and when the French were attempting all sorts of stratagems to keep Panasonic and Sony video recorders in warehouses in Poitiers rather than allow them onto the shelves of Paris department stores.

The American was being shown around the floor of the stock exchange in London by one of the organization's senior officials, when in the visitors' gallery there appeared some score of youngish and middle-aged Japanese businessmen. All were dressed in dark suits, white shirts, and dark ties, and most wore glasses. To the untrained eye of the Occidental, they seemed almost identical, each carrying a pad and what, at the distance, looked like a gold Cross pen and each furiously taking notes while listening to a lecture by one of the exchange's guides.

"Who are they?" the American asked, and the official replied that it was another group of Japanese investment bankers and brokers fresh off the JAL plane, there to study the City, London's financial district, "and see how we do things here." Gazing at the industrious crew, the American remarked that this might be one of the reasons for Japan's startling success: hard work, intelligence, seriousness, etc., but the Briton disagreed. "No," he said, "That's why

143

they'll never really make the grade. When the Japanese have a problem their first reaction is to learn how Americans and Europeans try to solve it, which is why they are here now: to learn from us. When Americans encounter a problem their reaction is to study it and see what can be done. The Japanese are here regularly; I've never seen a like American group in London specifically to see how we do things."

The suggestion was obvious. The Japanese are expert imitators, but are not particularly original (like this idea, it must be conceded). Let the Americans and Europeans produce some interesting item, be it an electronic calculator, videocassette recorder, television set, automobile, or electronic wristwatch, and it will only be a matter of time before the Japanese turn out versions that are better, less expensive, and, in the end, market successes, pushing the Occidentals off the retailing map. Just as Sony bested RCA and Toyota did quite well against General Motors, so the thinking goes, Hitachi, Fujitsu, and others would pose a more serious challenge to IBM than Honeywell, Control Data, or Digital Equipment.

Armonk likes to reinforce the idea; its spokesmen, from John Akers down, regularly and solemnly warn of Japanese industrial might, ingenuity, and power in the information processing industry.

The idea was summed up by Peter Drucker, recalling Japanese reactions to talks he gave on how the Japanese approach to management embodied native values. "Don't you realize we are simply adapting what IBM has done all along," was one comment, prompting Drucker to ask why this was so. The answer was simple enough: "When we started to rebuild Japan in the fifties, we looked around for the most successful company we could find. It's IBM, isn't it?"

But in all of this, one word often is omitted. The Japanese don't merely imitate and offer products at lower prices. They improve. Japanese manufacturers are experts and produce better *American* goods than can their counterparts in the United States. Losing is bad enough, but it irks when foreigners can best you at your own game. That's what the Japanese have done in a wide variety of consumer goods and now hope to do in information processing.

Perhaps so. Recently, hordes of Japanese businessmen, like clones of those investment bankers who turned up in London, have been seen touring California's Silicon Valley, Route 128 in Boston, and other American high tech pockets, looking grim, taking notes, and presumably working out their plans to make deep inroads into the American computer market.

Is there some way to discover what approaches they will take? Yes, and for three reasons. In the first place, the invasion has begun, and the strategic outlines are not all that difficult to perceive. Second, Japanese businessmen tend to react to challenges in ways consistent with their training and value system, and both have undergone considerable study in recent years. Finally, and most important, the Japanese have done this before—in silk, inexpensive gadgets and toys, steel, consumer electronics, and most recently and best known, automobiles. There are patterns that may be discerned in these instances that can be anticipated in information processing, and these patterns merit attention.

The Staging Area

The Japan that General Douglas MacArthur surveyed in late 1945 seemed as defeated as a country could be. "Never in history had a nation and its people been more completely crushed," he later wrote. MacArthur wasn't referring to the gutted buildings, which soon would be razed in preparation for rebuilding, but to the wounds of the spirit.

No other people save aboriginal populations were as homogeneous as the Japanese, who always had discouraged foreigners from settling for long, had safeguarded their isolation until the second quarter of the nineteenth century, and had believed themselves not only superior to the West but impregnable. Now Japan had been defeated by an Occidental power, which occupied their land; their Emperor, thought to have descended from the gods, appeared a prisoner in the Imperial Palace.

A quarter of a century later, when Japanese goods flooded the world and that country's labor force, managements, and government seemed impregnable, one might have been forgiven for asking the question: "Who won World War II?"

But there was a more important, less facetious query: What accounted for the Japanese success? The answer, as it always is to such apparently simple questions, is complex. But three elements must be considered, one of which—the Japanese knack for taking products of other lands and then improving upon them—has already been alluded to, and will be analyzed and demonstrated in some detail. There are two others of lesser prominence that should be mentioned.

One is the MacArthur vice-regency, a subject hardly touched upon by most scholars and popular writers during and after his reign in Tokyo. It was MacArthur who prevented a Soviet presence in Japan, who presided over the writing of the postwar liberal constitution, who managed to walk the fine line between accepting the old ways and pressing Japan into new ones. Had MacArthur truly forced the breakup of the old industrial oligarchies—the *zaibatsu,* whose more familiar members were Mitsubishi, Mitsui, and Sumitomo—Japan might have undergone a social and economic upheaval from which it would have been difficult to recover. Needless to say, the ejection of the emperor would have had an even more convulsive effect. As it was, "Maccasa-san," as the Japanese knew him, rejected such prodding, which came from American liberals. But at the same time, he won little applause from conservatives when he insisted upon women's suffrage and insisted upon land reform. As a result of his wise leadership, Japan underwent a relatively smooth transition from defeat to rebirth, and MacArthur went down in history as that country's most important leader in more than a century.

Curiously, America's two great World War II military leaders, MacArthur and Dwight Eisenhower, each presided over the affairs of a nation during the postwar period. While Eisenhower's presidency nowadays is considered more successful than it appeared in the 1950s, one might argue that his Pacific rival performed even better. That the American military could produce two such adept political leaders in one generation is a matter worthy of deeper analysis than it has received thus far.

The third element, an outgrowth of the first two, was the impact of the Korean War upon Japan. The stage was set by Joseph Dodge, a bland, colorless banker whose chief claim to fame had been a term as president of the American Bankers Association. Had it not been for World War II, Dodge might never have ventured far from his base in Detroit. As it happened, Dodge became one of MacArthur's chief economic advisors in postwar Japan. Whether he understood the Japanese or knew how to manage an economy is highly doubtful; Dodge was one of those figures whom Leo Tolstoy would have characterized as a hedgehog rather than a fox, in that he knew one great truth rather than many small ones. Dodge's great truth was his belief in balanced budgets combined with an abhorrence of inflation. In 1949, Japan's economy was plagued by both a budget deficit and inflation. That year, with MacArthur's support, Dodge initiated what came to be known as the "Dodge Line," a nine-point program to balance the budget, end subsidies to inefficient companies, and stabilize the yen at 360 to the dollar, making it undervalued in world money markets. The latter was done to stimulate exports and discourage imports.

The result was an immediate sharp recession, one of the worst in Japanese history, which resulted in widespread unrest and a swing to the political left. Stability returned the following year, however, just in time for Japan to benefit from the Korean War, during which it served as the marshalling base for the United Nations forces fighting on the Korean mainland. American procurement policies favored the Japanese, and this fact combined with the dollar-yen ratio provided a sharp spur to the economy, which boomed in the early 1950s. In the midst of all this, the United States and Japan signed a formal peace treaty, which went into effect in 1952, and the two nations entered a new chapter of a relationship begun almost a century earlier, in 1853, when Commodore Matthew Perry's famous black ships appeared in Yedo Bay and helped pave the way for the opening of the Meiji era.

The United States-Japanese treaty of 1952 permitted Japan a free hand in its own affairs. At the time, Japan's newly erected steel mills, shipyards, machine-tool shops, and factories were turning out ever-larger amounts of capital and consumer goods. The country's gross national product was still below what it had been prior to World War II, but growth was rapid. Part of this growth was provided by foreign trade, which was not yet of prime importance but was advancing smartly. In the year of the treaty, Japan exported $229 million worth of goods to the United States against $633 million in imports. Impressive recovery, perhaps, but not much more than that in the eyes of most Americans concerned with such matters—whose interests were attracted more to events in Europe than Asia.

Economic Miracles

Americans were barely aware of Japan's industrial growth during the late 1950s and early 1960s. At the time, all attention was focused on the German Federal Republic, in which the much-vaunted "German Economic Miracle" was unfolding, a miracle that was to provide both a prelude to and model for the Japanese experience. And some scholars were still writing about another, earlier instance of economic growth.

At the turn of the century, when the sun didn't set on the British Empire and London was the center of world finance, the British awoke to what might have been called the American Challenge. The United States had vast natural resources, a hard-working labor force, and energetic, imaginative entrepreneurs, who were supported by Republican administrations that erected tariffs to protect domestic markets against foreign competition. Even so, America started flooding the world with capital goods and consumer goods of a higher quality and lower price than their European counterparts; this was made possible by productivity of the new American factories that was higher then that of their European equivalents. While Britain and Germany prepared to do battle in the Great War, prescient observers in both countries feared that the only victor would be the young, vibrant, dynamic United States. And they were right, for a while at least.

For good and sufficient reasons, though, the U.S. victory came more rapidly than most believed possible. For one thing, the United States was so far away—across a vast ocean, which in those days seemed much more difficult to cross than it does today. Then too, the United States was essentially isolationist, populated by individuals who rejected Europe and were convinced that their civilization was superior to that of the old continent. Finally, the United States possessed a large internal market for its goods, and at the time at least, it appeared that this would occupy its manufacturers for decades to come. There are differences between the American and Japanese miracles, but striking similarities as well.

The German counterpart came after World War II. The growth of the German economy was in part, at least, the result of forces similar to those that were transforming Japan. The Basic Law there was drawn up in 1949, elections to the new Bundestag took place in August, and the new government, headed by Konrad Adenauer, was installed the following month, with full independence going into effect in 1955. Shortly thereafter, under the aegis of Finance Minister Ludwig Erhard, the Federal Republic underwent the equivalent of the earlier Dodge Line; the economy was decontrolled, the currency devalued, and after a period of dislocation, a boom began that surprised the western world.

As they later would flock to Japan, American scholars of that time made the trip to Germany and after quick tours returned to the United States to write, lecture, and above all scold their fellow countrymen who were accused of sloth, indifference, foolhardy behavior, and worse for permitting their recent enemy to seize important economic territory in such areas as machine tools, cameras, and automobiles. There was much talk of retaliation—tariffs, quotas, currency controls, and negotiations with the Germans to oblige them to erect factories stateside. There were also attempts to uncover the "German Secret," Americanize it, and then make changes in the way the Yankees did business.

If this sounds familiar, it is meant to, for virtually all the fears, discussions of reactions, and suggestions that greeted the Japanese Challenge, once the Americans became aware of it, which is to say, by the early 1970s, happened first with the Germans.

The German Miracle was real enough but insufficient to topple the United States from its position of preeminence, and for several reasons. The German Federal Republic is much smaller than the United States, is dependent upon the U.S. for military support, and lacks important raw materials. So, too, does Japan. Does this mean that Japan, like West Germany, will pose a temporary threat and then fizzle out?

As recently as two decades ago, informed Americans who read about Japan in newspapers, magazines, and the few books dealing with that country considered it a faraway place inhabited by a people who didn't particularly care to mingle with Westerners, a place that, at the time, seemed intent on satisfying its domestic markets. Even so, the Japanese Invasion had already begun, and in just the same way that the American Invasion of Europe had started in the early twentieth century—with less expensive, better goods that first had been turned out for domestic consumption. And with the cooperation of its government that would dwarf anything ever experienced in the United States.

Japan: The Fourfold Path

There have been four stages in the Japanese invasions of the United States markets, be those in shirts, steel, consumer electronics, or automobiles. There is no reason to expect a change in tactics for their invasion of the information processing industry.

First of all, the Japanese come to the United States to study techniques, make contacts, become aware of marketing problems, and uncover weaknesses. The second stage is marked by a return home to train workforces in the foreign ways, all the while adapting native Japanese practices to the new technologies and techniques and simultaneously entering into licensing agreements with the Americans. That is, they do so where such agreements are available. Occasionally, the Japanese firms will imitate without agreements, or—in the view of the Americans—violate patents, more on which later.

Most of the above is done with an eye on domestic markets, which is where the learning curve begins. In this period, the Japanese will erect tariff and quota roadblocks and, where this isn't politically feasible, put into place as many informal barriers to potential foreign exporters as possible.

During the third phase the Japanese unite, usually behind their Ministry of International Trade and Industry, and with that agency's assistance, make the initial foray into the American markets. They do so with superior goods priced as low as possible without incurring the wrath of the American companies or being charged with dumping. In addition, the Japanese establish superior sales and service networks and employ large-scale American-style advertising. When the American firms protest unfair tactics, the Japanese delay as long as they can, giving way in inches while consolidating their grip on the market, subsidizing the lower prices of exports by keeping prices on the same products sold domestically as high as they dare; these high domestic prices are possible due to the aforementioned tariffs and quotas. (New Yorkers are amazed to see Japanese tourists flocking to Times Square discount houses to purchase Sanyo, Sony, Nikon, and Panasonic products, since they are so much less expensive here than at home. This, while Japanese government spokesmen blandly claim innocence in the matter of dual pricing.) If necessary the Japanese will erect sales and service facilities in the host country in anticipation of quotas and tariffs, which in any event arrive too late to do much good for the by-then prostrate American companies.

The goal, of course, is market share. And when this is achieved, the Japanese businesses enter the fourth phase, that of upgrading and turning out new models while increasing prices, so that what in the beginning was a high quality, low priced unit is replaced by one that is upgraded but much higher priced. Thus, the 1968 Toyota Corona was deemed a better buy than the Chevy or Ford; today the Toyota Cressida competes with Cadillac and Lincoln.

The strategy worked well against the American shirt industry and then in steel, consumer electronics, and automobiles. Now a variant of it is being employed in information processing, where the going is rougher. The American computer industry is more complex than any the Japanese had encountered earlier and is dominated by what is one of the strongest and best-managed firms in the industry. Moreover, while the Japanese computer firms planned their invasion of the United States, they had to face the reality of a challenge at home, from the selfsame IBM.

IBM Japan

Japan had a data processing and computer industry in the 1950s. Sometimes known as the "Big Six," the manufacturers in order of importance at that time were: Nippon Electric (NEC), Hitachi, Fujitsu, Toshiba, Oki Denki, and Mitsubishi. Over time, the order would change, but the players remained the same. By the mid-1980s, the Big Six accounted for approximately 80 percent of all *native Japanese* manufacture of electronic components and about the same for mainframes.

The catch is that there is a seventh computer firm—or to be more precise, a third, since it now is the runner-up to Fujitsu and NEC in size—and that is IBM Japan, which would be the clear leader were it not for Tokyo's strong intervention in favor of the Big Six. As it is, IBM Japan had revenues in 1984 of $2.27 billion, behind Fujitsu's $2.86 billion and NEC's $2.37 billion, but far ahead of the others. Today Fujitsu is the main threat. Though less than a tenth the size of the entire IBM corporation, it is an aggressive competitor. More than half of its new midsize mainframe customers in 1984, for example, had formerly been devoted to IBM machines.

Like other World Trade affiliates, IBM Japan is as close to being a native company as possible. Its president, Takeo Shiina, was born and educated in Japan, as are all but some 450 of its approximately 15,000 employees. IBM Japan is also the third-largest World Trade company, behind the U.K. and German affiliates, and it accounts for approximately 5 percent of the parent company's earnings. There seems little doubt that without even stronger government intervention (not likely given fears of American retaliation) IBM Japan's position and share of profits will expand during the foreseeable future. By how much? During the first half of 1985 they rose by 30 percent, faster than both Fujitsu and NEC, and by late summer of that year it seemed virtually certain IBM Japan would be back in the number two slot before long. As it is, it is the clear leader in large mainframes. "What we are trying to do is catch up in other system areas," Shiina said. These include midsized office systems and personal computers, more on which later.

IBM Japan now operates under a new central organization, IBM Asia/ Pacific Group, headed by George Conrades, who prior to then had been an executive at the company's Information Systems & Technology Group. Conrades and some 250 other executives, most of them American, were transferred to Tokyo in 1983 with a mandate to work with IBM Japan and make it more competitive. That this would create conflicts was foreseen. "It's a loss of face," said one Japanese industry analyst. "They [IBM Japan] spent all this effort to create an image as a Japanese company, and now the Americans move in." Indeed, the arrival of Asia/Pacific more than doubled the number of American IBMers in Tokyo overnight.

Armonk realized this would create tension but in the light of the importance of the Asian market was prepared to take risks. Akers explained that "We're more involved by far in Japan because the problems there are bigger." Beyond Japan was the promise of the Chinese market. Asia/Pacific oversees operations in seventeen countries, and while the Chinese business now is relatively minor, it could become much more important by the late 1990s. Already the Japanese have made a major push there; one of Conrades's more important assignments is to make certain the American presence is felt on the mainland.

Well aware of Japanese sensitivities and rumors that his power has been eroded, Shiina devotes a good deal of his time to the firm's native image. In addition, IBM Japan has fashioned a network of alliances with as many Japanese companies as it can. This has been done for four reasons.

In the first place, Shiina is cognizant of the Japanese mistrust of foreign companies; entering into a web of alliances with several of Japan's major and young, growing concerns might help allay that problem. At the same time, such alliances would create projects that MITI and other government agencies would have to support, since failure to do so would harm the domestic firms. For years, any Japanese company wanting to purchase a mainframe computer from IBM had to justify the move to a government agency, which wanted to know why the order had not been placed with a native concern. "The government really put some clamps on us that legislated against our progress," Conrades said. Due largely to American pressures and fear of retaliation this practice has ceased. But here, as with so many products, IBM faces difficulties in overcoming a Japanese preference for products produced by Japanese companies. "We'll survive against IBM in our home market," a Fujitsu executive said, "because of the cultural factor."

Then too, IBM Japan was considering a wide variety of new products in the late 1970s and early 1980s, among them personal computers, which for the first time would place the company into the consumer market. In the past, the firm had concentrated upon commercial clients. Prudence dictated joint ventures so as to make the products more appealing to Japanese purchasers. As will be seen, the same problem was being dealt with by World Trade, which for quite a different set of reasons opted for a similar strategy, but the point was clear: IBM was more willing to enter into alliances in this period than at any other time in its history.

While IBM Japan's drive toward cooperative ventures began long before the well-publicized "sting operation" in which Fujitsu and Mitsubishi were caught trying to purchase IBM secrets (see chapter IX), continuation and intensification became more important as a result, so as to soothe ruffled Japanese feelings and unable the industry to save face.

Finally, the Japanese companies were engaging in some interesting research on their own, and IBM hoped to work with some of the leading firms to obtain insights into their thinking. But cautiously, with each company hoping to learn more than it taught.

On mainframes and related gear, IBM worked with Mitsubishi in both the software and hardware areas. This cooperation began prior to the sting and continued afterward. In 1981, IBM Japan entered into arrangements with Kanematsu-Gosho, a leading electronics distributor, to sell the 5150, its first entry into the micro market. This collaboration was followed two years later by an ambitious cooperative program involving IBM Japan's 5550 computer, the Japanese equivalent of the popular PC. The 5550 contains parts provided by a dozen or so home island companies, headed by Matsushita, which contributed the body frame and become the principal manufacturer. Oki Denki and Alps also participated; according to industry sources, the only important American component is the Intel microprocessor. Moreover, IBM Japan has purchased 35 percent of Japanese Business Computer, which provides technological input. The 5550 is offered through Nissan outlets and was introduced with a major advertising campaign featuring Japanese motion picture star Atsumi Koyoshi.

The 5550, which was introduced in 1983, arrived late; Fujitsu and NEC had personal computers on the market in 1980 and 1982 respectively. Conrades later conceded IBM Japan's lag in this market. "Could we have done some things differently on our own?" he asked, and then provided the answer: "Yes. We might have moved into the 5550 family faster." In addition the original 5550 was slower than the Fujitsu and NEC offerings. IBM Japan tried to compensate for this by offering more software than the others and through price competition. The crucial matter was speed, which by 1985 IBM conquered through changes in computer architecture and better software.

Yet much more remains to be done if Japanese word processing is to come up to the American version. One reason is flexibility, and this is an area in which up to now IBM Japan has lagged. A good American typist can churn out copy at the rate of one hundred words per minute. The best Japanese word processors, operating a 5500, can do slightly more than half that amount, and less with one of the older models.

There are approximately 7,000 characters in the kanji, although most literate Japanese have to know only 2,000 or so to get by. Still, so many characters pose an obvious technological problem. When the time came for Americans to create English-language word processors, the keyboard required only a few more keys than the familiar typewriter. In contrast, the early kanji keyboards resembled large mats. But not for long. In 1978, Toshiba came out with a word processor that used the simpler kana ideoforms. While more cumbersome and less flexible than kanji, a kana keyboard could be created with approximately fifty keys, and, later on, Toshiba created a system whereby the user could employ katakana, one of the two kana forms, after which the software changed it into kanji.

Others followed Toshiba's example, and by 1983 the field was dominated by NEC, Fujitsu, newcomers Sord and Micro Rickkei, and of course IBM Japan. But it wasn't a particularly large market; that year only 96,000 word processors were sold, but the figure was expanding rapidly. IBM Japan participated in this, initially through the 5500, and in 1984, the JX, produced largely by Matsushita, which featured color graphics and the ability to use either Japanese or English software. The JX drew upon the American experience in that, for the first time, IBM Japan offered its wares through retail outlets. "JX was the first product that IBM had to offer in the storefront," said Shiina in the summer of 1985. "We are still learning the process." But here too it had to play catch-up with Fujitsu and NEC, both of which had already invaded the market. Sord, which was founded in 1970 and now has approximately 15 percent of the personal computer market in Japan, has proven the strongest of the independents.
strongest of the independents.

In 1984 IBM Japan sold more than 80,000 micros, of which 6,000 were JXs, and at that was deemed a distant second behind NEC, which had some 80 percent of the market. It seemed a decent enough showing—but, in late 1983, IBM Japan set a goal of 120,000 machines, and so by Big Blue standards, performed poorly in this area.

Nonetheless, IBM Japan has managed to overcome much of its foreign image—this at a time when the Americans were concerned that Sharp, Panasonic, Sony, Sanyo, and other Japanese firms then invading their market would perform in home computers the way Toyota, Nissan, and Honda did in cars: namely, decimate the American ranks. Meanwhile IBM Domestic entered into cooperative arrangements with several Japanese firms. For example, it markets a copier manufactured by Minolta under the IBM nameplate and imports industrial robots from Sankyo Seiki. This arrangement hardly was a new idea: we have seen that Fujitsu had been doing the same in the United States through its relationship with Amdahl.

Japan and the Seven Dwarfs

Amdahl wasn't the Japanese companies' only American contact, however. Like the Europeans, the Japanese cultivated relationships with IBM's American rivals, without much better fortune.

Early on, the Seven Dwarfs were as eager to cooperate with the Japanese as they had been with the Europeans and for the same reason: they looked upon such alliances as an excellent method of obtaining partners in the global struggle against IBM. Thus, RCA licensed its patents to Hitachi, while General Electric sold its machines through a licensing arrangement with Toshiba. Honeywell entered into arrangements with Nippon Electric, and RemRand with Oki Denki. Other players—such as TRW, Bunker Ramo, and Westinghouse—developed reciprocal agreements with Mitsubishi. Fujitsu refrained from entering into such programs, but then entered the computer field through a joint venture with TRW, Spain's Secoinsa, and Consolidated Computer of Canada, and by means of arrangements with other Japanese companies was able to obtain needed information. And, of course, Fujitsu and the rest continue their licensing arrangements with others.

Not, however, with IBM, which is the only foreign firm actually manufacturing computers in Japan. MITI attempted to woo World Trade into affiliations with Japanese firms, to no avail. There were rumors that in some way the Japanese would oblige IBM to sell a minority position in its Japanese affiliate to local interests, but they ended when India tried that ploy and IBM withdrew from the country rather than submit.

The Japanese had no intention in the 1950s and 1960s of pushing IBM to that extreme, for they needed its computers badly for domestic industry. So Big Blue would license technology—carefully, usually when the patents were on the verge of becoming obsolete anyway—but eschewed closer relationships than that.

Just why this was so is a matter for conjecture, since IBM is typically closed-mouthed about its strategies, and the Japanese aren't talking. But it should be noted that as a matter of policy IBM has always tried to avoid joint projects with foreign companies and, until quite recently, with American companies as well. Furthermore, while the Seven Dwarfs were operating from a position of weakness, that wasn't the case with IBM World Trade. For example, Honeywell and RCA *needed* Nippon Electric and Hitachi in order to crack into the Japanese market; in the 1960s, IBM Japan was by far the largest factor in that country, and it led the pack technologically and in terms of placements during that period. IBM Japan also was the only significant

155

exporter of computers from the home islands, and seemed likely to remain so unless something dramatic occurred. Then, too, while the others needed capital to expand their computer programs, IBM was awash with liquidity. Finally, IBM understood the Japanese industry far better than did the others, since the firm retained the knack of making its foreign operations appear to be under the control and leadership of natives.

IX

THE QUEST FOR RATIONALE

The Japanese Strategy

Almost a quarter of a century ago, the Japanese fashioned a master plan to seize a dominant position in the computer industry. Ambitious, wide-spreading, and carefully worked out, it nonetheless had meager success in the face of IBM's power.

As early as 1961 MITI had created the Japan Electronic Computer Company, Ltd. (JECC), capitalized at $18 million, the initial goal of which was to study export possibilities and make certain that foreigners didn't obtain too large a share of the Japanese market. In addition, JECC purchased computers from domestic firms and placed them with users; thus it supported manufacturing, encouraged purchases and leases, and eased the inventory-bearing burdens of the young industry.

Initially, JECC would take machines that had at least 20 percent domestic content, but the figure was raised to 50 percent by the end of the decade. This effectively barred those American firms hoping to sell their wares in Japan while placing a protective umbrella over the Big Six. MITI's intention at that point was to safeguard the domestic market and then, when the time was right, expand overseas to the Common Market and the United States, with machines superior in design to IBM's, and at a lower price.

MITI also developed and funded several major projects that provided the domestic firms with needed work. The first of these, known as "FONTAC," was initiated soon after JECC's creation and was aimed at developing mainframes. FONTAC involved grants to Fujitsu, Oki, and Nippon Electric, which were supposed to cooperate on the design and manufacture of the mainframes, with Oki and NEC being responsible for peripheral gear, and Fujitsu, which became the project's leader, acting as the central processing unit.

FONTAC was followed in the mid-sixties by another program, which united these three firms with Mitsubishi, Toshiba, and Hitachi to develop additional machines with greater capabilities, which would be offered by Fujitsu and NEC. These machines were to be offered on the domestic market, in the hope they could take some of the play from IBM Japan. Little came of this. Moreover, it was during this period that the 370s arrived, with their greater power and lower price tags, and they savaged the Japanese companies, forcing them to think more in terms of retrenchment than expansion.

This led MITI into a new direction. For the time being at least there would be less thought given to the old plan of creating new lines of machines and software—that shoal upon which Univac, RCA, GE, and others had foundered—and more to creating IBM plug-compatibles for at least the next decade. Only later would the Japanese come out with the new machines and software, and then only when a superior and radically new approach was feasible. This approach would be the so-called "Fifth Generation Project," more on which later. For the time being, in the 1970s, Japan concentrated on becoming the leading supplier of plug-compatibles.

The powerful ministry concluded that none of the Six could compete effectively, and so it proposed mergers which would leave three competitors. Just as the automakers fought this ukase, so did the electronics firms. MITI promptly retaliated with a carrot and stick approach: it offered $155 million in aid for the development of new systems and withheld financial assistance from JECC. Unlike Toyota, Nissan, and the other car companies, the recalcitrant computer firms fell into line. They wouldn't combine, but each agreed to specialize in one segment of the field and cooperate with partners. Fujitsu and Hitachi were to produce large PCMs, Mitsubishi and Oki would concentrate on smaller PCMs, while NEC and Toshiba would go ahead with their own computer architecture. To complete the package, MITI funded the arrangement to the tune of $300 million.

Fujitsu and Hitachi developed the "M" line of large computers (out of which came Fujitsu's interest in Amdahl), Toshiba and NEC joined in the "ACOS" series, while Mitsubishi and Oki put together the COSMOS line. In varying degrees, all were successful, in large part due to MITI pressure on buyers and lessors to take them in place of IBMs. And there were other cooperative ventures, such as an arrangement between Fujitsu, Nippon Electric, and Hitachi to create the Japan Software Company, which developed and marketed programs and provided consulting services for other Japanese firms.

With all of this JECC had only limited success in subduing IBM Japan, which even found a way around its strictures. In 1981, the company formed a joint venture with Orient Leasing, the nation's largest factor in that field, which was to purchase and lease IBM mainframes to JECC. In this way, IBM Japan attempted to elbow its way into the Japanese inner circle. At the time, Tom Zengage of IBI, a Tokyo-based consulting firm, remarked, "They are making tie-ups all over the block to shore up their position in Japan." So it was. IBM was and remains the outsider against which the Big Six are arrayed.

Gene Amdahl and the Japanese

Meanwhile, Fujitsu attempted to mine Gene Amdahl's expertise; in effect, they hoped to obtain from him the concepts that would have gone into the next generation of machines he intended to create for IBM. Not that Amdahl intended to cooperate to that extent with the Japanese. He thought to use them for capital, just as they desired his ideas, and in the end each side got what it wanted.

Fujitsu was to manufacture components for Amdahl, share in technological developments, and participate in transfers of same. In 1971, Fujitsu established a small research laboratory at Amdahl (Hitachi was offered participation in this but turned it down) and two years later purchased some 24 percent of Amdahl's stock. The company didn't appear all that promising, but Fujitsu was patient—and present during the harsh years when Amdahl designed, manufactured, and tested his machines. On more than one occasion, the Amdahl treasurer flew into Tokyo to borrow funds to meet payrolls, money Fujitsu willingly advanced to its American client, while working with its Japanese partners on a national strategy.

Most important from Fujitsu's point of view was the fact that Amdahl was doing something the Japanese not only understood but at which they were highly proficient—especially in the areas of consumer electronics and automobiles—namely, taking an American or European technology and product and turning out a better, improved version at a lower price. With a difference, however. The plug-compatible business of the 1970s was dominated by firms that literally had started from scratch. Some, like Amdahl,

159

experienced tremendous growth in their first few years, requiring constant innovation and adjustment to a rapidly changing situation. That was not the metier of the leading Japanese companies, which function best in a more settled environment. Except at Sony and a handful of other companies, there is nothing in the Japanese experience to match what transpired in the newer areas of the information processing industries in this decade.

This hardly troubled Fujitsu, which, after all, was obtaining the needed technology. By 1974, this was sufficient for the Japanese firm to introduce its 370M in the home market, a frank copy of the 370 (but faster) with which it was plug-compatible. Hitachi followed with a clone of its own, which, given MITI's pressures on customers, helped shrink IBM Japan's share of the market by the end of the decade to 27 percent. In 1979, Fujitsu passed IBM as the nation's leading manufacturer of computers. As though to celebrate, MITI established a set of goals for the industry: by 1990 Japan was to have a 30 percent share of the world market—and an 18 percent share of the American market.

Then IBM countered with the more powerful 3033, which was followed by the 308X, and now its market share expanded once again—which illustrated one reason why IBM can meet and defeat the Japanese given "a level playing field," and even with the lack of one. Unlike the steel and auto industries, computers are rapidly evolving, so that any advantage is momentary. Imitating a Chevy or producing a better version of a Zenith television set is one thing; obtaining a secure advantage in an industry where today's products are obsolete tomorrow is quite another. Imitation doesn't work as well in data processing as elsewhere, and IBM is the toughest competitor the Japanese have ever encountered, as they—and Amdahl—were soon to learn.

IBM Swats Amdahl

In 1970, the big news in plug-compatibility was coming out of RCA, whose Spectra systems were supposed to do everything Amdahl hoped his machines would. Yet the Spectra systems hardly were roaring successes. Had Amdahl introduced his machines at that time there would have been a good chance he, too, would have failed. As it turned out, he was fortunate in entering the market when the initial flush of interest in the 360s and early 370s was over; users had become accustomed to them and were prepared to make comparisons.

Amdahl Corporation concentrated on research, development, and tooling up for the first five years of its existence. Then, in mid-1975, it introduced the 470 V/6, which was advertised as being compatible with IBM's largest system, the 370/168. In order to lure customers, Amdahl offered them a 60-day trial period.

Priced at around $5 million, which was some 20 percent below the cost of the 168, the machine was an instant success. AT&T took several systems, in part to indicate its independence from IBM (the Bell companies were IBM's largest nongovernmental customer), and placements at NASA, universities, and banks and insurance firms followed. By July 1976, it was estimated that Amdahl cost IBM some $40 million in lost business. For the year as a whole, Amdahl installed 35 systems worth more than $140 million, producing revenues of $93 million and earnings of $11.7 million, and was projecting placements at the rate of one per week for 1977. Amdahls manufactured by Fujitsu were being placed in Europe. Growing bolder, the firm was raiding IBM for talent, winning a real prize in Tom Simpson, one of the handful of top individuals in the field. Simpson's defection, along with that of other technicians and several key salesmen, indicated Amdahl's initial success was no fluke. More than anything else, these defections indicated a belief that Amdahl had discovered a weakness in the IBM facade.

How might IBM have stopped Amdahl (and by implication, Fujitsu) in its tracks? There were several ways, starting with the familiar ones of cutting prices or upgrading machines with no price increase. Then, too, IBM might have slashed leasing rates—encouraging clients to rent rather than buy—knowing that Amdahl lacked the financial muscle to engage in a struggle on this level. On the technological side, IBM could alter its internal microcode, so as to make the 470s incompatible with the 168s—at least until the new microcode could be deciphered. Then, too, there might be announcements of a new series out of Armonk—which wouldn't have been far from the fact, since one was being prepared—which could have crippled Amdahl.

Initially, however, IBM did none of this. In fact it went in the opposite direction and in mid-1976 entered into a cross-licensing agreement with Amdahl that covered substantially all patents relating to computer systems owned by each firm on a nonexclusive basis. The reason IBM did this had more to do with litigation than any market factor: IBM was defending itself in that plethora of antitrust cases, and it seemed prudent to have an industry situation in which other firms thrived, so as to be able to indicate in court that the firm hadn't blocked competition. That Amdahl had fine machines that were well-priced is undeniable, but it also had a major ally in the Justice

Department, which caused IBM to exercise restraint—but only to a point. Without this ally any company coming against IBM would have a difficult time of it indeed.

Nonetheless, Amdahl did prosper. By mid-1977, Gene Amdahl was boasting he had close to a quarter of the market for mainframes in his categories, and the company's revenues for the following year came to $321 million with earnings of $48.2 million. Amdahl's profit margin was higher and growth more rapid than those of IBM, and, in Fujitsu, Amdahl had a parts supplier prepared to cut prices in order to obtain market share.

Amdahl's successes encouraged others to enter the plug-compatible arena. Some were familiar firms like CDC, but most were newcomers, and these included Magnuson (whose executives included Gene Amdahl's son), Nanodata, Cambridge Memories, Storage Technology, Kardios, Citel, and Two Pi (a Dutch company).

The most important of the newer firms was National Semiconductor, a leading manufacturer of components as the name indicates, which in 1973 started manufacturing equipment compatible with IBM and NCR machines. Six years later National acquired Itel's sales and support operations, which it renamed National Advanced Systems (NASCO). Earlier, National Semi President Charles Sporck spoke out in favor of limiting Japanese penetration of the American computer market. "Successful domination of markets by Japanese companies has weakened or destroyed the corresponding industry in the United States," he said, citing examples such as motorcycles, calculators, television sets, and so forth. "Clearly IBM and every other computer manufacturer in the U.S. are under attack," he concluded, demanding that the Japanese exporters to America be treated in the same way as Americans who attempted to sell in Japan—namely, subject to trade restrictions to protect domestic industry. In 1979 he had changed his tune and for an obvious reason: Itel had an import arrangement with Hitachi, which NASCO inherited.

Soon thereafter, NASCO was selling the Japanese company's plug-compatible mainframes in the United States under its nameplate, and little on the subject of Japanese domination was heard from Sporck. Others were to follow, as the Japanese sought out stateside partners both in order to obtain technology but more important, as a means to penetrate the American market. A typical example of this was an arrangement worked out between Mitsubishi and IPL, a smallish Massachusetts-based operation that had revenues of less than $20 million. IPL's President, Steve Ippolito, dreamed of swamping the market with Mitsubishi's PCMs bearing his nameplate. "Put simply, we aspire to becoming the biggest and the best of the PCMs."

For a while, Amdahl, Itel, NASCO, and other manufactures of plug-compatibles did quite well. But at the same time, IBM was preparing its blitz, aimed at blasting them out of the market.

It began quietly enough, with IBM salesmen notifying customers of maintenance difficulties on IBM peripheral equipment hooked to plug-compatible mainframes and of software changes in the works that could make these machines less desirable. The big blow came in March 1977, when IBM introduced its 3033 mainframe—the first of the 303X series—which was almost twice as powerful as the 168, and which was sold or leased for two-thirds the price of the older machines. The debut of the 3033 was accompanied by an announcement of a 30-percent cut in the prices of 158s and 168s. Thus, IBM would clear its backlog of 360s and early 370s at knockdown prices to bring in cash, while leasing 303Xs so as to provide a future stream of revenues.

It was by then an old and proven technique, but one that shocked Big Blue's competitors, to say the least. IBM and other firms in the industry cut prices regularly, though never before so sharply. There could be no doubt that the move had been aimed at Amdahl. Perhaps IBM truly feared loss of market share, but more likely, having demonstrated entry was possible in the industry, it now was moving to put Amdahl and the others in their places. Yet Gene Amdahl didn't appear cowed; three days later he announced price cuts of his own, making the 470s, which were compatible with the 3033 and half again as fast, only three percent more expensive (this was made possible by Fujitsu's price concessions on parts).

The attack continued as IBM pressed its advantage. While orders poured in for the 303Xs, IBM announced the 4300 series, which slashed costs even more drastically. For example, the 4341 was as powerful as the 158 but sold for one-quarter of its price. This caused an industry shakeout; Nanodata simply threw in the towel and others cut back.

Amdahl attempted to keep up with these developments, but the pace was too grueling, and the company faltered. It hardly was beaten, but Amdahl's momentum was halted. Revenues for 1979 were $300 million, or $21 million less than the previous year, while earnings were slashed by two-thirds. In vain, Amdahl searched for merger partners to beef it up for the ongoing competition. In the summer of 1979, it appeared a merger might be arranged with Memorex, whose interests were in peripherals and telecommunications, but nothing came of it. A year later, talks began with Storage Technology, which in addition to turning out PCMs was a major producer of tape drives and related gear, but this too failed—significantly, because Fujitsu opposed the deal.

There was a pickup in revenues thereafter, but not in profits. In 1981, IBM released the 3081, a large machine that sold for between $3.7 million and $4.1 million. Placements were excellent until Amdahl came out with its PCM, the 5860, the following year. IBM promptly cut prices, and in a major coup displaced Amdahl as a supplier to AT&T with a $1 million per copy discount.

Amdahl was crippled. Sales came in at $462 million in 1982, but earnings were a mere $4.9 million. Soon after, Heizer sold its stake to Fujitsu, raising the Japanese firm's share of ownership to close to 50 percent, and Amdahl was being perceived as the Japanese firm's representative in the American market. More particularly so because by then Amdahl himself was gone, to organize a new company, Trilogy, which he hoped would give IBM another major worry. For the time being in 1979, however, IBM had its victory.

But at a cost. So severe was the price drop that it set off a flurry of activity among customers, who lined up for the new machines shortly after they were announced. IBM had believed the market could absorb twenty thousand 4300s; within three weeks of their introduction, the firm's salesmen had taken orders for 42,000 of them, with some deliveries scheduled for five years in the future.

(It later would be learned that not all of these were firm orders. Realizing there would be a long wait-time, and that IBM was prioritizing orders by drawing lots, a number of firms and individuals placed orders hoping to get a low number in the draw, and then they sold their places in line to genuine customers. Thus, IBM wasn't really certain just how many orders it had.)

Some industry observers, along with virtually the entire computer press, considered the 4300 pricing policy something of a fiasco, causing the firm to unnecessarily forego earnings. And in fact, this was one of the very few periods in IBM's history when it was strapped for cash and was obliged to borrow heavily to finance ongoing programs. In time, the 4300 sale-and-lease prices would be raised, which was taken as an admission of error. But significantly, the price increases occurred only after Amdahl, NASCO, and other manufacturers of plug-compatibles had been thrown back. In this regard at least, it must be counted as another IBM victory.

In 1978, Amdahl had been considered the one American firm capable of taking on IBM in mainframes. Such talk wasn't heard in 1983, by which time

Amdahl was reduced to being what amounted to the American branch of Fujitsu. That year NASCO ceased producing its own machines, to rely exclusively upon Hitachi products. As for Itel, its revenues, which had gone from $79 million to $564 million in three years, was savaged, and had filed for bankruptcy.

By early 1984, all of the domestic PCM manufacturers except Amdahl and NASCO had left the field, and their role had been diminished greatly. For example, the previous year IBM had shipped 2,500 of its popular 308X mainframes—the smallest of which went for approximately $1 million each—and even so couldn't keep up with demand. In the same period, Amdahl and NASCO sold 200 of their PCMs at some 10 percent below the equivalent IBM price, and they wouldn't have done that well had IBM been able to keep up with orders.

Even so, IBM continued to cut prices. In September 1983 there was a reduction of from 10 to 13 percent, and in August 1984, IBM announced price reductions of from 10 to 16 percent on the 308Xs, which took the industry unaware since demand remained strong. The reason for this was evident; at the time IBM was preparing to bring out a new line of mainframes, known as the Sierra, early in 1986 and was attempting to clean house of the 308X inventory.

Amdahl and NASCO doubtless will ready their own versions of the Sierra PCMs, but given the 308X experience the outlook hardly is promising. Nonetheless, the fact remained that by mid-decade in the American market, the contest was between IBM and Futjitsu and Hitachi (the companies behind Amdahl and NASCO), with the BUNCH far behind and losing ground. Given the results to that time, it was little wonder that the Japanese were dismayed at the prospects for them in the fourth generation of the computer market, and some were looking forward to the fifth round in the struggle.

A Quartet for Trilogy

Gene Amdahl was not around for much of this. A stockholder revolt, tacitly supported by the Japanese, who by then seemed to think that they had milked him dry of ideas, led to his ouster in 1979 and replacement by Eugene White, under whose leadership Amdahl became more of a Fujitsu satellite than ever. Amdahl was cheerful enough; in fact he had been thinking of leaving for more than a year, unhappy that he had so little of the firm's stock, having sold off so much to get the company going. Vowing never again to permit this to happen, he already was planning a new entry, one in which he joined with his son Carlton, who had recently left Magnuson Computer. Together and with some associates they formed Acsys Corporation, intending to start out by bringing to market PCMs, but then going on to more ambitious undertakings. Within a few months, the name was changed to Trilogy Systems, and Gene Amdahl was talking about a typically ambitious attempt to re-invent the computer.

Amdahl certainly couldn't be faulted for lack of vision and daring. He now planned to replace the scores of chips used in big computers with several large-scale complex units etched on fairly large wafers. If successful, Trilogy would be able to produce machines four times as powerful as their IBM counterparts for approximately the same costs. Moreover, these machines would be simpler to service, smaller in size, and more rugged.

Amdahl had no trouble raising capital. From Sperry, Digital Equipment, Cii-Honeywell-Bull, and Control Data came $80 million, not necessarily because these firms hoped to share in Trilogy's growth but rather because they wanted quick access to any new technologies Amdahl might develop, to be used in the struggles with IBM. Another $85 million came from venture capitalists, and $55 million from limited partners. In November 1983, Trilogy offered shares to the public and raised $55 million in that fashion. Thus, Amdahl had more than a quarter of a billion dollars for his venture, from individuals and institutions willing to gamble on his credentials. And why not? After all, Amdahl Corp. had been a viable concern, and was still a major force in the European and American market. It seemed a good opportunity to participate in a development that conceivably could change the face of computer technology.

Amdahl created a $35 million research facility to which he attracted some of the industry's top talent. A like amount of money went into the acquisition and design of a manufacturing site in Ireland, from which he planned to deliver his first computers by 1985. But snags developed. Amdahl was unable to overcome several technological hurdles, the most important being developing a method to dissipate heat generated by the wafers. Time and again experimental units burned out, causing a series of redesigns, none of which worked. Delay followed failure, and then the process repeated itself.

Amdahl conceded defeat in June 1984, throwing in the towel and announcing Trilogy was abandoning its computer project and would concentrate on creating wafers for use by others. Two months later, he admitted a failure in wafers. Thereafter Trilogy would develop and market more conventional chips. The firm was little more than a holding operation, and in late 1984 Trilogy appeared doubtful it would be able to continue on independently for more than a year or so.

This was a blow to the quartet of partners, all of which were obliged to take large writeoffs, and of course Amdahl's dream of besting IBM at its own game was once again derailed. More than ever before, it appeared that the Armonk Monster was unbeatable. Certainly it was so insofar as its American and European rivals were concerned. They would survive for a while, but mergers and further combinations seemed inescapable. Some spoke of the inevitable showdown that was to come in the late 1980s, with *Economist* speaking for them by observing it would be "between IBM on the one side and Fujitsu and Hitachi on the other," with the Japanese the decided underdog. "IBM holds many advantages," thought the magazine. "Its size, financial strength, marketing experience and technological prowess favor it." But more than that there was the matter of sheer size. In 1983, IBM's mainframe revenues came to over $10 billion, or approximately three times that of Fujitsu and Hitachi combined. The firm's total revenues were better than $40 billion, which was twice that of the Japanese firms. Moreover, IBM was growing more rapidly than were its rivals. Given this situation, what could they hope for in the future?

The Sting and the Stung

In the early 1980s, Hitachi, and to a lesser extent other Japanese firms, become involved with the theft of IBM research—there is no other way to put it, for subsequently Hitachi and Mitsubishi admitted they had done so. This was not the first time this had happened. In the late 1970s, when Japan was behind the United States in microchip research and manufacture, Japanese 16K chips appeared that were all but direct copies of one turned out by Mostek, and there were other examples. But none was so dramatic or caused as much commotion as the theft that caused the IBM sting operation.

It will be recalled that Hitachi had refused Fujitsu's offer of playing a role at Amdahl, and like so many others in the plug-compatible business, the firm appeared reduced to awaiting the next IBM series, then scurrying around to analyze the machines, and finally creating copies, by which time IBM would have been well on the way to developing yet another series. It was a frustrating game, always trying to catch up, never really succeeding, and knowing that by your actions you were conceding IBM's innate and everlasting superiority.

There were four alternatives, of which the first—abandoning plug-compatibility, ignoring IBM, and going on to design and develop better and lower-priced machines and software—no longer was feasible. The second, a move to leapfrog IBM with startling new technologies, was the long-range goal.

The third was to work with individuals who knew IBM, thought like IBMers, and perhaps had actually been involved with the firm, hoping in this way to steal the march on the company. After all, if your operation was staffed by IBM clones, it might come up with IBM ideas before the parent. Fujitsu attempted this through the Amdahl connection; for a while Hitachi's efforts were bent at hiring as many former IBM scientists and technicians as it could obtain, turning them loose, and hoping for the best. In fact, there was nothing illegal or unusual about this. Ever since the dawn of the industrial revolution almost two centuries ago, firms have been involved in attempting to pry secrets from one another, often skirting the law in so doing.

The fourth way was the aforementioned theft of IBM research, in which Hitachi became involved.

In 1980 Raymond Cadet, a middle-level IBM scientist, quit the firm to take a position at NASCO. It appears that prior to leaving IBM's Poughkeepsie installation Cadet had taken ten of the workbooks on the 308X project. By some means—the actual details are in dispute, but it seems Cadet's NASCO supervisor, Barry Saffaie was involved—copies of the workbooks came into the possession of Kenji Hayashi, a senior engineer at Hitachi. At the time, Hitachi had a working arrangement with another former IBMer, Maxwell Paley, who offered to provide Hayashi with some legitimately acquired information on the 308X. Unwittingly Hayashi revealed he already had the information. Suspicious, Paley contacted a friend at IBM, Robert Evans, and told him of the encounter with Hayashi. Evans alerted IBM's internal security force (IBM spends more than $50 million annually in safeguarding its secrets), which contacted Paley, who agreed to work with it to uncover the suspected theft.

What came out of this resembled a classic "sting" operation, in which IBM and Paley set out to trap Hayashi. Paley told the Hitachi scientist he might be able to provide him with additional workbooks, and the two arranged to meet in Tokyo to discuss the matter. At that time, Paley convinced Hayashi he needed to see the first ten books so as to make certain he was delivering the genuine article. Hayashi agreed to let Paley see them. Paley then gave the ten workbooks to IBM's security forces, who turned the matter over to the Federal Bureau of Investigation.

Next, undercover FBI agents, operating through a phony consulting firm called Glenmar Associates, attempted to sell Hitachi purported IBM secrets, making certain that the Japanese knew they had been stolen. Hayashi was quite enthusiastic about the prospect. As a sign both of good faith and their ability to deliver the goods, the undercover agents arranged for Hayashi to photograph a supposedly secret IBM disk drive then being tested at United Technology's Pratt & Whitney installation. Meanwhile, Hayashi and other Hitachi employees were paying for the information, the total coming to around $600,000 for Hitachi and $26,000 (a down payment on what was to have come to more than $1 million) during the period from November 1981 to June 1982, for what they believed were tens of millions of dollars worth of company secrets. And all the while, the FBI was drawing the net tighter, making certain that Hitachi's top management, not just a few overzealous scientists, were involved in the theft.

On June 18, 1982, Fujitsu announced a new computer that was plug-compatible with the IBM 3081K. "The era in which many little stars revolve around the great IBM sun is coming to a close," Fujitsu Chairman Taiyu Kobayashi was quoted as saying by the *Nikkei Computer.* "Thus a new era in international business in dawning."

The FBI sprung the trap on Hitachi four days later. Eleven top Hitachi executives were involved, including Kisaburo Nakazawa, head of Hitachi's largest computer installation, whom a special prosecutor later was to characterize as its "leading computer developer." The government had an airtight case; after trying to deny the charges, the Japanese gave in and plea-bargained the charges down, so as to keep publicity to a minimum. In February of the following year, Hitachi was fined $10,000 on criminal charges and Hayashi another $10,000. There were several other minor payments.

Far more important was the civil case IBM brought against Hitachi. This was settled in a manner that mortified the Japanese. Hitachi had to return all stolen IBM documents and agree to pay what has been reported as $300 million for its transgressions. In addition, the company had to allow IBM to preview forthcoming Hitachi hardware to satisfy itself that no secrets had been used in their design.

There was an interesting sideline to this. In addition to the indemnity, Hitachi and Fujitsu were to pay $2 million to $4 million per month to IBM in software and licensing fees for customers' use of software, and $42 million to cover past illegal use of software. While some outsiders concluded that these payments might put to rest the old canard that Big Blue was technologically backward and dependent upon its superior sales force for placements, others perceived Hitachi's and Fijitsu's cooperation as evidence that the two firms feared IBM had additional information regarding attempts to purchase stolen documents and that they were paying the fees to safeguard against disclosure.

As though to underscore this possibility, IBM instituted an amended complaint against Hitachi's American partner, National Semiconductor, asking damages of from $750 million to $1.5 billion for having stolen computer secrets. Though the case was settled out of court, few industry observers believe the episode won't put a crimp into PCM sales and further cast doubts on the Japanese ability to fight the Armonk giant. It hardly could be claimed that developments emerging from the damage actions will knock the Japanese out of the box. That in the future they will be more wary of copying IBM hardware seems obvious.

In 1981, Hitachi spent 10 percent of its R & D budget on software; three years later the share came to 30 percent. Nothing—not the sting nor the harsh feelings created—would stop the Japanese drive in this direction. And the MITI-created Software Association received still larger grants and moved toward closer cooperation. "We don't want to copy IBM [software]," said Hisao Ishihara, managing director of the Association, in 1984. "We want to beat IBM." Thus, the goal remains the same.

What of Big Blue? IBMers were understandably angered on learning of the thefts but also proud. "They came to us for the secrets," one technician said, "because they knew we lead the industry."

The Sting "Shokku"

The Japanese were as much angered as embarrassed by these events. Such sting operations are illegal in Japan, and so it was roundly condemned. The fact that Paley had done business with the Japanese before, on an entirely ethical basis, and then "lured" Hayashi into making the offer was deemed a sign of American duplicity. "Japanese feel that when they are hitting someone they are in a fight, and when they are shaking hands they are friends," wrote one journalist. "Hitachi's losing out to IBM is a clear example of the drawbacks of Japanese-type one-handed boxing." During the trial, trucks equipped with loudspeakers appeared outside IBM Japan President Shiina's house, blaring out messages that he was a traitor, calling him "Yankee Shiina!" and "Go back to America, Shiina!"

Still, Hitachi was mortified, and this could be seen at the company's annual meeting the following June, at which President Katsushige Mita was obliged to devote more than an hour to answering questions about the thefts. Finally Mita said, "We did our utmost to solve the problem, and we have punished ourselves, including myself. We would like to do our best from now on too," indicating he hoped to put it all behind him. Could this happen? Given the Japanese sense of honor, it doesn't seem likely.

Few Americans seemed to realize that the revelations constituted a shattering blow to the Japanese psyche. Fujitsu's Kobayashi, in an address before a world electronic conference, had spoken of his country's reputation for product reliability, adding: "Japan must have similarly excellent traits in creativity before it is recognized as a world pacesetter. . . . When Japan becomes the equal of Europe and the United States in the matter of innovation, I shall be able to declare without hesitation that Japan can properly be called the pacesetter of the world." What of that, in the light of the admission of stolen documents?

Will this kind of information-buying continue? Doubtless it will, but probably without such scandals. Americans can count on Japanese computer companies to be less trusting in the future when they attempt to purchase technology.

The implication of all this was clear: Japanese firms would know what to expect from the duplicitous Americans and be on guard in the future, and the campaign against IBM Japan would intensify. Kenichi Saito, director of equity research in Japan for McKinsey & Co., thought that in time Hitachi might look upon the payment not as a fine but as "tuition" in a very difficult school, and that it would come out of the experience with new plans.

What might these be? The Amdahl situation could provide the paradigm. Japanese electronic and computer firms would purchase interests in small American high-tech firms and use them as listening posts. As noted, this approach could already be seen in Silicon Valley, where Japanese faces at local watering holes are quite common, and where information is passed about quite freely and is available for the listening. In 1977, Nippon Electric purchased Electronic Arrays, and NEC Electronics has its own offices there. Toshiba bought Maruman Semiconductor two years later and entered into a joint venture with LSI Logic. More of this can be expected in the future.

United States vs. Japan

But not too much, for the episode made an impact in America as well. Now

171

more aware than ever of the need to block the Japanese in data processing—and in the aftermath of the dropped antitrust suit—Washington seemed more willing than ever before to meet Japanese trade restrictions with equal if not more severe measures. Anti-Japanese sentiment was growing in the United States by the mid-1980s, as it was in Europe too. This hardly was unusual, and was not necessarily the result of the sting operation. Americans were—or should have been—familiar with the phenomenon, for it resembled the anti-Yankee sentiments of the 1950s and 1960s. At that time, the United States was the world's leader in many if not most industrial areas and the "ugly American" was a caricature created by those who resented American power. In the 1980s, Japan was the rising power, and that anti-Japanese feelings were stirred should have caused no surprise.

Nor should the thefts have been so shocking. In the context of Japanese-American rivalry in the 1980s, when leaders on both sides of the Pacific spoke of "trade war" as though it was somehow similar to the Soviet-American conflict, it might even have been anticipated. In a typical comment reflecting this view, one American scholar, William Davidson, wrote that the United States is engaged in a two-front war against specialized rivals. "We compete against the Soviet Union in the military arena, and against the Japanese and others in the industrial arena. Both are specialized rivals. The USSR neglects its industrial activities to focus on military development; Japan neglects its military to concentrate on industrial endeavors. If the United States is to retain leadership in these arenas, it must dominate those sectors that are critical to success in both arenas. If the United States does nothing else, it must do this. Its leaders know it, and they have taken appropriate actions."

(That the USSR was engaged in spying on the United States was generally accepted in this period, and the estimate by U.S. Navy Rear Admiral Edward Burkhalter, Jr., that the Soviets had stolen more than two-thirds of their military technology from the United States was verified by examination of captured Soviet military gear.)

To Davidson and others like him, the analog to the Reagan military buildup against the USSR would be trade restrictions against the Japanese. This at a time when some were comparing the theft of IBM's secrets to the Japanese attack on Pearl Harbor on December 7, 1941. Japanese-American relations were at a low point when the sting was revealed, and with it they fell even lower. That this negative attitude might deepen is one of the most dangerous problems in the Western world today. One might say that Washington is divided into two camps as to what constitutes the greatest danger to the United States in the foreign policy policy arena: an erosion of relations with the USSR, or a drawing apart of the United States and Japan.

The sting dramatized what up to now has been the single most surprising failure on the part of the Japanese in the technology and marketing areas; namely, their inability to seize a larger share of the information processing market than they did. After their successes elsewhere, it had been assumed that the struggle between "Japan Inc." and IBM would be in full swing by now, with IBM on the defensive. Throughout this period, IBM portrayed itself as beset by powerful rivals, always in danger of being engulfed. In 1980, CEO John Opel told IBM's stockholders of these fears:

> In addition to the many veteran companies in our industry, we see new and growing competitors all around the world, especially the Japanese. They come to the market alone, and they come with American and European partners.
>
> Then we see the PCMs—the plug-compatible manufacturers. They are proliferating. They are the kind of companies that offer equipment in substitution for IBM products interconnected with IBM systems.
>
> AT&T and other telephone companies, both here and abroad, are expanding horizontally into our business.
>
> The semiconductor manufacturers are integrating vertically into our business.
>
> Even an oil company, Exxon, is diversifying into information processing.
>
> A greater number of well-managed business enterprises in the United States, as well as around the world, often supported by their governments, continue to enter our industry.

While Opel didn't mean it as such, it perhaps is revealing that he spoke of "our" industry, for even then it appeared IBM owned it.

X

THE AMERICAN RESPONSES

The Micro Revolution

IBM seemed to rule supreme in the early 1970s. DEC was troublesome and Control Data had an entrenched position in large systems, but IBM dominated the vital center of the market. Or at least so it appeared at the time. Something was germinating out there, a force that IBM didn't seem to understand, and because of this force it would have to alter sharply its view of the industry, reshape the corporation, and even tamper with its renowned approaches to merchandising and service.

The Armonk leadership had assumed that computers were tools for businessmen and scientists, and had covered both markets quite successfully. Apparently no one of consequence at headquarters or in the field ever put in a serious effort to explore whether small computers—micros as they came to be known—might be marketed to individuals, such as independent businessmen, professionals, and students. Indeed, IBM had never shown much interest in these markets. During this period, a writer desiring to purchase an IBM electric typewriter might have found it difficult if not impossible to make a purchase or even be granted a demonstration. IBM simply had little interest in selling to such individuals, who more often than not had to get their machines from secondhand dealers.

Others would mine this market in ways that put one in mind of how the young Henry Ford placed his simple Model Ts when the nation's best seller was the more expensive and luxurious Buick, and driving schools for chauffeurs were sprouting up all over the country, headed by entrepreneurs who were convinced the average man would always lack the savvy to handle so complicated a piece of machinery.

This was where computing was in the mid-1970s, and this was one time when the usually astute IBMers missed the boat. That they did so indicated that even the industry's best-run firm could stumble, and that imaginative companies not only could enter the lists against the leader but perform well in the face of competition from so formidable a production and marketing force. It was a close call. Looking back from the vantage point of a decade later, it seems clear that IBM almost overlooked what might yet become the largest and most important computer market of them all. But when IBM's response came, it was powerful and well-informed. In the process, IBM altered its public image to a greater extent than ever before, and in ways that might have shocked Tom Watson, Sr.

The movement began in 1971, when Marcian "Ted" Hoff, a designer at Intel (one of the leading manufacturers of electronic gear), designed and then created the world's first "computer on a chip," better known as a microprocessor. He had done this for a Japanese customer, Busicom. Known as the 4004, it had limited use and was considered little more than a curiosity. Before long, however, the implications of the invention became manifest, and others entered the business.

While microprocessors were used for a variety of purposes, many acting as what one researcher called "a built-in traffic cop to make certain the flow of information is proper" within a computer, there seemed no reason why they could not perform as the heart of a small computer, which naturally enough was soon called a "microcomputer." Mulling this over was a group of scientist-entrepreneurs at a small New Mexico-based electronics firm, Instrument Telemetry Systems. In 1975 they created the Altair (named after the bright star in the constellation Aquila, which in the popular "Star Trek" television series was the sun of a fictitious planet) 8800, in a kit form, intended for hobbyists, who paid $400 for the basic materials, the most important of which was the Intel 8080 microprocessor. The hobbyists would also pay another $2,000 for peripheral equipment.

The Altair had limited appeal, since it required expert knowledge to assemble. ITS didn't engage in advertising or promotion, yet 1,500 of the kits were sold within a year, most of them through a small chain of hobbyist stores known as The Byte Shop. The name is significant, for in those days only an engineer or someone who liked to fiddle around with computers knew what a byte was.

The news got around, encouraging others to enter the field in the late 1970s. From Commodore International came the PET, while Heath, a major manufacturer of build-it-yourself kits, offered micros through its mail-order catalogue. Radio Shack, a chain of electronic supply stores, turned out the TRS-80, which was sold for $499, and which turned out to be the first of the major commercial successes in the subindustry. However, none of these companies was able to combine technical skill with marketing know-how, though, as will be seen, Radio Shack came the closest. It remained for Apple to provide the breakthrough.

The Amazing Young Men of Apple

Steve Jobs and Steve Wozniak, two young scientists who were working at Atari and Hewlett-Packard respectively, appeared to be typical technology-oriented Californians of the time. Both were natives of that state and had been involved in several cultlike organizations and activities before their mid-20s. Thus they combined interests in Oriental philosophy and a deep involvement with high technology in a way that seemed peculiar to California, especially the Silicon Valley, which is located around Palo Alto, Santa Clara, and San Jose.

Along with other hobbyists at a group called "The Homebrew Computer Club," Jobs and Wozniak had played around with electronic gear and were interested in the Altair kit. Eager to construct a microcomputer for their own use, not particularly flush, and hoping to save a few dollars, they obtained some parts from their companies, purchased others, and in the spring of 1976 turned out a crude model that they called the Apple, which as Wozniak said, "was designed strictly on a hobby, for-fun basis—not to be a product of a company."

Why the name? The answer depends on whom you ask. Several at the firm claim Jobs selected it to commemorate a summer devoted to picking apples in the Northwest, while others observe that he had spent time in India, and returned a confirmed vegetarian, and thought it sounded "nice and friendly." Wozniak wrote that "Apple is an odd name. It came from the days when you picked an interesting, fun name for a company. You do that when you're on a hobby basis." When the advertising agency they took on tried to come up with a different name the partners protested. "We took the attitude that Apple was a good name. Our computer could be friendly—everything an apple represents: healthy, personal, in the home." Perhaps without meaning to do so, the partners captured the essence of the new product and provided the rationale others, IBM included, would imitate.

Jobs and Wozniak demonstrated the machine to friends at Homebrew, who made suggestions for refinements. Several of them wanted to buy one, and production began, though it might be more accurate to say that Jobs and Wozniak started turning them out to order. And the orders rolled in. "Sometime about the fall of 1976, I realized that the market was growing faster than we could grow," recalled Jobs six years later. "We needed some more money."

Funds were obtained by selling copies of Apple I to the Byte Shop, and Wozniak attempted to win support from Hewlett-Packard while Jobs did the same at Atari; neither company was interested. So the two men opted to go it alone.

The pattern for them to follow was quite familiar in Silicon Valley, where for every ten or so small firms there appears to be at least one venture capitalist. These individuals prowl the area, seeking out start-up operations or rumors of highly regarded engineers considering going off on their own. In return for financing and guidance, venture capitalists expect a sizeable chunk of the equity. In the previous five years, they had founded more than 200 such firms, most of which followed the formula set down when Heizer helped finance Amdahl; now Jobs and Wozniak sought a similar arrangement.

They found their venture capitalists in the persons of Don Valentine, who raised some money, and Mike Markkula, Jr., a former marketing expert at Intel, who added more. Markkula became chairman; the firm moved into a small factory and soon after was producing a new machine known as the Apple II. Jobs and Wozniak, who knew nothing about running a firm and had no desire to learn, took positions as vice-chairman and vice-president for research respectively. Michael Scott, a hard-bitten veteran (at thirty-three he was the oldest of the group), who had been director of manufacturing at National Semiconductor, came in as president and chief operating officer.

As has been suggested, the Apple II was to personal computing what the Model T was to autos, namely the means whereby a formerly esoteric product was brought down to the average person. It was both relatively inexpensive and simple to operate, and it was ready for the market in a few months; in fact, the Apple II was demonstrated at the West Coast Computer Fair in April

1977, and orders were taken at that time. The company grew exponentially thereafter—$2.5 million in revenues for fiscal 1977, $15 million for fiscal 1978, $117 million in 1980. That year Apple sold its first issue of stock, taking in more than $100 million and leaving the 25-year-old Jobs with shares worth $165 million while the 28-year-old Wozniak's holdings came to $88 million. By then, the home computer industry's revenues topped the billion dollar mark for the first time. Radio Shack was the industry leader, but Apple was closing rapidly. The following year—when IBM announced it was preparing to offer a micro of its own—revenues stood at $335 million.

What some have called the "Apple Revolution" was on in full force by then, at which time Wozniak spent far less time at the office and factory and more in other pursuits, while Jobs attempted to rationalize what had happened. In the course of an interview granted to *Computers & People* in the summer of 1981, he put it this way:

> The whole concept is this: for the same capital equipment cost as a passenger train, you can now buy 1,000 Volkswagens. Think of the large computers [the mainframes and the minis] as the passenger train and the Apple personal computer as the Volkswagen. The Volkswagen isn't as fast or as comfortable as the passenger train. But the VW owners can go where they want, when they want, and with whom they want. The VW owners have personal control of the machine.
>
> In the '60s and early '70s, it wasn't economically feasible to have the interaction of one person with one computer. Computers were very costly and complicated; 50 people had to share one computer. Back then, you could have the passenger train but not the Volkswagen. But with the advent of microelectronics technology, parts got smaller and denser. Machines got faster. Power requirements went down. Finally, electronic intelligence was affordable. We finally had the chance to invent the personal computer. . . ."
>
> Basically, Steve Wozniak and I invented the Apple because we wanted a personal computer. Not only couldn't we afford the computers that were on the market, those computers were impractical for us to use. We needed a Volkswagen.

Wozniak had a somewhat different view of Apple's ability to excite interest and take so great a share of the market so rapidly.

> Our success was due to a number of factors. First of all, we had never

manufactured computers before. We couldn't look back and say, "Here's how computers earned a lot of money in the '60s and '70s, that's the style to do." All we thought about was what was going to work out in our own homes. Our motivation was what would be good in the end. If there were a known formula for what would make a successful product and what would make a billion dollars, all the big companies were a lot smarter than we were. What we had was luck. We did the right things with the right coincidences of timing and the right people in the right place together.

Their attitudes are typical of the way the young microcomputer companies acted and spoke in the late 1970s. In a way it was a wedding of the kind of political activism that was fashionable in the 1960s with "star wars" fantasizing. There was also a liberal dollop of the ideas associated with the then governor of California, Jerry Brown, and philosopher E. F. Schumacher, whose "Small Is Beautiful" might have but did not happen to refer to micros. How different this was from the geometric perfection so admired at IBM, the tough-minded engineering found at DEC and CDC, and the earnest—albeit fumbling—efforts of RCA and RemRand! IBMers were dedicated; Apple's young men and women were "mellow," "with it," and "involved." It wasn't only a technological difference; there was what must have appeared to Jobs and Wozniak a cultural gap of Grand Canyon proportions between Armonk and the Silicon Valley garage in which Apple was born. Nor was this unique; in 1984 Wozniak calculated that out of the Homebrew Club sprang "something like 21 companies. We managed to bring the computer revolution home!"

There was an underside to all of this, one which is worth mentioning. The traditional American companies are much concerned with the "bottom line." Harold Geneen of ITT, perhaps the most admired manager of the 1960s and early 1970s, always insisted that each quarter's result better those of the previous year; this was a clear indication that short-run financial results, not long-term technological ones, were of primary importance. Not to those young people of Silicon Valley, who, while not unconcerned about success, were prepared to wait it out, to ignore stockholders (and they were large holders themselves) if necessary in order to obtain technological satisfactions. To his credit, Geneen recognized the value of this approach and indicated as much in his memoirs—after leaving ITT. So do the Japanese. The long-term approaches they are famous for and the ones of the Silicon Valley entrepreneurs derive from different sources, but are quite similar. Thus, the new

American technology, born in California and spreading throughout the land, is yet another problem for those Japanese companies thinking of breaking into the computer and information processing and transmission industries.

It remains to note that with all of this novelty there was something familiar in the atmosphere at Apple in the late 1970s, a sense of excitement redolent of what had been going on at Control Data and Digital Equipment two decades earlier. Just as Jobs and Wozniak planned to turn out micros for the masses, so had Bill Norris and Seymour Cray attempted to create huge mainframes capable of performing any task imaginable. And Ken Olsen's and Harlan Anderson's minis were not that different from the micros of the 1980s, though they targeted scientists. Indeed, DEC started out by putting together boards for other companies, and this was Apple's experience too. And, of course, imaginative venture capitalists made both firms viable. The time, place, and scope were different, but the ambition was the same. All three firms were successful in coping with IBM, since this kind of almost romantic and poetic approach was in short supply at Armonk, and hadn't really been seen since the days of the 360.

Whether this lack represented an IBM strength or weakness is a matter of opinion, for though it occasionally prevents Big Blue from taking daring steps, it has saved it from gaffes as well.

The Siliconized Culture

Yet there surely was more to it than that. A new, young, electronics-based culture was developing in the Far West, one that tended to look across the Pacific to the Orient—unlike the more staid and older culture in the East, which was Atlantic-oriented. If it puzzled American Easterners, the California approach absolutely baffled the Japanese, to whom it posed both problems and possibilities.

For one thing, the Silicon Valley pioneers were at the same time more loosely organized and imaginative than their counterparts at, say, Burroughs, NCR, and Honeywell, and so were more difficult for the generally stolid and often imitative large Japanese firms to keep up with. At the same time, the Pacific orientation often brought with it a willingness to work with Japanese firms, even to the point of entering into joint ventures (as with Amdahl). There was a far stronger Japanese presence in Silicon Valley, for example, than along its eastern counterpart, Boston's Route 128.

Apple's pioneers were as typical of this cultural type as one might have found in the late 1970s. They rejected the corporate mentality that they believed to be a hallmark of the older computer companies, but since their experiences had been limited to California they had no real standards against which to judge the established firms. Certainly they couldn't judge IBM, which most of the people at Apple deemed to be the quintessential old-line firm. But more than any of the others, IBM was flexible and prepared to shift ground, and in Frank Cary possessed a CEO ideal for the task.

IBM/West

Cary was a Westerner himself, a graduate of UCLA and Stanford, who had joined IBM in 1948 as—what else?—a salesman, worked his way up, won battle stars in the 360 campaign, and in 1969 was named to the select Management Review Committee, which formulates policy and carries out decisions. By then, too, he was an obvious candidate for the top spot, which he took in 1974 on Vince Learson's retirement.

Mention has been made of Cary's impact upon the firm, but not of how he further dismantled elements of the Watson Sr. superstructure that were out of place in the 1970s. One of his early decisions was to take apart the organization Tom Watson, Jr., and Learson had put together for the 360 campaign and reshape its General Systems Division, the Atlanta-based unit out of which had come Systems/3, one of IBM's early experiments with small computers. Into General Systems he placed most of the firm's mavericks, individuals conceded to be brilliant and imaginative but who found it difficult to work within the traditional IBM structure. General Systems was to remain in Atlanta, but its most important facilities were in Boulder, Colorado, and in San Jose, right smack in the heart of Silicon Valley. By mid-decade General Systems had acquired the nickname of "IBM/West," while the San Jose installation was filled with bearded young men, clad in jeans and sportshirts, padding barefoot through the halls, looking for all the world like refugees from one of the newer high-tech firms.

A decade earlier, these oddballs might not have been considered worthy of an interview at IBM. It was a tribute to a vibrant American industrial climate that Jobs and Wozniak were able to succeed as they did, and to the flexibility of IBM that it proved capable of moving the mountain to Muhammad and accepting as much of the California culture as it did, so as to succeed in this new area.

Thus, while Jobs, Wozniak, and others disdained the older companies, not without reason, they might have omitted IBM from the crowd. As much as any young Silicon Valley firm, IBM was prepared to compete with the Japanese, and when the time for it came, to do so in microcomputers.

The IBM Version: Success

IBM introduced its PC (Personal Computer) amid much ballyhoo on August 12, 1981. It was a highly publicized event, well-covered by the press and television, quite unlike the release of the first news regarding the 360s and perhaps the closest IBM ever came to doing anything quite so dramatic.

The reason was obvious. Whereas data management vice presidents could become excited by large mainframes, hundreds of thousands of potential customers were awaiting the PC, and most of these weren't big businessmen but professionals, students, and owners of relatively small enterprises. In 1981 Apple would sell more than 150,000 computers and Radio Shack some 80,000. Now the market would expand, or so went the thought. At IBM some were talking confidently of selling a half million units by 1983 or 1984 at the latest.

They were wrong. In its first full year, $2 billion worth of PCs were sold, and at that there was a waiting line at the retailers. Sales for 1983 topped 600,000 and would have been more had IBM been able to turn out machines fast enough to meet demand. The million mark was passed the following year, by which time IBM was the leader of the subindustry.

The PC turned out to be a quite conventional machine without extraordinary software. What was unique—for IBM at least—was the way the program was put together, and once again the comparison with the 360 might be instructive and an indication of how flexible the firm can be when needs dictate.

First IBM carefully studied the industry, attempting to discover the whys and hows of the micro businesses; the company concluded that the main competitor was Apple.

Then, in 1980, Armonk organized a team, headed by engineer Philip Estridge, gave it a rather ramshackle single-story building in Boca Raton, promised financing, and withdrew—there was virtually no interference from headquarters. "We were allowed to develop like a start-up company," Estridge said. "IBM acted as a venture capitalist. It gave us management guidance, money, and allowed us to operate on our own."

Thus, IBM proved capable of learning and imitating when necessary, something for which the Japanese are so famous.

What Big Blue failed to do was consider how the PC would fit in with other hardware. Stated simply, it was not designed to interface with mainframes and so remained squirreled in the micro niche. Eventually other PCs would come to market, none of them capable of the kind of networking that compatibility would have made possible. Of course there were other possibilities IBM did not perceive at the time, one example being the telecommunications potential. As will be seen in the following chapter, while starting to acquire Rolm in 1983 IBM recognized much earlier that it would soon enter telecommunications, and it should have realized the importance of compatibility. Permitting Estridge to go off on his own brought immediate results; not having him work in tandem with others meant that IBM lost the chance to erect telecommunications networking much earlier than it did.

On the other hand, IBM was quite prepared to consult with others outside the firm when it came to software and even hardware. From Intel came a 16-bit microprocessor (the 8088), for example, this at a time when most of the other micros utilized 8-bit microprocessors. The hard disk drive came from Seagate, Miniscribe, and Onyx/IMI, the floppy disk drive from Tandon, the hard disk controller from Xebec, and the system board assembly from SCI Systems (the only major supplier east of the Mississippi—SCI was headquartered in Alabama). Texas Instruments and the Mostek division of United Technologies provided semiconductors. And there were dozens of others, firms who contributed, as IBM obviously attempted to encourage industry-wide cooperation on the project. In fact, it even gave some contracts for floppy disks to former archrival Control Data.

Once the PC's success was assured, backup sources were established and the Boca Raton plant was expanded by more than one million square feet and the workforce beefed up by 2,500. The installation was the closest to a factory assembly line the industry had seen to that time. Manager David Wilkie claimed that a PC rolled off the line at the rate of one every 45 seconds. But, in fact, the plant, too, was a copy—of a smaller but highly efficient Apple II facility.

Needless to say, all of these suppliers derived reputations and status as well as profits from their participation. "It's credibility, it's revenue stream," said Xebec's Stan DeVaughn, "if you can tell a potential customer that you are an IBM supplier. It says a lot about who you are."

IBM released the PC specifications to any and all who were interested in writing software and promised to cooperate to the fullest extent. Microsoft, which provided the PC's basic operating system called MS/DOS, was permitted to sell it to others, helping bring into being a new group of plug-compatible companies, such as Compaq, Columbia, Corona Data Systems, and Eagle. This idea was not original; Apple had been doing the same thing for several years.

Gradually, it became evident that IBM was following the old game plan—let others pioneer and then step in and do it better than they can. Again, this was the hallmark of the Japanese as well. Gene Amdahl was irate. "IBM wants everything," he said. "It's their policy to wait until a market gets big enough so they can deal with it in their own *modus operandi.* Now they are helping themselves to the fruit that Apple grew." One journalist went so far as to write that "The only thing IBM contributed to the PC is the name and logo." But of course there was more: behind the PC was the awesome IBM reputation.

The firm was prepared to change image and strategy when the situation demanded, but at no point since its beginning was so drastic an alteration required as with the personal computer. IBM had been erected around salesmen who had been trained to serve and service business and governmental clients. An individual whose life had been spent outside these circles would have known of IBM, but his or her sole direct contact might have been limited to receiving checks printed on one of the firm's ubiquitous cards. Not only had the company failed to cultivate the general public, but it seemed to harbor a positive dislike of the thought of doing so.

Now it was seeking to sell these very same individuals machines with the IBM logo and maintain them as customers for software and related services. The task required a major study, which ended in near-complete success.

IBM opted for a triple approach in the distribution area. In the first place, there were now IBM showrooms, less than a half dozen in that first year, all located in the business districts of large cities. Established prior to the PC introduction, they now became salesrooms as well. Initially they did not do as well as IBM had hoped, and for reasons that were easy to fathom. The general public respected IBM but didn't feel comfortable in that environment. As Charles Pankemier, who directed the PC advertising program put it, "We were dealing with a whole new audience that never thought of IBM as a part of their lives."

In order to change this, the firm launched a massive advertising campaign, the most costly the industry had ever known. It began with an internal search for a product image, which in that period meant a spokesperson to appear in televised commercials, which, too, were something new for IBM. Others were doing it with actors who had developed "images." Alan Alda, the popular star of "M*A*S*H," spoke for Atari; William Shatner, the Captain Kirk of "Star Trek," was there for Commodore; while Apple hired Dick Cavett, a well-known talk show host believed a trifle more cerebral than most. Bill Cosby, a gentle comedian much loved by middle-class Americans (and who had a proven track record in the commercials market), was the Texas Instruments selection.

Looking over the field, IBM's advertising agency considered a wide variety of individuals and images, ranging from the Muppets to French mime Marcel Marceau, before settling on the aforementioned Charlie Chaplin lookalike, in an attempt to obtain that "friendly" reputation. Their choice worked quite well. According to surveys, the Charlie Chaplin "tramp" created sentiments of warmth, empathy, and affection—which were just what IBM wanted and needed. IBM also trained a new sales force, individuals who were geared more to the retail market than to offices and government agencies.

For a while there was talk of setting up a nationwide chain; those who believed this would happen apparently could not imagine IBM agreeing to share store space with other firms. Once again IBM proved flexible. Thus, would-be purchasers could buy their PCs at the likes of Programs Unlimited, the Computer Factory, Computerland, and so on. Or they could go to 47nd Street Photo in Manhattan, a major discounter that sold the machines in their original cartons.

(In its early months Apple sold the I and later the II at the Byte Shop, but problems soon developed and Jobs sought to modify the arrangement so as to be able to use other retailers. Byte refused to give in, so Apple terminated its agreement, upon which the store refused to pay for its more recent shipments and each side sued the other. The matter was eventually settled, but in the meantime Apples were offered by a wide variety of retailers.)

Finally, IBM entered into agreements with Sears Roebuck, Macy's, and more than eight hundred other established retail stores to establish computer centers, and the machines were sold from these stores by non-IBM employees.

The idea of students and small businessmen lining up at 47th Street Photo to pick up IBMs as though they were so many TV sets would have sent Tom Watson, Sr., reeling; the knowledge that his company had to turn to outside salesmen to offer IBM equipment would have been flabbergasting.

In Armonk in the mid-1980s, one often heard statements beginning with the words "The old man [Watson Sr.] would turn over in his grave if he knew . . . ," followed by yet another innovation. The veterans recognized the need for change. IBM was venturing into unfamiliar waters in marketing to

186

the masses rather than the familiar business and governmental clients and needed a new kind of support and assistance.

The change could be seen in product areas other than personal computers. In September 1984, Armonk announced that its factory automation equipment would also be offered by outside vendors, the reason given being the need to husband scarce resources such as the sales force. "We think our whole business capability will be made more effective by bringing more resources to bear on this market," said national sales manager Dean Arnold. Others noted that IBM not only needed to reduce expenses but thus far had turned in a poor performance in this field and required assistance.

John Opel was finely tuned to these new markets and set down a new rule, one that existed in practice but now became official company dogma: zero defects. It was a concept usually identified with the Japanese, but many American firms had utilized it decades earlier. It had become a necessity with the PC, however, since Opel did not visualize a major service operation for the line.

Due to all of this the machine became an industry bestseller and the standard against which the others were measured. And there was a bonus, in that the PC stimulated sales of other IBM equipment. "They're following the Trojan-horse strategy," said Frank Gens of the Yankee Group, a major industry-watcher. "The executive sits down at his self-contained PC, but pretty soon he decides he needs to plug into the company's mainframe. Suddenly three hundred executives want to tie into the mainframe—and the corporation has to buy more mainframe capacity."

The European Blitz

IBM Europe began turning out PCs soon after they were introduced domestically. Soon the factory at Greenock, Scotland, into which came components from suppliers in all the Common Market countries, was on double shifts to meet demand. The strategy that worked so well in the United States was duplicated in Europe. IBM Europe's CEO, Kaspar Cassani, signed contracts with as many of the large department stores as would set up computer shops under their roofs; within a year and a half he had more than 14,000 outlets. When it appeared that sales were lagging, Cassani cut prices and they perked up once again, to the utter frustration of competitors, who in common with their American counterparts slowly realized that Big Blue's corporate culture was changing. "We are dealing with a different IBM today," said Elserino Piol, Olivetti's executive vice president for strategy and development. "They never discounted; now they are discounting. They used to be predictable; today they try to use any kind of marketing tool."

The results were roughly those of the American experience. In 1982, Commodore held a slim lead in personal computers in Europe, based upon its price/performance ratio, and was followed by Apple, Olivetti, and Acorn (a U.K. company). The following year, Apple grabbed the lead with 21 percent of the market, with Commodore second at 18 percent; IBM Europe was next in this, the PC's initial year. By the end of 1984, it appeared that IBM Europe had approximately 25 percent of the market, Apple 18 percent, while Acorn and Olivetti came in at 12 percent each, and a slipping Commodore fell to 9 percent.

The success wasn't all that it implies, however. In the first place, Europe is a small market compared to the United States. In 1984, IBM believed 2 million PCs would sell domestically, while the figure for the entire Common Market was around 300,000. More important, in recent years several of the European companies—Olivetti, Nixdorf, Siemens, and ICL among others—had come out with small office systems that were well received. While IBM Europe had a robust 70 percent of the market in mainframes, its share of smaller systems in which four or five operators are tied together was in the 17–20 percent range. Intent on increasing its share, IBM Europe looked upon the PC not only as a product that would win the small businessman, but as the entering wedge for a larger system to be introduced the following year, the AT, which was aimed at the heart of this market. The first ATs made their appearance overseas in late 1984, and it is too early to make any judgments on them.

The IBM Version: Failure and Recovery

It worked the other way around too; IBM and IBM Europe had their eyes on professionals and others who might be interested in a smaller machine. Suppose that executive wanted to compute at home? In 1983, IBM provided the answer: the PCjr (known during the preparation phase as the Peanut), which could run almost all software used on the PC and was smaller, lighter, and less expensive.

Industry forecasts for huge sales didn't materialize, however. "We are very pleased with the success of our IBM Portable Computer," said company spokesman Jeanette Maher. "Demand is strong, and we are continuing to increase our manufacturing capabilities." But the fact was that a Compaq plug-compatible, released soon after as an alternative to the PCjr, was outselling it by four to one in the summer of 1984. "There is an extremely important lesson in this," said Enzo Torresi, a marketing expert in micros. "Even the big three letters are not sufficient to push a product to market if it is not a substantial step ahead in technology or price performance."

What had gone wrong? It appeared that the firm had priced the PCjr too high (in the $800–$1,600 range for the stripped-down box), in the hope that the machine would not cannibalize sales from the PC. It turned out that the machine was too expensive for students and not powerful enough for many businessmen; for example, it couldn't run such software as the Lotus 1-2-3 financial spreadsheet, which many considered vital. Computer consultant Peter Norton argued that the PCjr "may well be targeted at a gray area in the market that just does not exist." In addition, the smaller unit had an uncomfortable keyboard, the hard rubber keys resembled Chiclets gum and looked fragile.

Finally, the machine suffered in comparison with the Apple IIc, a $1,295 product released in early 1984. Moreover, the Apple Macintosh, which came to market in force the previous year, was a clear success, leading some analysts to wonder whether it might capture ground from the PC itself. "Apple has very neatly bracketed the PCjr," said Tony Morris of Morris Decision Systems, a New York retailer. "Those who are fearful of spending $1,600 on a fully-equipped PCjr may turn instead to the IIc or to the original Apple II."

In early summer 1984, Opel acknowledged that the machine "has not been as successful as I would have liked," and he said he planned to do something about it. So he did; once again IBM demonstrated its ability to recoup. A few weeks later the company announced sharp price cuts combined with the offer to replace the keyboard free for anyone who did not like it. This was combined with a large-scale advertising effort. It was a major public relations success, and thereafter PCjr sales rose substantially. Despite this, it did not live up to its expectations and production was halted in the summer of 1985.

The PC sharply altered IBM's image, or perhaps a better way to put it would be that it provided Big Blue with its first public persona insofar as the average person was concerned. While hardly the only important product out of Armonk in the early 1980s, PC sales came to over $2.5 billion in 1983, better than 5 percent of total revenues, making it the company's single most important computer. Still, other parts of the empire were doing as well, though they were less publicized. The corporate culture was changing, this seen not only in the PC project but also indicating that IBM was prepared to carry its new policy of cooperation with others to new heights.

They were also ready to compete more fiercely than ever, a thought which sent shudders through the industry. The anticipated shakeout began, with such giants as Texas Instruments and once-vigorous firms like Atari throwing in the towel. That others would follow seemed inevitable.

XI

ON THE ACQUISITIONS TRAIL

The Intel Connection

In December 1982, IBM announced it had purchased a 12-percent interest in Intel for $250 million. As has been noted, Intel (the name comes from *Int*egrated *El*ectronics) is a pioneer in microprocessors and other integrated circuits, and at the time its 8080 chip was the standard for the industry.

The move was at the same time surprising and to have been expected. The surprise came from the fact that this was a new experience for IBM. The corporation had made some relatively minor acquisitions and engaged in joint projects occasionally. But now it was taking a major equity position in an independent corporation, placing a member on its board, while averring it had no intention of going much further than that—at least for the time being.

So much for the surprise. The expected was that IBM would integrate backward into microchips in this most sensible fashion.

IBM was and is a major manufacturer of 64K Ram chips and a leader in many other categories. When American journalists were panicking readers by noting that Japan had taken the leadership in the *sale* of chips, they neglected to note that that country's lead in 64Ks was due to the fact that the American companies had opted to turn out a more sophisticated version, one that conformed to the needs of the military—always a major consideration for firms deriving much of their sales from that source.

While the Japanese enjoyed a 2-1 margin over the American firms in 64Ks, the United States led in the faster growing market for 16-bit microprocessors, even supplying most of the Japanese companies with them. Such firms as Intel and Motorola are far ahead in the powerhouse 32-bits, which are capable of handling from 2.5 to 8 million instructions per second. NEC, for example, manufactures 16-bits under an Intel license, and currently is attempting to create a microprocessor which might replace Intel's, so that customers could switch to it without difficulty. Which, as has been often noted, is a Japanese forte—producing a better and less expensive model of an item American firms pioneered with, especially if the technology has become fixed.

Microchip production is one area in the business electronics field in which this familiar Japanese approach appears to have worked. For example, in 1983 Zilog, an American subsidiary of Exxon started by a group of engineers who had left Intel, had the lead in the 8-bit market with its Z-80. Then the Japanese entered the scene. Soon after, Zilog accused Nippon Electric of having copied several of its more popular chips. Nothing was ever proven one way or the other, but many customers preferred the less expensive NEC chip and observed that the Japanese company had better quality control. Today Zilog manufactures a number of products under NEC licenses.

In the 128K and 256K RAM markets the Japanese and American firms appear to be neck and neck in the area of manufacturing—with much of the interesting technology coming out of IBM, Texas Instruments, and Intel. However, the Japanese companies have 90 percent of the market for 256Ks and 54 percent of that for 64Ks. In all, the Japanese companies account for more than a third of worldwide microchip revenues, estimated to be close to $19 billion in 1984.

The reason for this apparent disparity is that IBM—and Bell Labs, GE, and other American firms—are substantial component manufacturers that use all their production in their own products. In 1982, the year it took the interest in Intel, IBM accounted for $2.1 billion of the approximately $4.1 billion in "captive manufacture" of semiconductors. In contrast, the world's leading manufacturers of semiconductors that year were Motorola ($1.3 billion), Texas Instruments ($1.2 billion), NEC ($1.2 billion), Hitachi ($1 billion), and Toshiba $810 million). Yet with all of this IBM doesn't turn out sufficient chips for its own use and has to turn to outside vendors, the most important of which is Intel. "IBM is trying to make sure its suppliers are lined up and adequately financed," observed a Dataquest (a major market research operation) analyst. "It wants Intel to stay around in the form that it is now."

There was more to it than the naked numbers. IBM is a major chip manufacturer, to be sure, but it concentrates on mass production of conventional arrays, often configurations pioneered by others; this an ancient company tradition. No less than the Japanese, IBM engages in licensing advances pioneered by others. This is where Intel comes in. That firm specializes—indeed, earned its reputation—in custom chips and is at what the trade journals like to call "the leading edge of technology." In aligning itself with Intel, IBM has associated itself with pioneering while not being obliged to engage in the practice itself.

Under terms of the agreement IBM was permitted to up its equity holdings to 30 percent, but not go further for eight years. The stake was raised to that 30 percent figure the following year, by which time industry observers were coming around to the belief that IBM would take over Intel completely in 1991. IBM denied this, with some at the company pointing out that the $250 million stake hardly was large by Big Blue standards. David Stein of the Gartner Group, the leading IBM-watcher, remarked that such a sum "is about equivalent to building a semiconductor factory," and a low price considering what IBM was getting from the deal. Yet the rumors of a takeover persisted, as will be seen for good reasons.

What did Intel expect to obtain from the association? The company needed capital to fund its ongoing and extensive research and development operation, especially in the face of intense competition from the Japanese. Andrew Grove, the engineering Ph.D. who is Intel's CEO, had been complaining bitterly about unfair Japanese competition and welcomed the IBM connection. Along with others in the industry, he recognized that its economics dictated such marriages and seemed pleased to have wound up with such a partner.

Time was when as a result of the learning curve the ratio of rejects to accepted units fell rapidly, as did price, but the latter not so fast as to prevent companies from making substantial profits, which would be used to create the next generation of chips. Such had been the experience with the 1K, the 4K, the 16K, and the 32K. Things changed with the 64K, for the Japanese mounted a worldwide offensive, slashing prices across the line in their drive to capture market share, and this obliged Intel, Motorola, and other chip manufacturers to form alliances with others, if only to share research and development costs. In 1982, Intel expended $130 million for capital investments and a like amount on R & D; the corporation's 1981 earnings had come to $27.4 million. Thus, the equity sale to IBM made abundant sense.

It does not mean, however, that Intel occupies a special position in the IBM universe when it comes to supplying components, for such would fly in the face of American antitrust law. For example, in the summer of 1984, IBM introduced its powerful new AT personal computer, which sent shock waves through the industry due to its versatility and low price. Known by the code word "Popcorn" during development, the AT was priced between $4,000 and $6,000 and was capable of performing several computations at the same time and permitting three people to work at it simultaneously. IBM released the AT at a splashy party in Dallas, highlighted by a magician who made computers—and executives—appear and disappear with a wave of his wand. (Was Watson Sr. revolving in his grave at that?) "You said the customers wanted to be able to do far more," said cowboy-hatted Philip Ethridge to the assembled retailers. "We are partners. We are listening."

Ethridge revealed that the AT is constructed around an Intel 16-bit 80286 microprocessor, which appears to be well on the way to setting new standards for the next two to three years—a generation in such matters. The chip, which cost around $200 in the autumn of 1984, is one of the most complex and powerful now in use. David House, Intel's general manager, notes that "The circuitry we have put on the 286 would have filled three big five-drawer filing cabinets in 1971 and cost half a million dollars." And behind the 80286 is the 80386, a 32-bit microprocessor that will provide IBM PCs with the power of medium-sized computers.

Undaunted, Motorola formed a relationship with Apple, which uses its 32-bit 69020 microprocessor in its popular Macintosh. Burroughs employs a National Semiconductor chip. Other alliances are forming in the United States, and all are watching the Japanese with no little interest. "We are scared to death they will get something established," says Intel founder and CEO Gordon Moore, indicating why the IBM-Intel relationship will become closer.

That this closeness was in the works became manifest in 1984. Soon after the introduction of AT, it was learned that IBM intends to produce 80286s in its own facilities under an Intel license, and in addition will purchase them from American Microdevices and Siemens, all three operating as Intel licensees. The first important collaborative effort between IBM and Intel was off to a roaring start.

The Promise of Telecommunications

The evolution of the industry and IBM's ability to move with it demanded that IBM take another important equity position, which gave it an important stake in telecommunications and may be the prelude to a confrontation with the one domestic company that could offer it a difficult contest: AT&T.

Telecommunications and data processing had different origins, of course, but by the early 1980s they were coming together, and out of this union would come a new subindustry, which at the time was known as distributed data processing.

There are a handful of young, rapidly growing firms in the field—Rolm, Datapoint, Northern Telecom, Mitel, Hayes, and Four-Phase are some of the better known players. Digital Equipment and Data General are making strong efforts too, and several of the BUNCH companies were there; Burroughs is creating SWIFT for the Worldwide Interbank Financial Telecommunications, to link computers in 700 of the world's largest banks. Sperry established Distributed Communications Architecture, and a consortium of DEC, Xerox, and Intel planned local networking programs. Tymshare had Tymnet, GTE had Telenet, and so it went.

The most important player was AT&T, then in the process of being dismantled and set adrift in a competitive environment. The AT&T entry was known as Advanced Communication System (ACS), which when completed will put data banks in all parts of the world at the disposal of users of its terminals. Moreover, the new AT&T planned to enter the computer field, and in fact already was doing so. The clash with IBM seemed inevitable, especially since at the same time Big Blue was deploying into telecommunications.

IBM's interest was natural enough, since like the other computer manufacturers it was getting deeply involved with data transmission—the movement of information between computers. Cary became attracted to the concept in the late 1960s, and in 1971 sent CEO Learson a memo stating: "The market will move toward remote computing, and non-central processing unit equipment will be a continually increasing portion of the business."

To go in that direction was a gigantic undertaking, even for a firm with IBM's power, and allies were needed. Thus, in 1973 IBM purchased a majority interest in CML Satellite Corporation, the initials of which derive from those of its founders, Communications Satellite Corporation (Comsat), MCI Communications (AT&T's most important rival in long distance telephony), and Lockheed (then and now an important entry in the software area as well as a major military contractor). CML had been established to create a worldwide telecommunications network to rival that of AT&T, but it was not working out well, and the partners were willing to sell a controlling interest to IBM for $2.5 million each. In this way, IBM not only for the first time entered a field regulated by a government agency, but initiated its confrontation with

AT&T. IBM's interest in CML was a small beginning, however, and IBM was prepared to write it off at a loss if the technology and markets did not develop.

Soon thereafter, Cary initiated a program known within the firm as AQUARIUS (A Query and Retrieval Interactive Utility System), which had only limited success and appeal. AQUARIUS was downplayed for the next few years, so at its inception IBM fell behind in the distributed data processing (DDP) field.

By mid-decade, however, Cary revamped AQUARIUS, and the new program, Systems Network Architecture (SNA) became IBM's entry into the field. SNA was constructed around a large host computer (usually a 360 or 370) to which was added peripheral equipment of various kinds, while terminals at several locations were linked by wire. In 1978 IBM announced the 8100 computer, which was designed specifically for distributed data processing purposes. With no little hyperbole, industry expert Larry Woods wrote that the new machine may mark "a turning point in the general direction of worldwide computer development. With the 8100 introduction IBM legitimized the concept of DDP, and gave notice to the rest of the industry that it is serious about entering this marketplace."

Meanwhile IBM continued developing CML. In 1974, it announced the creation of a joint venture with Comsat to provide satellite transmission to customers by means of antennas on their roofs, and soon after they were joined by a third partner, Aetna Life & Casualty Insurance, with which they reformed operations into a new company, known as Satellite Business Systems (SBS). Cary spoke of a time when computers in all parts of the world could be linked by satellite, with data travelling across the continents in the twinkling of an eye. In 1981, a SBS market study indicated that within four years data communications revenues would exceed those for data processing, and that business communications would be a $100 billion market.

IBM's strategy was clear enough: it would wed SNA with SBS and offer customers a system in which all of its computers, together with as many terminals as were required, could be tied together on a worldwide basis. And all of this system would be in competition with AT&T. One more link was needed: a manufacturer of hardware, and this was in the process of being added.

The Rolm Connection

In 1983, to augment the strategy, IBM purchased 15 percent of the common stock of Rolm Corporation for $228 million and named one of its own executives to Rolm's board. As noted, Rolm is a manufacturer of sophisticated telephonic equipment and like Intel is domiciled in Silicon Valley. The company was founded in 1969 by four Stanford University electrical engineers—Gene Richardson, Kenneth Oshman, Walter Loewenstein, and Robert Maxfield—and its name is an acronym of theirs. These men hoped to turn out a line of rugged military computers. Rolm limped along for the first few years. As recently as 1977, the company reported revenues of $30 million and an income of $4.5 million. Then, as Rolm turned to telecommunications and its products caught on, both figures expanded exponentially, reaching $503 million and $69 million respectively by 1983.

Like many of its Silicon Valley neighbors, Rolm practices the relaxed life style known by some as "California laid-back." There are hot tubs, tennis courts, and Jacuzzis for all the employees; there is no dress code nor set working hours. Rolm employees are given twelve-week sabbaticals every few years. Not only did this win the loyalties of valued scientists, CEO Oshman said, but it turned out to be a good investment in that the satisfied workers turned out to be more productive. This is an approach different from IBM's traditional one, certainly, but with the same objectives.

Rolm's most important products are private branch exchanges (PBXs), switchboards that route telephone messages to various locations, usually within an office or company. If SNA can be likened to the brain and SBS to veins and arteries, Rolm's PBXs can be considered capillaries, reaching the individual within the organization, generally seated at his or her terminal. In 1983, there were 3.4 million advanced digital PBX shipments, of which Rolm was the leading force, accounting for 718,000, or around 21 percent of the total. (AT&T was in second place with a market share of 16 percent, followed by Northern Telecom [14 percent] and Nippon Electric [13 percent]). Thus, Rolm was competing against Ma Bell and a Japanese firm, having this in common with IBM. PBXs are a $2.5 billion market in the United States alone, one expected to come in at around $3.5 billion by 1988.

Why was IBM interested in Rolm? Because in a little-publicized effort in the 1960s IBM attempted to enter the field on its own, with models geared to the European market; it was an effort that met with limited success. IBM then tried a joint venture with another PBX manufacturer, Mitel, which turned out badly. Knowing of this, Rolm's leaders approached IBM, asking to be considered for an Intel-style investment. The firm was in need of additional capital. Moreover, Rolm wanted an assured purchaser of its equipment and its research and development, which is to say that it was in a position similar to that of Intel at the time IBM took an interest in that firm. The previous year,

Rolm's profits had fallen to a mere 6 percent of sales, or $38 million, obliging cutbacks in R & D to $25 million on a revenue base of $350 million, quite low as such things go. Approximately $49 million was earmarked for R & D in 1984, and there was some question as to how Rolm would come up with that much money. Even so, this was less than half the expenditures of Northern Telecom (a Canadian outfit, but one with an important American presence), an indication that without a strong partner Rolm would fall behind in the high-tech race. Thus the search for a parent, and the approach to IBM, knowing that any arrangement was bound to enhance its reputation as well.

So it did. After the initial purchase was announced, James Carreker of Dataquest wrote, "Thanks to the IBM connection Rolm is a safe choice [for buyers of telecommunications equipment] in the way the phone company [AT&T] used to be." But it seemed little more than that. Rolm's products were well-considered, but within the industry thought somewhat stodgy and on the point of becoming obsolete. The hunch in Silicon Valley was that, unlike the Intel experience, this time IBM had aligned itself with a drab performer. "Rolm was benefiting from IBM's prestige," said industry consultant Dixon Doll, "but IBM was getting very little out of its minority position."

A few months later when Rolm announced the CBX II, a PBX that appeared in advance of anything in its category, IBM's rationale became clearer. Almost simultaneously IBM upped its investment to 17.7 percent while adding another of Big Blue's nominees to the Rolm board. The IBM-Rolm union became firmer as additional fruits of the collaboration came to market. One of the more promising of these is "Mesquite," which combines a telephone with an IBM PC to provide voice recognition and a display of phone messages for the user. This kind of device, combined with multiple work stations, is estimated to have the potential of becoming a $200 million market before the end of this decade. Rolm is the clear leader at present and, if it remains so, would become an important purchaser of IBM PCs, thus adding to the demand for the popular machine.

More ambitious operations were to come. Armonk organized Telecommunications Products Division, comprised of Rolm and Satellite Business Systems, which was taken as a sign that IBM was moving closer to a conflict with AT&T. The TPD was deemed a weak entry by IBM standards. Rolm was promising enough, but SBS had lost $114 million in 1984 and by even the most sanguine estimates wouldn't turn a profit for three or four years. IBM had the hardware and software and Rolm the telecommunications gear.

Needed now was an equally strong entry in transmission. So IBM set about searching for a third leg to the triad.

By 1984 it had become evident that other American semiconductor and telecommunications equipment manufacturers would have to seek partners, and so they did. Convergent Technologies entered into arrangements with Burroughs and NCR, Northern Telecom worked out deals with Sperry and DEC, American Microsystems sold itself to Gould; earlier, Honeywell had purchased Synertek, Schlumberger took over Fairchild Camera & Instrument, and United Technologies bought Mostek. Wang had 15 percent of Intercom, and NCR owns 17 percent of Ztel. As noted, Intel already had several partners when IBM made the purchase, one of which was Burroughs, while IBM was developing integrated circuits for telecommunications purposes with Texas Instruments.

The Rolm connection was followed by a commitment to a much smaller company. In 1984, IBM purchased $6 million worth of convertible debentures in Sytek, a small, young Silicon Valley company that had been awarded a contract to produce networking systems for the IBM PC and had run low on cash. Soon after, Sytek announced its development of a local area network (LAN) by which mainframes, minicomputers, and personal computers could be linked so as to swap information. The Sytek system, known as PC Network, is capable of bringing together on the same line as many as seventy-two IBM PCs. Sytek is a rapidly growing company whose revenues have more than doubled every year of the 1980s, rising from $1.2 million in fiscal 1980 to $30.6 million in fiscal 1983. But the firm has had only one profitable year; it lost $1.7 million in fiscal 1983 and is expected to show more red ink well into the late 1980s. Clearly IBM didn't make its commitment in the expectation of profits, but rather to have a share in a firm that is one of the leaders in an interesting new technology. Dataquest's Carreker believes that by the end of 1985 more than one million personal computers in the United States alone will be connected through networks, which at $1,000 per PC would work out to $1 billion in revenues. "We believe PC Net could be as significant a product for IBM as the PC itself was three years ago" he stated.

Other alliances followed. In February 1984, IBM united with Sears, Roebuck and CBS to form Trintex, which will provide owners of minis with a wide variety of information and entertainment as well as electronic shopping. The following month came news of a joint venture with Merrill Lynch to offer stock market information to brokerage houses. C. Michael Armstrong, head of IBM's Information Systems and Communications Group (ISC), saw a fine mesh in the making. "If someone needs to operate an IBM/Merrill Lynch brokerage terminal over IBM's Information Network using Rolm switches and employing facilities from Satellite Business Systems, we'd be very happy."

Important signals were being sent out by the Rolm, Intel, and Sytek connections: IBM is creating a community of companies to support its endeavors. This was to be the path taken by others as well. But no one thought it would go much further, certainly not to the point where IBM would actually acquire one of these or some other company.

John Akers: The Next Generation

Or would it? The answer came on Tuesday, September 25, 1984, which turned out to be IBM Day insofar as business news was concerned, as Big Blue treated the Street to a triple play that may indicate the direction the company is taking.

First came the announcement that President John Akers would become CEO the following February. The charismatic, avuncular, and gregarious Akers came to IBM in 1960 as a sales trainee after graduating from Yale and service in the Navy. His career was a model of its kind. Akers began as a marketing representative in New England, did well enough to become a member of the Hundred Percent Club, and went on to join the Golden Circle, whose members are the elite of the firm and are targeted for better things. Promotions followed regularly, and in 1971 Akers was at Armonk as Frank Cary's administrative assistant. From there he was promoted to industry director at the data processing division, and then on to Los Angeles as vice president and regional director for the DP division.

By then Akers had been recognized as a possible candidate for the top spot, and his star rose even higher in 1974 when he was named president of the division out of which came the PC and its cousins, products that have obliged the firm to stress consumer rather than office sales for the first time. He is the kind of person who would have received appreciative nods from Tom Watson, Sr. "When a project at IBM is a success, the team succeeds," noted James Immershein of the Gartner Group. "IBM recognizes the team, spreads money over them and holds parties for them. It's only when something fails that IBM picks out an individual and pins the tail on the donkey. Akers has never been a donkey." He became IBM's president in 1983, so the CEO appointment wasn't a surprise, even though several others, including Vice Chairman Paul Rizzo, were considered possibilities. But at this time IBM requires a person with Akers's personality and marketing experience for the top post.

The second item regarded the introduction of a new line of PC software. IBM has been encouraging free lancers to submit their creations for consideration under licensing agreements, and doubtless this will continue. But it was inevitable that the firm would make a major move of its own into this market.

The last and most intriguing story was that IBM intended to take over Rolm. The price? $70 per share in convertible subordinated debentures, which works out to around $1.26 billion face value for those shares not already in IBM's hands.

One could see a link between the Akers appointment and the software and Rolm announcement, viewing them as yet another move on IBM's part to secure its strong position in the PC market and its emerging and rapidly developing interest in telecommunications.

There is one worrisome aspect to the Rolm takeover. Not since the early 1920s has the firm undertaken a major acquisition. For the past six decades, IBM has refined its corporate culture, the most homogeneous in American big business. Now it will have to explore means of dealing with the quite different people at Rolm and decide whether to permit them leeway or attempt to transform them into IBMers.

Management consultant Larry Stessin saw few problems, noting that the 8,500 Rolm employees "will have more security as part of IBM than they had on their own. IBM rarely fires anyone, and the takeover could lift morale and with it productivity and performance. Besides, it isn't in the IBM tradition to force its way on others. Note that under the arrangement Rolm will retain its name and senior management. Finally, IBM appears to like Rolm the way it is. Why change a winning combination?"

What did this imply for IBM's famed corporate culture? As might have been expected, rumors immediately developed that Intel would be the next to come under the IBM umbrella. When asked about this, Intel CEO Grove quipped, "God, I hope not. I only own one white shirt." But he couldn't have been serious since IBM's San Jose facility was staffed by men all of whose shirts were every color except white. Sytek president Michael Pliner wasn't concerned, noting that any bid on the part of Armonk to acquire his company was bound to be cordial. Besides, General Instrument already owned 51 percent of the company and hadn't indicated any desire to sell, and IBM's interest, if equitised, would come to only 5 percent. "In any case IBM isn't a predator," Pliner said. "In general, an unfriendly takeover isn't realistic in a high tech company—people walk, and when people walk you lose the whole drive of the company." But a takeover of either or both isn't out of the question. International Data Corporation consultant Joseph Levy remarked that "With the Justice Department off their backs and with IBM's inevitable quest for domination, the world is their oyster. If I were Intel, I would wonder if Intel is next." Cornell professor Alan McAdams, a long-time critic who testified for the government in the antitrust suit, stated, "It isn't bad in itself, but it's also an omen of what likely is to come. Intel can't be far behind. IBM wouldn't have attempted this during the antitrust suit." Levy and McAdams were echoed by Wall Street stock analyst Sanford Weill, who asked, "Why stop at Rolm?"

The once stable IBM culture was evolving more rapidly than ever before, to the point where industry insiders were speculating that some time in the near future IBM would absorb an Intel, a Sytek, or two—or three, or four, five, six . . .

The MCI Connection

In the summer of 1985 IBM shocked both the industry and the investment community by announcing it was taking an important interest in MCI Communications, the second largest force in the nation's long distance telephone market. Founded in 1968 by William McGowan, a feisty, independent-minded individual who liked to boast how he would smash AT&T's monopoly, McGowan not only cracked into the field and held on, but sued AT&T for $17.4 billion in damages for anticompetitive practice in earlier years. While the courts decided in MCI's favor, the award was for only $113 million, and this was accounted an AT&T victory. "We should have gotten a lot more," McGowan said, as he prepared to appeal the decision.

MCI had 2.5 million customers and 8 percent of the market at the end of 1984 and reported revenues of $2 billion, on which it earned $59.2 million, with McGowan predicting that by 1990 the company would have 10 to 15 percent of the market. To do this he would have to have funding and a strong partner, which is where IBM came in.

In 1984 Comsat signaled its intention to sell its share of Satellite Business Systems to IBM, and it appeared that Aetna, whose only interest is financial, would soon follow, leaving IBM in total control of the company. As of

November, IBM owned 60 percent of SBS, which, after absorbing $1.3 billion in capital, had yet to turn a profit and didn't seem likely to do so in the immediate future.

Rather than simply buy out Aetna, IBM entered into a complicated deal with MCI, proposed to its vice chairman, Paul Rizzo, by McGowan that spring. In exchange for a debt-free SBS and the agreement to invest up to $400 million in MCI, IBM was to receive 45 million shares of MCI plus an option to purchase another 7 million at $15 per share. Thus, IBM rid itself of a company that was absorbing capital for approximately 18 percent of the promising and strengthened MCI, and should the option be exercised as seemed likely, even more.

McGowan was delighted. He would still have control of MCI, but now with a new business and ally. "They [IBM] haven't had much experience and much success in telecommunications services like we have. We needed stockholders, preferably wealthy, preferably who are going to stay around for a long time. It's a perfect fit for us." With IBM behind it, MCI would be a more credible company. "I believe the large, sophisticated user will be more comfortable working with MCI now," he said. Noting that IBM and AT&T were just beginning to square off, McGowan added, "We've been the most successful competitor to AT&T. We'll bring that to IBM in our joint efforts."

MCI is a small company when compared with IBM; it has 11,000 employees against Big Blue's 400,000. But it is an important player in its own niche and fits in clearly with IBM's overall strategy. "We've said clearly we continue to be interested in the telecommunications service industry," said an IBM spokesman, adding that its position in MCI "is indicative of our interest."

Will MCI eventually be absorbed into IBM? The betting was that this would happen, probably before the 1990s, with the first step being the exercize of that option. Given its telecommunications abilities and those of Rolm, IBM might link up customers around the world in a massive network unlike anything yet seen or, until recently, even imagined. This is yet another sign of the forthcoming struggle between IBM and AT&T.

XII

LESSONS LEARNED
AND TO BE UNLEARNED

Setting the Stage: Consumer Electronics

As we have seen, Japan employs a distinctive strategy when entering overseas markets, and it is one from which the computer industry appears to be deriving instruction. To recapitulate, the Japanese study the market, license technology when necessary, and then produce low-priced, high-quality goods, the aim being market share rather than immediate profits. This done, the Japanese upgrade, expand profit margins, and await the inevitable complaints from the domestic companies. They counter threats of tariffs and quotas by establishing cooperative agreements and opening factories in the host country.

Perhaps the clearest and most striking examples can be seen in consumer electronics (such as portable radios, television sets, and tape recorders) and automobiles. An analysis of Japanese strategy and tactics in these may provide insights into what might be expected in data processing. But no clear guide, for several reasons.

In the first place, there are the obvious differences between marketing a $25 radio or tape recorder, a $200 television set, or a $13,000 car, and marketing a $100,000 or even $2 million computer. Furthermore, radios, TVs, and autos are consumer items, while computers in the mini range and above are purchased as capital goods; individuals bring different attitudes to the market when shopping for the latter. Next, the rate of technological change was far slower in autos, though less so in consumer electronics after the 1960s, than

205

was and is the case with information processing. Japanese companies, whose characteristic approach is to produce a superior and less expensive version of an already-existing product, are better attuned to a fixed environment.

Finally, there were differences in approaches and attitudes between RCA, Ampex, General Motors, and Ford on the one hand and IBM and Apple on the other. The consumer electronics and auto makers blundered badly. They lagged in the introduction of transistor-powered radios and retained old designs simply to squeeze a bit of extra profit out of them, while the Japanese came to market with more modern models. The Americans sold licenses freely; of the 236 agreements in the electronics area in 1970, for example, 89 were in tape recorders, players, and related gear and a like amount in semiconductors, tubes, and components utilized directly or indirectly in consumer electronics products. Not that this was not lucrative; at one point RCA was earning more from consumer electronics licenses than from sales of products.

The American computer manufacturers were and are much more wary on this score, and in any case, the pace of change is such that by the time the license agreement is implemented, the product or process covered more often than not is on the road to obsolescence.

The situation in television sets, perhaps the most notable Japanese triumph prior to that in automobiles, is fairly typical of the experience. During the late 1940s and through the early 1950s, the American industry engaged in intensive and costly R & D programs, honed their manufacturing and marketing skills, and turned out products that each year seemed to be better and less expensive. RCA and CBS developed competing color television systems, and a struggle developed that was won by RCA; in 1953 the Federal Trade Commission approved its version.

At the time, RCA was the dominant force in television set manufacture and a clear leader in research. Had the firm acted to expand upon its base, the Japanese might not have been able to make a serious dent in the market. But RCA wavered, and research and development slowed down. The move from the tube-powered to transistorized models was slower than should have been the case. Reception for the color models and technologies remained strong, the manufacturers seemed to have concluded. In such a situation, why change? The major firms eyed one another warily. Had one or two of them made the move, the others doubtless would have followed. But there was no leader, and so the industry competed in terms of advertising rather than technology, and the stage was set for decline.

By the end of the decade, manufacturing was in poor shape, with the American companies putting up with inferior quality controls and with marketing arms noted for their arrogance. Service was generally poor. The reasons for this malaise were clear enough: the market was still expanding, there seemed no need to seek additional share through aggressive merchandising, and the thought of strong, meaningful competition from overseas seemed far-fetched.

Meanwhile the Japanese had developed their domestic industry and were prepared to enter the American market. The reason for this selection was clear enough. During this period, Japan suffered what many believed would be a chronic negative balance of trade with the United States—in 1952 exports came to $229 million and imports, $633 million. MITI and other government agencies sought products that might be exported to redress the balance, and initially found them in steel and textiles. Toward the end of the decade, however, the agency had targeted consumer electronics and autos as key export possibilities. In both, as in virtually all other growing industries, there was the licensing of technology, an investigation of manufacturing techniques, and a meticulous study of the American market, the largest in the world.

Why the United States rather than Europe? For a variety of reasons—the enormous size of the market, the proximity of the market, which meant lower shipping costs, and the personal wealth of American customers. Entry presented little difficulty. The United States had emerged from the World War as the unquestioned paramount economic force in the world and felt no need for tariff restrictions or quotas. Additionally, the domestic market was so large and wealthy that companies in most industries gave little thought to foreign sales. So the United States had erected few barriers to trade, and indeed welcomed it, while foreigners understood that they had little to fear from American competition in their own markets once their economies recovered.

Under MITI's guidance, the major manufacturers came together to form the Television Export Council and the Television Export Examination Committee, which coordinated the effort and established prices. The idea was to sell the sets for as low a price as possible—significantly lower in fact than they were being offered for in Japan. All of this was carefully done with a view toward creating a defense against American charges of dumping, which had been illegal for almost half a century, an allegation certain to be raised by the domestic industry when and if the Japanese challenge became significant.

The Japanese TV invasion began in the early 1960s, when Sony attempted to sell a small, fully transistorized set. By 1962, Japanese TVs were being marketed to Americans for a third less than the same size sets being turned out by RCA, Zenith, and Motorola, and although it was not recognized at the time, they were more advanced and better constructed as well. Still, the going was slow at first.

The breakthrough came in 1963. That year Sears, Roebuck attempted to purchase black-and-white TVs from RCA and Zenith for use as "house brands," meaning they would carry the Sears nameplate. The American firms felt sufficiently secure to reject the deal, reasoning that Sears would be forced to accept whatever nonfinancial terms it could get from the two leading firms in the industry. They were wrong. Sanyo learned of the situation and sent representatives to Sears with an offer: not only would they provide the retailing giant with as many sets as it wanted that conformed to Sears specifications, but would do so at prices lower than that offered to RCA and Zenith. After some initial hesitation, Sears agreed. The deal proved advantageous to both companies and, more important, gave the Japanese their first important TV market in the United States. From 1963 to 1977, Sears purchased 6.5 million Japanese TV sets (most from Sanyo and Toshiba) worth more than $700 million.

Given this situation, why didn't some of the American firms respond? Lack of perception and poor leadership were factors, but there was another factor as well insofar as the most important company in this industry, RCA, was concerned. We have already seen what happened to RCA in this period—it turned to non-TV receiver areas, the most important of which was computers. As hundreds of millions of dollars were poured into this and other new product areas, the television business stagnated. RCA did not even make an effort to get into the TV camera business, it entered video tape late, and seemed to have lost interest in the product area.

So it was that the Japanese were able to obtain market share without a serious defense from the leader. Not that the Japanese won all of their battles, but they made the effort, rectified errors, and came back to the field with improved models, which carried attractive prices. For example, in 1964 Sony introduced in the domestic market a 17-inch vacuum tube color set that proved defective. The model was withdrawn; Sony consulted with American researchers—and obtained guidance from several, especially GE—and in 1968, came out with a new, transistorized model using a Trinitron gun, a vast improvement over all else on the market. The following year Sony Trinitrons, selling at premium prices, were gobbled up by Americans, and the Japanese were well on their way to victory. In this way, the Japanese were starting to upgrade in their drive to take command of the more lucrative upper end of the market.

By 1971, the Japanese had half the American TV receiver market, and had obliged ten American manufacturers to leave the field, directly or indirectly forcing some 100,000 workers from their jobs. Along the way there were charges of dumping, several of which proved justified, but at the same time a significant number of allegations ended with vindication for the Japanese firms. Japanese firms purchased American plants and, in the case of Motorola's Quasar Division, an entire company, the buyer being Matsushita—the price, $100 million.

Today Japanese firms dominate the American market, as they do most other areas of consumer electronics. Additionally, the Japanese were able to transfer their industrial *élan* to American workers, so that factories in the United States proved competitive with those in Japan despite the significant wage differential.

Victory in Automobiles

There was a similar and even more striking experience in automobiles. Japan had a minuscule auto industry prior to World War II and nothing at all in the immediate postwar years; as recently as 1959, total production came to a mere 79,000 passenger cars—against 158,000 of the more popular, less costly three-wheeled vehicles. In 1950, Hisato Ishimada, a governor of the Bank of Japan, thought there was no future for his country in autos. "It is meaningless to develop the motor vehicle industry in Japan," said Ishimada. "Now is the time of international division of labor. As we can get inexpensive motor vehicles of excellent quality from the United States, why don't we rely upon them?" Nor was Ishimada unique in thinking this. Suehiro Nishio, who was in the cabinet of Prime Minister Tetsu Katayama, believed there was no prospect for a Japanese automobile industry, saying: "Japanese motor vehicle manufacturers cannot compete internationally because equipment is too obsolete and production methods lag behind those motor vehicle manufacturers in advanced countries."

The Bank of Japan rejected the notion of supporting the industry, and for a while, at least, MITI agreed. Indeed, throughout the postwar period MITI and the manufacturers have been at odds with one another, clashing repeatedly, with MITI convinced that amalgamation of smaller companies into a third entity (to go along with Toyota and Nissan) was vital, and the companies rejecting the notion. MITI did all it could to prevent Honda from entering the passenger car business, failing by a hair.

(Americans and others who've become convinced of the business acumen of MITI on all substantive matters might consider that the agency has been wrong and the companies correct on most important issues; those who believe that MITI dominates Japanese business should note that the companies have been able to sidestep its policy repeatedly.)

The Japanese industry received a boost from the Dodge Line and the Korean War, during which Japan became the staging area for the military effort, and Americans purchased cars and trucks from the domestic industry. Meanwhile, as prosperity returned, consumers lined up for autos. Initially, they appeared to prefer American products, perhaps because they were status symbols of a kind, the vehicles produced by the people who, after all, had defeated them in war. But gradually they took to the Toyotas and Nissans. The industry's capital investment doubled from 1951 to 1952, and in the following year produced almost 50,000 cars, with some 1,000 going overseas.

Consideration of overseas markets began soon after, with the United States receiving the most interest for the same reasons that motivated MITI in the case of consumer electronics. Some within the industry thought Europe might be a better target. Europeans were accustomed to the small cars Japan was turning out. Would not that suggest Europe might have been a better starting point? Perhaps, but the Europeans had placed high tariffs on cars while the Americans had not, and so for this reason and the others the United States became the prime target.

That the Japanese thought they might achieve a measure of success in America was due in large part to the Volkswagen experience. The small, buglike car known as "the Beetle" was well made, inexpensive to buy and run, and unusual both in appearance and technology. Volkswagen had good quality control and had established a strong dealership network, supported by accessible spare-parts depots. The car's reputation spread by word of mouth. More than 120,000 Beetles were sold in the United States in 1959, up dramatically from the 20,000 of four years earlier. VW led the import field by a wide margin, but even so it was a very small portion of the total American sales of 5.6 million. Detroit was hardly concerned; the feeling there was that the unusual Beetle appealed primarily to oddballs and intellectuals who wanted something different. The vast majority of Americans still wanted larger, more comfortable and powerful Chevys, Fords, and Plymouths, and dreamed of Cadillacs, Lincolns, and Chryslers.

The Japanese attempted to combine the strength of the VW with the advantages of the Chevy, which is to say offer passenger cars that were well-constructed and inexpensive while at the same time being more conventional than the Beetle. But just as with consumer electronics, there first had to be a sizeable base in the Japanese domestic market so as to achieve realistic economies of scale. And there could be no thought of blitzing the market, not for a Japan that still bore the scars of defeat and that was still dogged by the reputation for producing shoddy goods that it earned prior to the war.

The beginning was made in 1958, but it was not auspicious. *Business Week* observed that "Japan is plunging into the foreign car market here with two entries, Nissan's four-door Datsun and Toyota's somewhat larger Toyopet Crown. With over 50 foreign car makes already on sale here, the Japanese auto industry isn't likely to carve out a big slice of the U.S. market for itself." The outlook was bleak, especially when the Crown turned out to be unsuited for American high-speed traffic and was plagued by breakdowns. Moreover, while the Japanese clearly attempted to imitate the VW distribution and service network, they had not done so yet, so customer dissatisfaction was high.

Both Nissan and Toyota retained their beachheads and beefed up service operations, while readying different models for the American market. What was needed was a small car that was not radically different from the Chevy, but with luxury features, and at a bargain price. Toyota's answer was the Corona, a car that had been introduced in the domestic market some years before, was thoroughly "debugged," and so had some hope of a favorable reception. Exported to the United States in 1963 and selling for under $1,800, it appeared at a time when the VW Beetle had become an aging design and Detroit had just about abandoned its earlier attempts at bringing out compacts. Nissan, which in that period outsold Toyota in the United States, had its counterpart in the 600.

This time the strategy worked, though the going was slow. In 1960, the Japanese produced 165,000 passenger cars and exported slightly more than 7,000. Exports wouldn't reach the 100,000 level until 1965, at which time production came in at close to 700,000. Fewer than 26,000 of those exports, or one out of every four, went to the United States; the Germans sold 377,000 cars to Americans that year, while Detroit's total reached 9.3 million. The leading import remained the VW, with 323,000 cars, while Nissan's Datsun shipped only 10,000 to the United States. Still, Datsun's prospects were good—better, in fact, than VW's. This could be inferred from a 1965 rating by

Consumer Reports, the touchstone for many American car buyers: "There is no question as to which car is most like U.S. cars—it is the Datsun, with its familiar arrangement of components, its comparatively quiet running, its relatively soft ride, full equipment, and a level of quality that would put many U.S. cars to shame."

Japanese penetration of the American market continued throughout the decade, as it became apparent that they had both learned the secret of success and were implementing it. As the Beetle declined, Toyota and Nissan expanded their share of the foreign car market. By 1971, when the Japanese sold 703,000 cars in the United States vs. the German 771,000, it had become clear that the former would displace the VW in short order. And so they did; five years later the Japanese figure was 695,000, while the Germans sent 370,000 passenger cars to the United States.

More significant than the overthrow of VW was Japanese penetration into the GM, Ford, and Chrysler market shares. By 1981, when Japan displaced the United States as the world's leading manufacturer of motor vehicles and Detroit was in disarray, Congress was besieged with the same kind of arguments heard in consumer electronics—charges of dumping, talk of tariff boosts, and demands for quotas. It seemed a crucial matter, far more significant than the situation in TVs and hand calculators, since the automobile industry is the nation's largest. In 1980, one out of every three cars sold in the United States came from overseas, and the total value of these imports came to $16.6 billion—of which $8.2 billion went to Japan, which accounted for three out of every four import sales.

The Japanese response to American complaints was not unusual or unexpected; they turned to production in the United States and to upgrading to achieve higher profits. That $8.2 billion had been earned on sales of 2 million cars; in 1984, as a result of "voluntary" restraints, Japan sent 1.8 million cars to America—and took in $12.4 billion, this largely due to the fact that they were sending upgrade cars to the United States, like the Toyota Cressida and Nissan Maxima.

Thus, the Japanese, who started out by taking aim at owners of VW Beetles, Chevys, and Fords, were seeking out purchasers of BMWs, Cadillacs, and Lincolns. Ironically, by 1985 the Americans once again dominated the economy car field, but by default, since the Japanese were sending over so few of their low-priced models. Finally, Toyota will soon be turning out cars in conjunction with GM from a California plant, Honda has its facility in Ohio for the manufacture of Accords and Civics, and Nissan has its operation in Tennessee.

The Japanese victory in autos is not as sweeping as that in consumer electronics, but the Japanese pattern was the same, beginning with real and perceived weaknesses on the part of American companies, entry at the bottom of the market, and a rise to the top of it afterward.

Can the same strategy work in computers?

Up till now, IBM has performed superbly in all of the areas in which the American consumer electronics and automobile companies were weak, which is not to say that IBM alone possesses this talent. Many other American companies, ranging from Texas Instruments through Minnesota Mining & Manufacturing and Procter & Gamble, have been able to meet Japanese competition and triumph. The talents found in the executive suites of these companies often were lacking among their counterparts at consumer electronics and auto firms.

The American information processing industry possessed yet another advantage. The Japanese challenge in this area began *after* their pattern had been discerned, and the United States was on guard against repetitions. The slack attitude on the part of industry and government demonstrated in radios and cars will not be duplicated in information processing. In the past, Washington has proven an unwitting though important ally of the Japanese by refusing to impose tariffs and quotas, domestic content legislation, and the like, while threatening antitrust prosecutions against successful American competitors. At the same time, the American companies were sluggish in responses to threats to their domestic markets. That time has long passed. It will not help the domestic steelmakers, who pleaded for government aid while the Japanese were practicing patently unfair competitive practices in the 1950s and 1960s. But the lessons learned in consumer electronics and automobiles in the 1970s will benefit the Americans in information processing in the 1980s and beyond.

Japan Pushes Overseas

One of the more puzzling aspects of all this has been the failure of American firms of the immediate postwar period to mount aggressive sales campaigns overseas. One can understand the preference for cultivating the vast domestic market for the first few years until the demands pent up during the Great

Depression and the war were satisfied. But why didn't the American companies turn overseas afterward?

The domestic consumer electronics companies, led by RCA, Zenith, and Ampex, traditionally had relatively little exposure to foreign markets. RCA did not ship its radios to Japan prior to World War II or after, nor did the others have much exposure to that country. Thus, Sony, Panasonic, and other Japanese manufacturers knew they had no reason to fear invasions of their own markets. As for the automakers, GM has strong representation aboard, but this was through local companies, whose efforts were not well coordinated with that of headquarters. Ford abroad was even stronger, but not until the 1970s did it make any important attempts to draw upon its overseas companies for expertise and technology. This is not the case with computers; the Americans have been trying to make headway in Japan and, as has been demonstrated, none so much as IBM.

This difference between information processing on the one hand and consumer electronics and autos on the other is of paramount importance, and one not considered carefully enough by the Japanese, who embarked upon their overseas campaign with mainframes as though they were not that different from consumer products.

First of all, the Japanese cultivated the domestic market so as to obtain experience, benefit from the learning curve, and realize economies of scale. Then they expanded slowly and at first tentatively into areas of opportunity—less developed countries where lower prices on PCMs might bring placements. As with steel, consumer electronics, and autos, the Japanese were willing to accept lower profit margins so as to obtain market share; in Hong Kong, for example, Hitachi offered PCMs at half the IBM price in order to displace Big Blue's machines.

The Japanese initially concentrated on public sector clients, offering those large discounts so as to obtain major deals. Once these were won over, the struggle would commence for the commercial accounts, and then on to smaller users.

It was slow going. There were successes in Spain, Brazil, Australia, and several other countries, but slim pickings elsewhere, especially in Latin America, Africa, and Europe. By 1979, Japan was still exporting only 7 percent of its domestically manufactured machines—by way of contrast, half the nation's car production was sent abroad that year. Japan had less than 15 percent of the world market for mainframes in the early 1980s, and there seemed little hope for additional progress. By then it appeared evident that

Japan was not going to make much of an impact with its domestically produced mainframes, and it started to concentrate more intensely on those manufactured through joint ventures.

The American market proved virtually impenetrable; just about the only Japanese machines placed there carried the Amdahl, NASCO, or other captive label. There were several reasons for this, the most obvious being the presence of IBM and strong representations on the part of BUNCH companies. Equally important was the fact that the Japanese could not offer the kind of service support for their products that the others already had in place. Then too, why purchase a Fujitsu when Amdahls were just about the same? The lack of a wide variety of software hurt; as recently as 1983 Fujitsu and Hitachi had less than 25 percent of the software by volume as did comparable IBMs.

Finally, there was the matter of distribution, which was much more complex for computers and related gear than for television sets or automobiles. With the former, the Japanese relied upon traditional retail outlets, and for the latter they had the Volkswagen experience upon which to draw. Mainframes hardly could be sold in department stores, and the only examples upon which the Japanese could draw were domestic, IBM in particular. But the BUNCH companies had been trying to emulate IBM for years without much success. How could Hitachi and Fujitsu hope to do better?

In such a situation, the Japanese were obliged to fall back on an alternate strategy, one which would take decades to come to fruition. They would start with peripherals (such as disk drives, printers, copiers, and the like), become entrenched there, and then hope to work their ways up to mainframes. In 1978, Masateru Takagi of NEC commented, "We want to establish our reputation for reliability and quality with the printers and then move up," conceding that the time was not ripe for a head-to-head confrontation with the Armonk Monster. This was viewed as a rather defeatist attitude, but the Japanese had little choice in the matter. Thus in the late 1970s, NEC was supplying disk drives to Honeywell and selling its Spinwriter printer in computer stores. Hitachi sold tape and disk drives to NCR, Itel, and others, while Fujitsu supplied a variety of American customers with peripheral equipment. "Competing with a company like IBM is like fighting with Muhammad Ali," Takagi said. "But remember—Ali has been beaten. Though he has very big hands, we can get him in special places."

It would appear that Takagi had in mind a variant on the experience with autos and consumer electronics. As has been seen, the Japanese did well in consumer electronics because the American firms were unwilling to innovate in that rapidly evolving market until they had wrung the last dollar in profits out of existing products. Sony and Panasonic offered customers high quality, advanced TVs, radios, and videos, and so won them from RCA, Zenith, and Magnavox. In the case of autos, there were no important innovations in the 1970s, and Toyota and Nissan defeated GM and Ford with higher quality and lower prices.

It was different in mainframes. In this area, change was rapid (like consumer electronics) and IBM was prepared to innovate, forcing the Japanese to continually play catch-up. In short, unlike the TV manufacturers, IBM was capable of moving ahead into new areas, and unlike Detroit, it had no problem with quality and, when necessary, price.

The Micro Shows the Way

Personal computers might appear a product ideally suited for the Japanese exporters. If the lessor of an IBM 4300 could not be lured to Fujitsu and Hitachi, perhaps a businessman, a writer, a student, or others in the market for a micro would respond better. This was an entirely different market, more akin to that for electric and electronic typewriters than computers, a market that the Japanese understood and one in which they had some experience. IBM was selling its personal computers through Sears, Macy's, and other retail outlets as well as its own stores. So were other American manu-facturers—Kaypro, DEC, Apple, IBM compatibles, and so forth. In addition, individual and chain-operation computer stores were proliferating, becoming as much a part of the scene as McDonald's or Burger King, and these would be willing to take on lines of Japanese micros. Moreover, their customers were not purchasing agents or vice presidents for data processing, but rather everyday kind of people who hadn't much knowledge of computers, probably had played some video games, were interested in them to perform specific tasks or "to give the kids a leg up in school."

In other words, the vast majority of those in the market for micros were the sorts of individuals whose purchases of consumer durables had brought them into contact with Sanyo calculators, Seiko watches, Ricoh cameras, Sharp copiers, Sony TVs, Hitachi tape recorders—who may have driven to the store in a Toyota or Mazda. That is to say that they were presold on Japanese quality and value. Indeed, considering the situation one wonders why the Japanese companies couldn't essay the step of moving up from the ubiquitous hand-held calculators—a market they controlled—into micros. Why didn't firms such as Casio, Sharp, Unisonic, and Panasonic, which dominated the small calculator market, do as well in microcomputers?

Several answers come to mind, all of which in one way or another are related to innovation and perception, two areas in which the Japanese have proven quite weak in the past. In all other products, they had searched out the proper model—a company or group of companies to emulate and products to turn out and market. Whatever the Americans or anyone else could do, so the thought ran, we can do better and less expensively. But first others had to blaze the path with perception and innovation, and the subindustry and products had to settle down to some recognizable form. The Japanese needed a fixed target, and this one was constantly moving.

The matter of perception is more subtle. Begin with the simple question: Just what *is* a micro? Steven Jobs was trying to answer this question when he spoke of how the Volkswagen often can do the work of a locomotive at a much lower cost and with greater freedom for the user, by his analogy indicating that the micro can perform the same function as the mainframe. Yet there is yet another way of looking at the product; the micro may be viewed as an upscale version of the hand-held calculator. In other words, the subindustry might just as well have developed out of a more complex version of the small calculator, which is a smaller and less complex variety of computer. In the late 1970s, the calculator manufacturers, American as well as Japanese, simply did not give sufficient attention to the possibility of expanding upward to computers. Their perception of the market proved too narrow. In their failure to upsize they left the way open for computer manufacturers to downsize, and so capture a market that might have been theirs.

There were some programmable calculators on the market in the mid-1970s, most from American firms like Hewlett-Packard and Texas Instruments, and the step from these to minis would have been a small one. Had it been taken the industry today might look quite different. For example, today's micros would have been less expensive and less powerful, while word processing would be a separate rather than integral part of the business. Micros would be sold in variety stores and catalogue showrooms, the kinds of places one goes to now to purchase a programmable calculator.

The Japanese calculator manufacturers failed to recognize the opportunity early on, and by the time they had recovered it was too late—Radio Shack, Apple, Commodore, and, of course, IBM had beaten them to the market. But the calculator firms were in the United States in force in the early 1980s. Even so their efforts met with little success. For example, John McDonald, CEO of

Casio's American operation, believed his company would make a sizeable impact on the market, believing as he did that micros would appeal to owners of his firm's popular hand calculators, of which some 800,000 per year were being sold. "Every major department store from Sears to K mart will be in computer retailing," he predicted, going on to say that Casio America preferred department stores. "When you go through Bloomingdale's or Macy's, there is a sense of theater that is lacking in computer stores."

What McDonald seemed to be saying is that he expected purchasers of Casio computers to be relatively unsophisticated, just as those who took the calculators.

Yet Casios did not sell well, and other Japanese models also met with cold receptions in 1981–83. The reasons were soon known. By then the micros were perceived differently from what McDonald considered them to be, namely large, more elaborate calculators; the product had evolved downward from the minis of the 1970s rather than upward from the small, programmable calculators.

Price certainly was a major consideration, too, as was complexity. The hand-held calculator might be mastered in a matter of minutes; the software for micros often was quite complex and documentation crucial. Most of the early Japanese machines were not IBM-compatible, and they came with poor instruction manuals. The failure to come up with IBM-compatibles earlier was and is one of the major errors committed by the Japanese, and in the light of their experience, one that defies explanation. The Japanese could not agree upon a common operating system, the key to libraries of software. Most settled on CP/M (a product of Digital Research), which meant that the owner of one of these machines could have access to programs already written for that system. But others did not, and this created some confusion, which in turn hurt sales. Moreover, the IBM PC used MS/DOS (created by Microsoft), which meant that owners of Japanese computers could not run programs written for IBMs and those machines compatible with them. The Japanese continued to seek the proper formula in software, turning to Microsoft when the CP/M experiment seemed to be working poorly, and out of their collaboration came MSX, an operating system that most Japanese firms have accepted. But it would appear too late in the game for this to work.

Even if the Japanese come up with solutions to other problems it appears that the software difficulties will remain. "This is a culture business," remarked Kazuhito Nishi, implying that the Japanese have not been able to fathom the difficulties of language, something unimportant in TVs and cars. Nishi is in a position to know: he is executive vice president of Ascii, a computer design and publishing company affiliated with Microsoft.

Distribution: The Radio Shack Blunder

The second perception problem involves distribution, and the Japanese might have studied the VW example in autos, their own experience in consumer electronics, and the American way in micros for clues to how to act.

The Germans correctly recognized that two earlier methods of retailing foreign cars to Americans—through supermarketlike operations and as adjuncts to non-Big Three distributorships—were unsatisfactory, and they insisted upon independent, separate units, with well-trained mechanics, offering a level of service superior to that to which most Americans had become accustomed. There was no such difficulty with consumer electronics, which for years had been sold from a wide variety of retail stores; all the Japanese had to do was to gain floor space, which was no great problem. The American micro experience was by far the more pertinent, for it offered not only examples of how to succeed, but, in the case of Radio Shack, a warning of pitfalls.

As has been seen, the Altair was offered in kit form from Byte Shop locations, many of which became hangouts for hobbyists. The first Byte Shop had been opened in 1975 by Boyd Wilson and Paul Terrell, hobbyists themselves, in Mountain View, California, smack in the middle of Silicon Valley where scores of customers might be found. When Jobs and Wozniak began operations, they fabricated computer boards to gain funds, and they looked to The Byte Shop for customers. Later on, when they turned out their Apple I, they once again brought wares to that operation, were told to redesign the case and did so, upon which The Byte Shop took them on. The Apples were a huge success by the standards of the time, so that within two years Wilson and Terrell had seventy-five outlets as well as a claim to being the world's first computer store and chain. Soon after, Apple and Byte Shop parted ways and bitter litigation followed. Byte Shops now offer a variety of micros and supplies, but had the Apple connection remained intact, they might have evolved into a computer facsimile of a VW or Toyota distributorship.

That is one way to describe Radio Shack. In the '70s, a distributor of radio supplies to hobbyists (and a producer and distributor of leather goods made by its parent, Tandy Corporation), Radio Shack opened a home computer retail outlet in the basement of its Fort Worth headquarters in 1977. Why at that time and in that way? Because Radio Shack had committed itself heavily to citizen band radios, which for a while enjoyed a vogue. The boom collapsed that year and, seeking another product, the firm's managers settled upon the micros. In other words, the powers at Radio Shack lacked a devotion to micros (as did those at Byte, for example), but rather looked upon it as just another electronic device to sell. Then, too, there was the matter of the name, Radio Shack, something which might easily have been rectified in the early months but wasn't. IBM has stood for power and service for as long as most Americans can remember, and as seen, Apple was considered a friendly, comfortable designation. The name Radio Shack seemed to signify hobbyists dealing in transmitting-and-receiving equipment, certainly not a milieu reassuring to businessmen and others interested in bringing computers into their lives. Still, the company forged on, at a time when it was being portrayed as the biggest player in the subindustry.

It was not long before Radio Shack was integrating backward, namely by purchasing components, assembling them into micros, affixing the Radio Shack nameplate, and selling them through its chain of stores, which at one time were expanding more rapidly than McDonald's. There are some 9,000 of them today, of which almost 500 are computer centers and another 800 have departments at which computers are offered. Radio Shack might have become to home computers what McDonald's was to hamburgers, namely the industry leader, were it not for a series of blunders.

The first was an inability to recognize that the vast majority of micro purchasers were quite different from the hobbyists, that they needed instruction and hand-holding as well as a vast array of support products and services. This is to suggest that Radio Shack's view toward the market was more like that developed by DEC than the one utilized by IBM in the 1960s. IBM was the quintessential hand-holder back then, while DEC concentrated upon a more sophisticated clientele, offering lower prices but fewer services. But the potential micro owners needed education and instruction and little was available at Radio Shack, many of whose salespersons seemed to specialize in the kind of technical verbiage that frightened shoppers and sent them scurrying out the door.

The Radio Shack computers (known by designations such as TRS-80 and so forth) were rugged enough, but the software was second-rate compared to that turned out by others in the early 1980s, and this hurt too. More important, however, was its reaction to IBM's entry into the field in 1981. We have already seen that Apple opted to go head-on against IBM, able to do so because of its size, reputation, and most important, the vast array of software available to its customers. Another manufacturer, Commodore, was able to do the same for a while, due to its market penetration and position in several specialized markets, schools in particular. But most of the others decided early to concentrate on IBM-compatible machines, advertising that their units could run the plentiful software being churned out for the IBM PCs. It was a respectable enough path; Franklin and a few others became Apple-compatible, so that within two years it had become evident that the micro universe soon would be divided into two spheres—IBM and Apple, with their compatible companions.

Evident to all, that is, except Radio Shack, which continued to turn out machines that would run only its own still-inferior software. Customer traffic through the stores dwindled, as did revenues, profits, and market share. Not until 1983 did Radio Shack start offering computers made by others (its popular Model 100 portable is manufactured by Japan's Kyocera), but under its own nameplate.

In December of that year, the company presented the Tandy 2000, a micro notable for two of its aspects: the 2000 could run some IBM software, and it was known as a "Tandy" and not offered under the TRS label. The following summer Radio Shack unveiled the Tandy 1200, which is close to fully compatible, and which CEO John Roach went so far as to call "an [IBM] XT clone." The machine received excellent reviews and, priced at $3,000, was $1,000 less expensive than the XT. Had Radio Shack moved more quickly it might have been a formidable competitor to IBM, right up there with Apple. What was required was the proper combination of hardware, software, and availability. In 1982, Radio Shack had only the third part of the triad, and so it stumbled. And now it is becoming a laggard in this area too. "We are going to give the customer a level of service and support no other manufacturer can offer," Roach said recently. But as he spoke there were almost 3,500 retail outlets selling and servicing micros, and of these, 1,700—400 more than the Radio Shacks—featured IBMs.

The Japanese Dilemma

This provided a warning to the Japanese. At one time, it might have been possible to follow the VW and Toyota rubrics in distribution, but the moment had passed. Did this mean the example to imitate was that of the consumer electronic companies? Not necessarily. Perhaps a better way would be to attempt to learn from the IBM experience, but this did not appear viable in the mid-1980s, due to another factor that merits attention, more because it was deemed important by some American writers than any true significance. That factor is the lateness of the Japanese entry. There weren't many Japanese micros in the United States until 1981, and for two reasons.

In the first place, the major Japanese companies lagged in the development of small machines, with none being produced in that country until 1979. Then the subindustry took off, and two years later there were more than sixty Japanese firms in the field, which by then appeared as promising as that for transistorized radios had been in the early 1950s.

The Japanese firms were then more concerned with the domestic markets than exports because the American manufacturers, unlike their counterparts in consumer electronics, had invaded Japan. Apple and others were starting to move into that market, too, with their micros, and IBM was preparing its push for the 5500. How could the Japanese hope to sell their personal computers in the United States when it was not even certain they could dominate their home turf?

The traditional response—import controls, tariffs, and other devices to keep American machines out of Japan—would not work, for Washington, acutely aware of the trade deficit with Japan, and awake to the importance of a strong computer industry, was more than willing to take retaliatory steps. The experiences of Magnavox, RCA, General Motors, and Ford served to help IBM, Apple, and other American micro manufacturers. "One of the reasons Fujitsu and Hitachi have a low profile in the U.S. is to protect Japanese auto exports," one industry consultant said.

As it turned out the Japanese had little to worry about on their domestic front. With the exception of IBM, the American firms were making small headway in Japan. Apple mounted a concerted effort to sell its micros there, but in 1983 was able to place only 45,000 for a market share of 1 percent, and the Macintosh, introduced to great acclaim in the United States, has yet to make an important impression. "Mac is not the direction of computers in Japan," observed Shigehiro Tanaka of that country's *Business Computer News,* implying perhaps that neither country would do well in the other's market. Perhaps so, but still, IBM's 5500 was leading the field when he wrote.

The major Japanese firms were waiting for the export markets to settle down. The trouble was that while they waited not only were American firms being organized and becoming powerful but there was also activity in Europe, especially in the United Kingdom, where Sinclair and Acorn were lively and interesting entries. The moment was coming, however, and ironically, when the Japanese received the needed signal; it came out of Armonk.

As noted, the introduction of the IBM PC was welcomed by some micro manufacturers. Not that they wanted the competition, which in any case they knew was on the way; rather, since all expected IBM to set the standard for the industry, it meant they might concentrate on making what amounted to plug-compatible machines. This is to suggest that the very force that crippled Radio Shack and cemented Apple's industry position provided the Japanese with their signal to launch their invasion.

Toshiba and Panasonic made the first move, announcing in January 1982 their intention of exporting their micros to the United States. By then, however, American companies were expanding rapidly, innovating at an accelerating pace, showing none of the malaise of the auto firms when they were challenged or the blindness of the American consumer electronics industry when faced with Japanese competition. Once again, the experience of these industries had not been lost on the domestic manufacturers; for example, the Japanese announcement probably had the effect of causing IBM to move up its introduction of the PC by several months. And here, too, the Japanese were slow. As noted, the PC had a 16-bit microprocessor, causing many other American firms to make the switch; the Japanese remained with the 8-bit versions until early 1984.

The Japanese had decided to market their machines through the computer stores that carried a variety of brands—the analog of the foreign car super-markets of the 1950s—and department stores, where they would stand beside and be compared with IBMs, Apples, and their compatible counterparts. The comparisons weren't favorable, in part because IBM and Apple had excellent reputations by then, but more important was the matter of selling both a technology and a product. The person who test-drove a Toyota in the 1970s probably had owned a Chevy or Ford; the shopper for a Sony color set a decade earlier had an RCA or Zenith at home. Not so the first-time purchaser of a micro, and as it turned out, he preferred the familiarity of a domestic model.

Then there was the matter of dedication to the product. American firms concentrating on micros clearly had it; Apple, Commodore, Radio Shack, and others had no desire to move up into larger computers, though in time the power of micros might rise to the point where challenges would be made. Even IBM and DEC exhibited a genuine commitment to micros. During these years the Japanese companies proved unable to convince purchasers that they harbored the same feelings. Atsushi Asada, executive director of Sharp's Industrial Equipment Group, indicated as much by stating that while micros were a significant market, his eye was on bigger game. "How well Sharp does in personal computers will determine whether we sell larger machines," he told a *Business Week* reporter. So while Sharp turned out and marketed fine machines for American buyers, it lacked the kind of support and publicity earlier given to Panasonics and Datsuns. And of course, the American micros, too, were excellent products. Shoppers would compare the Apple II or IBM PC with their Japanese counterparts, see little to commend the latter, and wind up buying the American version.

Nor were the Japanese able to even make a stab at the kind of price-quality approach that worked so well in TVs and automobiles, namely, starting out with low-priced goods and working their way up to high-priced products. The larger the machine, the more important were software and support, which the Japanese could not provide. What little success they had in PCs came through the path pioneered by Sanyo with Sears in TVs—by selling to Americans machines that would bear American nameplates. Mention has been made of the arrangement between Kyocera and Radio Shack. There was also one between Mitsubishi and Sperry, while Kaypro, a small but aggressive company whose homely but rugged Kaypro II won acceptance as "The VW Beetle of the micro field," entered into a similar agreement with Mitsui.

This hardly is what had been expected. Still, Japanese manufacturers observed that success in TVs, tape recorders, and autos had taken many years, and that it was too early to make a judgment about micros. Certainly there was reason for hope. By mid-decade the Japanese had made headway with their printers, disc drives, and display screens—but not with the micros themselves, which remained an American preserve, dominated, of course, by Big Blue. In 1984, the Japanese in the aggregate had some 5 percent of the American market for micros, which was less than Apple (27 percent), Compaq (10 percent)—and IBM (39 percent).

So at the moment the Japanese hardly are an important challenge to IBM in this rapidly growing area of the market. This young industry is being driven by technology, not marketing or even manufacturing. The new ideas are coming out of Silicon Valley, not Armonk, and recognizing this, IBM cultivates contacts with the young entries, encouraging them to submit ideas and write software for IBM products. As noted, the PC was fabricated out of parts manufactured by dozens of suppliers. The Japanese industrial environment is not as conducive to encouraging such operations, though, of course, there have been and will continue to be outstanding exceptions to the rule.

Finally, one has to take into account the yeasty, innovative American computer microculture, one in which hundreds of young scientists were fiddling at their workbenches, dreaming of becoming the next Steve Jobs, knowing that armed with a hunch and a short track record they could win backing and go from zero to $100 million in sales within a few years. Why not? Dozens of others, from Apple to Tandem to Compaq had done so. Aggressive American engineers tend to dream about starting their own companies. (Gene Amdahl started two.) Consider the case of John Podulska, for example. After cofounding Prime Computer and becoming irritated at what he considered the bureaucratization of that firm, he left in 1979, drew up a plan that micro engineers might use in graphic and design work, and within a week had raised $1.7 million in venture capital from Sutter Hill Ventures of Palo Alto and Venrock, a Rockefeller family operation. With this he organized Apollo Computer, which is located near Route 128, and started turning out his work stations. In 1981, Apollo posted revenues of $3.4 million; the firm joined the $200 million club three years later, by which time that $1.7 million stake was worth $350 million in stock. This rapid rise was made possible by the fact that Podulska had virtually created the market for powerful work stations that could be networked and now controls about half of it.

Such is the innovation and creativity that market the micro industry, and for all their excellent attributes, these are qualities rarely found in the Japanese business scene. Of course, the situation in Japan is changing, but it is questionable whether that country's micro industry can make so great a leap. Amdahl's and Podulska's Japanese counterparts more often than not plan for well-ordered careers at existing large entities. So it is that the Japanese perform superbly when it comes to seeking entry into a mature market but, as computers indicate, don't do as well in those markets that are evolving swiftly. Ernest von Simpson of the Research Board put it this way when comparing the computer experience with that in automobiles: "I don't think the Japanese are in the same game this time. The computer industry is much less monolithic, because it's all those guys in the garages that push the industry." Professor Tohru Moto-oka of Tokyo University believes otherwise. "In the United States individuals are very strong, but some new scientific fields have become very complex. To create new breakthroughs, the cooperation of a group is needed. One person alone cannot change these fields very much anymore."

Moto-oka concludes that "In the future Japan may be better suited for big jumps in complex fields. A cooperative society may be well suited for basic developments."

Professor Moto-oka's thoughts on the matter are most important, for in addition to his academic duties he is chairman of the advisory council for the Fifth Generation Computer, a project that, should it prove successful, could make Japan the leader in the field—while failure would assure IBM's supremacy well into the twenty-first century.

XIII

IBM VS. JAPAN INC.

The Future of the Fifth Generation

In the first half of the 1980s, Americans who monitored things Japanese might have read several dozen works dealing with that country's history, economy, and culture, but the most accessible of these concerned its success in industry. Consider some of the titles, selected at random: *The Japanese Challenge to U.S. Industry; The Japanese Mind: The Goliath Explained; How Japan's Economy Grew So Fast: The Sources of Postwar Expansion; Japanese Manufacturing Techniques: Nine Hidden Lessons in Simplicity; U.S.-Japanese Economic Relations: Cooperation, Competition, and Confrontation;* and more ominously, *The Japanese Conspiracy: The Plot to Dominate Industry World-Wide and How to Deal With It;* and *The Amazing Race: Winning the Technorivalry with Japan.*

Japan-watching has become a cottage industry in the United States, with publishers, universities, corporations, and lecture circuit agents seeking specialists, many of whom would become instant celebrities. That was understandable, but many were little more than "instant experts."

The reasons for seeking out such people are not difficult to fathom. The Japanese were doing so well in so many industries that Americans yearned to learn their "secrets" so as to be able to make the proper adjustments and meet the challenge posed by that country's industry. Ironically, many Americans apparently wanted to imitate a people whose most developed quality, so they were told, was the ability to imitate others.

227

No two peoples in the industrialized world are as different as the Japanese and the Americans; no two peoples are so alike.

It is an unusual situation, even amusing were it not so serious. American readers assiduously pore over all they can find in print about Japanese business, while energetic Japanese middle-management personnel enroll in graduate programs at leading American universities to delve into American management and technology. In 1981, Fujitsu president Takuma Yamamoto thought Japanese companies lacked the "dynamism and creativity" of American counterparts, adding, "Japan can only follow Western science." He went on to observe that his firm spent 10 percent of its sales revenues on R & D, far less than IBM, and that young Japanese engineers often defer to their elders rather than seek their own answers to problems; Yamamoto concluded that the Japanese educational system discouraged creativity and that it nudged students into a "no risk" attitude.

Nor is Yamamoto alone in this belief. Katsushige Mita, his counterpart at Hitachi, concedes that the Americans devote more attention to R & D. "The reason we can get away with less," he said, "is that we are still pursuing the Americans in basic technology. If we ever become front runners in advanced technology, we will have to spend far more on research than we are doing at present." To which MITI's Seiichi Ishizaka adds, "Manufacturing and processing technology is all we really have. The rest is imported."

Exaggerated? Surely, but sincere nonetheless. And at the same time that American readers were placing books on Japanese management on the bestseller lists alongside tomes on how to lose weight or make a million dollars in real estate, scores of American businessmen were touring Toyota, Nissan, Sony, Toshiba, Mitsubishi, Hitachi, and Fujitsu factories, listening politely to Japanese managers explain just how they went about their business. Each country looks at the other and sees a colossus; each looks at itself and sees a flawed entity. This is one of the more intriguing paradoxes of our time.

One of the aforementioned group of books about Japan is *The Fifth Generation: Artificial Intelligence and Japan's Computer Challenge to the World,* by Edward Feigenbaum, a leading American expert on the subject and professor of computer science at Stanford University, and Pamela McCorduck, a New York-based science and technology writer. It is an altogether admiring study of one of the more important Japanese projects in the area, together with a warning to Americans that scientists in Japan are on the verge of leapfrogging over the West in what used to be called computers but now might better be termed information processors or—in their view—generators as well. *The Fifth Generation* received good reviews, won respectable sales, and was one of a number of books and articles in business and trade magazines on the subject. If one wants to know about the Fifth Generation project, one needs only go to library catalogues or data banks to find more than one needs to achieve a comprehensive view of the subject.

Before proceeding, here's why the next generation of machines is called the fifth. As we have seen, the early computers were based upon vacuum tubes, which were replaced by transistors, and then integrated circuits—these were the first three generations. The fourth, which we are in the midst of now, is erected on very large-scale integrated chips (VSLI), hybrids of the integrated circuits, which lead some industry analysts to believe it would more accurately be called "Generation Three and a Half."

All four generations proceed out of the rubric established in the 1940s by John von Neumann, in which a central processor, a memory, programs, and input-and-output peripherals process information a step at a time. You'll recall from the first chapter of this book how von Neumann stamped his philosophy on those early machines and set the path along which IBM and all the others traveled. The industry's drive since then was to create machines that could accelerate the process, always doing so according to the von Neumann formulation.

According to the Japanese (and Feigenbaum and others), the Fifth Generation will abandon this approach and process information along parallel lines; in addition, it will be capable of making judgmental decisions as well as merely processing information. Beyond this, the essential feature will be a far closer interface between user and machine than is possible under the von Neumann formulation, since communications will then be possible on a very high plane that will combine verbal with mathematical analysis.

In addition, the Fifth Generation machines are to possess the ability to solve problems rather than simply process information. Thus, they would achieve artificial intelligence, the aspect for which Feigenbaum's book became famous. As he put it, "These will be computers that can learn, associate, make inferences, make decisions, and otherwise behave in ways we have always considered the exclusive province of human reason."

Those involved in Fifth Generation projects talk of the end of information processing—a von Neumann concept—and its replacement by *knowledge* information processing, or KIPS. Professor Moto-oka is typical of Fifth Generation supporters in claiming, "In the 1990s, when Fifth Generation computers will be widely used, information processing systems will be a central tool in all areas of social activity, to include economics, industry, science, culture, daily life, and the like, and will be required to meet those new needs generated by environmental changes."

The implications of all this are both revolutionary and a trifle arcane, which is to say that at the same time one can be dazzled by the prospect and skeptical of its utility in the foreseeable future. For one thing, if Fifth Generation machines do appear they will have limited use, at least initially, and the von Neumann hardware and software will continue to be used to solve most problems in small, medium-sized, and large computers. Comparatively few processes now being used call for the capabilities of forthcoming Fifth Generation machines. Moreover, the technology may turn out to be less complex than imagined. There are two ways to create supercomputers: one can be designed as a unit, or it can be cobbled together—the industry term is "multiprocessing"—by piling one computer upon another. Most of the large Cray, Control Data, and Fujitsu machines are of the former type (though the new Cray II employs four central-processing units), but dozens of powerful units have been assembled through the "multiprocessor" approach at a far lower cost. This technique has the added virtue of flexibility since, theoretically at least, one can tack on additional units or remove them as needs dictate.

Any thought that a supercomputer can be fashioned simply by piecing together micros should be cast aside, however. Some of the most powerful supercomputers are capable of running a billion calculations per second, against the Apple IIe's 500,000. Thus, it would take 2,000 of the latter in parallel to equal a supercomputer. On the other hand, there seems no reason why several large machines, such as the IBM 3081, couldn't be used in multiprocessing. Multiprocessing is relatively simple and may make more sense in the long run. If this is so, then the future of supercomputer architecture would be quite different from the way that scientists at Japan's Fifth Generation project and Cray assume it would be.

Nonetheless, the more enthusiastic Japanese proponents of Fifth Generation systems talk of them replacing the VSLI computers, just as the automobile made the horse and buggy obsolete. A more reasonable analogy would be the relationship between the helicopter and the airplane and the auto, which is to say that the supercomputer will take over certain computer functions and perform them better, but will not be universally adopted.

The development of Japan's program hardly was secret. Readers of business magazines learned of it as early as 1978 when Bro Uttal of *Fortune,* to cite one example, wrote of MITI's interest in "a technological breakthrough that would allow the Japanese to turn out hardware superior to U.S. products [and] could multiply their success in distributed processing and data communication. . . . The point is to leapfrog IBM's next generation." William Givens of Twain Associates, a consulting firm, warned that "If they can achieve their goals with computers it could ensure their general economic dominance well into the twenty-first century."

Rumblings on this topic have been heard out of Japan regularly ever since. Under MITI's guidance, the Japan Information Processing Center (Jipdec) was organized as a clearing house for information. In 1979, Jipdec was charged with developing a two-year study on the Fifth Generation, which under the leadership of its Committee for Study and Research on Fifth Generation Computers was completed in 1981. Official notification of the program came in October of that year, when Soicho Nagamatsu, then deputy director of MITI's electronic policy division, announced its intention to budget $450 million over the next decade—with a like amount contributed by the companies involved—for Fifth Generation projects. The Institute for New Generation Computer Technology (ICOT) was organized the following April and charged with coordinating efforts. According to Nagamatsu, the first stage, that of experimentation, was to run until 1984, the second—establishing the architecture and erecting facilities—to 1988, with the third phase—placement—to be completed in 1991. Out of all this is to come a single line of computers, the result of a unified joint effort.

While ICOT constantly proclaims its belief in the new technology and has invited cooperation not only by Japanese firms but American and European as well, there seems little doubt that the major objective is not scientific or technical, but commercial. The goal is the defeat of IBM, which remains essentially wedded to the von Neumann approach, with the Fifth Generation as the means. For should the Fifth Generation become a reality, it will be IBM's turn to attempt to create PCMs—and follow the lead established by Fujitsu, Hitachi, and others in the next turn of the wheel of the information revolution.

Yoneji Masuda, one of Japan's most respected computer scientists and author of *The Information Society,* put it this way when asked why Japan has placed so much effort into the Fifth Generation. "One reason is that Japan wants to have an independent computer industry," he replied. "Over the past 15 years we have struggled to catch up with IBM—for government and business, this has been our most important objective in the computer industry. Now our technology is almost competitive with the IBM machine. And the time has come for Japan to change strategy, not just to follow IBM but to do better." Somewhat disingenuously he joined with Jipdec in calling for IBM's cooperation. "It is hoped that IBM will join," he said, adding that "IBM is a giant, of course, and we hope to gain the benefit of their knowledge."

IBM has expressed interest in Fifth Generation concepts, and the company, which despite all the cultural changes of the past decade remains secretive about R & D, doubtless has been engaging in experimental work along these lines.

It is worth knowing that while MITI talked of a $900 million Fifth Generation budget for the 1980s, IBM will expend well in excess of $30 billion on R & D during the decade. Indeed, of the $5.8 billion spent on R & D by American computer corporations in 1983, IBM accounted for $2.5 billion—more than twelve times the $472 million of runner-up DEC. Of course, this includes all work on all projects, but the enormity of the sum indicates that if IBM believed in Fifth Generation concepts it would be able to outspend and—given its record—outperform any rival. It would appear, however, that the firm is not about to make a major push in that direction. In fact, there are those within the company who indicate a suspicion that the Fifth Generation is little more than a diversion, that the major Japanese move will come from a different and more conventional direction, namely, the creation of supercomputers utilizing the familiar von Neumann architecture.

In any case, there is an American response to the Fifth Generation Project coming from three sources: the universities, the companies, and the government, with academia perhaps the most important.

Any thought that the Japanese have pioneered in Fifth Generation concepts should take into consideration that the initial work on the subject came out of the Massachusetts Institute of Technology in the early 1970s, from Professor Jack Dennis in particular. Dennis theorized about "dataflow" machines with arrays of microprocessors, each functioning independently of the others, with routing systems to enable them to communicate with one another—and possibly to learn and create knowledge in the bargain. In 1982, Dennis embarked upon the creation of just such a mainframe, what the people at MIT call a "connection machine," which will incorporate a million chips, each of which can communicate with the others. Others are following this path; Professor James Browne of the University of Texas has actually constructed a parallel-processing machine known as the Texas Reconfigurable Array Computer (TRAC), which features four processors and nine memories. Denalcor, a small company, has a supercomputer that also utilizes four processors. At the University of North Carolina, Professor Gyulo Mago has designed a different kind of mainframe but with the same objective in mind. There are ongoing projects at some fifty other American universities besides those mentioned. The academic concern with artificial intelligence is so great as to make it the most serious threat to Japanese dominance in this area.

The British are at it too; a team at the University of Manchester is at work on a Fifth Generation mainframe. There are at least a half dozen Fifth Generation programs in the United Kingdom and the United States that at this writing are ahead of the Japanese Fifth Generation program. All have significant contacts with computer manufacturers, especially IBM.

The Japanese who are involved in their country's program know this. At an international Fifth Generation conference in Tokyo, it became evident that they were still far behind the United States and the United Kingdom. "I use the analogy of hop, skip and a jump," said Kazuhiro Fuji, a leading researcher in the Japanese challenge. "We have merely completed the first step, hopping. We are not saying that Japan is No. 1, but merely stating the outcome of our efforts, including those efforts in fields in which we are not mature yet." Professor Faye Briggs of Rice University concluded that "This is an opportunity for them [the Japanese] to get up to speed. The U.S. is not behind in any sense. They are probably where we were five years ago."

And so the Japanese hope to learn from the West, just as they once did in consumer electronics and automobiles. Dennis traveled to Japan in 1980 to deliver a series of lectures on the subject, and his input and those of other Americans was most welcome there. But some American computer businessmen, especially several at Control Data, call for limitations on cooperation. For example, there are more than 14,000 Japanese students studying in American universities, of whom 30 percent are in graduate schools, primarily in high technology studies. Hewlett-Packard founder and chairman, David Packard, recently noted that "Japan is highly dependent on U.S. basic research and skilled in taking the know-how and putting it into imaginative products. It's about time we found some way for them to help pay for it." Others would take more drastic action. CDC chairman William Norris has gone so far as to speak of the desirability of expelling those involved in computer science from centers conducting significant research, an indication not only of his fear that the Japanese will purloin secrets, but of his respect for the quality of research being conducted at the schools. "They [the Japanese] have imposed quite stringent barriers on their export of technology," a CDC spokesman explains, "but it's grab and run with whatever they can get here.

'Go out there and rape and pillage, but don't let anyone see our girls,' is their attitude."

Robert Rutishauser, a CDC vice-president, would not go as far as Norris, but has come to the same conclusion. "They have access to the basic technology that comes out of some of our leading universities.... The bulk of foreign graduate students remain in this country—but my impression is that the Japanese are a clear exception to that. Japanese students come over here, get their advanced training, learn everything they can, and for the most part, go back to Japan." Indeed, the leading Japanese companies have provided student grants and scholarships, with the likes of NEC and Hitachi in the forefront. And there are other methods of obtaining glimpses of future plans. The MIT industrial liaison program, which for a fee of $30,000 offers access to ongoing research programs, has 297 members, of whom 45 are Japanese.

Rutishauser and his counterparts at other BUNCH companies have demonstrated their belief in the high quality of university research by raiding the computer science departments for talent. Some observers believe that such raids weaken the schools. "There's no question there is a shortage of university AI people," says Lawrence Harris of Artificial Intelligence Corporation, one of several score of young companies now in the field. "The quality of people who left was high, and they have left a vacuum."

IBM takes a different approach, preferring to fund research and reap rewards, thus placating administrations while enjoying the fruits of campus-based work in the field. This hardly is a new policy; we have seen how in the 1930s Tom Watson, Sr., maintained close connections with Columbia University, eventually funding a major research facility there. Among its many commitments, IBM has made a grant of more than $15 million to Brown University, $20 million to Carnegie-Mellon, and, together with DEC, has placed $50 million in MIT's "Project Athena," a highly ambitious computer network. Virtually all colleges and universities with computer science programs know they can receive substantial discounts on IBM hardware and software. But this too is a long-standing program, one that other computer manufacturers also employ. That this is so is one of the more convincing bits of evidence that corporate America is conducting more research into this area than has been reported, and that a nexus exists between the companies and the universities, though no firm has exhibited as much dedication as IBM. Brown, Carnegie-Mellon, the University of California at Berkeley, Stanford, and other favored institutions have created programs by which virtually all students will become computer-literate—and that computer will come from IBM. "The key is tying together all the corners of the campus," says David Wasley, who has designed a system for Berkeley that will link the IBM PCs of some 30,000 students. Nor will IBM be the only beneficiary; its partner, Sytek, will have a share in this new market by providing circuit boards needed to make the system work. "The card we are delivering to IBM has more power than the PC itself," says CEO Michael Pliner, who concedes that the IBM connection is one of his firm's most important assets.

All of this has raised some important questions at the universities involved, which have traditionally insisted upon their independence. In several of the projects, IBM has obtained the right to copyright and license technologies and programs developed under the grant programs, leading critics to raise issues of academic freedom and independence. "When you dangle $20 million before a university the rules sometimes change," noted Professor Clement Markert, in charge of Yale's committee on cooperative research. Recalling campus protest during the Vietnam era, he goes on to say, "It's a cop-out to say that the benefits outweigh the principle of open research. There is no difference between keeping a company's secrets and keeping the Pentagon's." Professor William Shipp of Brown responds that his university's program is designed to suit its needs, and not those of IBM. "We have every intention to influence the course of IBM's future products," he says, conceding that "If we are going to do that, we have to play the game. You can't plant a garden without getting dirty." Douglas Van Houweling of Carnegie-Mellon believes the relationship is mutually beneficial, and that nothing has been lost by either side. "We have all gotten pretty good at building walls between our academic work and our commercial work. The trick is to see if they will stay up."

This is accomplished with IBM's cooperation; William Filip of IBM Academic Information Systems observes that the firm encourages publication of information derived from these projects. "The only thing that universities do not freely share is proprietary information about products that have not yet been announced, and universities rarely receive such information." It remains to be noted that, along with other IBM-connected universities, Carnegie-Mellon will be turning out generations of bright young technicians who have learned their craft on IBM hardware and are familiar with its software. This is bound to give Big Blue an edge in future placements, not unlike the one obtained when the Watsons did the same with mainframes in the 1950s and 1960s.

The Japanese Supercomputer Challenge

While the Japanese Fifth Generation program has received a great deal of publicity, of more immediate interest is another, lesser-known program called the National Superspeed Computer Project. Like the Fifth Generation Project, it involves government-industry cooperation; it is funded to the tune of up to $200 million per year by the Japanese government, in addition to substantial sums from the companies involved.

The Japanese Big Six, led by the National Electrotechnical Laboratory, has embarked upon an eight-year program (to be brought to fruition in 1989) to create gigantic machines capable of operating at up to a thousand times the speed of the most powerful computer in existence in 1981—limited production models from Cray and Control Data—and which will utilize chips with 10 million transistor-equivalents. Gene Amdahl's work at Trilogy may be considered part of the supercomputer development as well, and his machines—which, of course, were never produced—would have been almost as powerful and would have occupied only half the space of a 308X. The concept is staggering but, as with the Fifth Generation, may be too ambitious by half.

That there will be a demand for such machines from weather bureaus, the military, the space programs, and a handful of commercial concerns seems likely. There is evidence that large universities with specialized graduate programs in the sciences would like to have them. Firms involved in oil drilling and industrial design may use them profitably, but for others to do so would be akin to employing an ocean liner as a fishing boat, which is to say that it would be wasteful of all that power.

Then, too, smaller machines are getting more powerful all the time; some desktop micros have one-third the computing capacity of the first Univacs. For example, the massive Cray X-MP can do about a billion calculations per second. In contrast, there are medium-size machines that run at a speed of 50 million cps, and offer much better value for investment. So the list of potential supercomputer customers seems rather small compared with that for the present big machines, such as IBM's top-of-line Sierra mainframes placed in September 1985. Perhaps time-sharing, the concept that became familiar in the 1960s, would be the best approach for supercomputer customers—at least until, and if, a single organization develops a need for its full-time use.

According to informed estimates, there are some 130 supercomputers in operation world-wide. A number of analysts have predicted that by the end of

236

the 1980s the number will be somewhere between 700 and 1,000. Consider that, according to one estimate, the Japanese companies will turn out approximately 150 such machines by 1990 and that the Americans will manufacture and place four times that amount. Since no European company currently produces or intends to produce supercomputers, that comes to around 750 of them, at a price in 1985 dollars of from $8 million to $20 million per copy, for an average of $14 million. Thus, the total revenues from supercomputers will come to $10.5 billion. Of course all of these are crude figures, since we have so little experience to guide us.

Now consider that former IBM CEO Opel and others have estimated that by 1990 information processing and distribution revenues will exceed $1 trillion. Assume that both figures are at least close to target. If so, then the supercomputers will account for slightly more than 10 percent of industry revenues. Or put it another way. The total estimated revenues from supercomputers between 1985 and 1990 will be less than IBM's revenues company-wide for four months in 1985.

Yet there always is the possibility that this situation will change. Two years ago Peter Gregory of Cray told a reporter that "We don't know what the total marketplace is, but we know that our success has attracted competition. The Japanese have said they see a market for about thirty machines. Today there are only three supercomputers in Japan, two of them made by Cray." Gregory may have a rather narrow definition in mind; writing in early 1984, science writer William Broad thought there were approximately 85 in use throughout the world. Of these, Cray had accounted for approximately 65. At mid-year, however, the firm's backlog of orders stood at 22. Now consider that those 65 were placed over an eight-year period, at an average rate of slightly more than eight per year. Clearly the pace of orders is accelerating.

The concept of supercomputers, then, is hardly novel with the Japanese; as indicated, Cray and Control Data turn them out and are still deemed pioneers in the area. Most computer scholars consider the Cray I, introduced in 1976, to be the first of the supercomputers. The most powerful machines turned out by an American company are the Cray X-MP and the CPC Cyber 205. Both companies are working on units twice as powerful; the Cray II, one being developed by ETA Systems, a company in which CDC has a dominant equity interest, will combine with the Cyber 205. However, the Fujitsu FACOM VP-200 is the equal of the American machines in most respects and superior in others, and is the fastest nonexperimental machine now in existence. Updated versions of this machine were introduced into the American market as the Amdahl 1100 and the 1200, both of which are IBM-compatible, in 1985.

The reason is quite familiar: Fujitsu has drawn upon American technology. As Steven Orzag of M.I.T. put it, "Fujitsu has taken the best features of Cray, CDEC, and IBM architectures and put them all together." But most important and significant, unlike the X-MP and Cyber 205, the VP-200 can run most IBM programs. "They're clearly thinking about the IBM market," thought Nobel Laureate Kenneth Wilson of Cornell, who entertains some doubts. "The only way we'll find out for sure is when we actually get machines over here and start running standard problems on them. If the Japanese have really achieved IBM compatibility with their machines and can manufacture large numbers of them, they will get into serious competition with IBM with serious results for the United States." Apparently the Europeans are convinced of this. Fujitsu entered into agreements with ICL and Siemens to sell VP-200s there and in 1983 announced intentions of placing at least forty of them through those British and German companies through 1988.

None of this can be news at Armonk. The idea of customers purchasing or leasing VP-200s in order to run IBM software more rapidly is galling, and most industry watchers appear to believe that IBM has its own version on the shelf, prepared to release when and if the market calls for it. This seems likely and, if so, would hardly be the first time IBM utilized this strategy.

The American Response

During the 1984 American presidential campaign, one of the economic side issues involved a debate over the wisdom of an "industrial policy." The issue was raised by Democrat Walter Mondale and was a product of his brain trust, one of whose members, Lester Thurow of MIT, had been advocating such a policy for several years as the American response to the Japanese export assault. What Thurow and others seemed to want, and Mondale embraced, was an American version of MITI, the assumption being that one of the major reasons for Japan's success was its coordinated industrial effort.

Opponents of industrial policies replied that in their view Japan's great victories in a wide variety of product areas owed more to the nature of the workforce, the currency ratios, the relatively small amount of governmental interference with the industrial processes, and the slack antitrust laws. And so the debate went on, unnoticed by most voters whose concerns were on more immediate and better-publicized issues. One would have assumed that a Reagan victory would have meant a rejection of the notion, while had Mondale won, the United States would embark upon the greatest peacetime experiment in industry-labor-government cooperation since the New Deal.

What went unsaid in all of this is that the United States already has an industry policy, that cooperation between the three elements is both ongoing and significant. In the main, however, it is improvised rather than planned, created to meet specific challenges rather than to implement the ideas of some social planner or another. Certainly a policy emerged for automobiles in the late 1970s. And soon after, in recognition of the Japanese challenge in information processing, one emerged in that area as well.

This is recognized in Japan if not in the United States. The Japanese see the dropping of the IBM antitrust suit and the failure to challenge the Intel and Rolm investments as a sign that Washington is prepared to smile on Armonk and considers IBM the American entry in the race.

This is a vast oversimplification. The Japanese assumed that more thought and planning had gone into the situation than truly was the case. As with all such improvisations, complexity, not simplicity, is the result. In fact, there have been several responses, and IBM has figured importantly in only one of them. Rather, the initiative for a policy has come from government, the BUNCH companies, and leading electronics firms.

The Pentagon's Defense Advanced Research Projects Agency (DARPA) is the oldest and best funded of these programs, having begun in the early 1960s and since then expended some $500 million on projects related to the military. Typically, DARPA will provide all the funding for equipment and concepts that can be used by the Armed Forces—among these are supercomputers and experiments concerned with Fifth Generation concepts.

That DARPA will remain the largest and most important cooperative American effort in this area seems likely given the state of the Cold War, but significantly, in recent years more funding has been provided for R & D in areas where America is encountering Japanese competition. DARPA has to apply to the Administration and Congress for funding, this is in a period when both call for balanced budgets and the White House scrutinizes requests for added funding most carefully. Nonetheless, in 1983 Congress authorized the Strategic Computing Program, funded at $250 million, to develop "superintelligent" computers that can deal with symbols instead of numbers. While not spelling it out, SCP is really the main American response to the Fifth Generation program. DARPA would like to obtain an additional $100 million for a special supercomputer project, but this request was bottled up in subcommittee the following year.

Potentially more important, though smaller, is the Microelectronics & Computer Technology Corporation (MCC), inspired by and organized in 1982 by William Norris, that perennial Japan-basher. It was established by CDC and eleven other computer and electronics companies, including Honeywell, DEC, National Semiconductor, Harris, Motorola, and RCA, each of which anted around $150,000. Since then, seven more companies, led by Eastman Kodak, have joined in with fees of $500,000. In 1984, MCC's budget came to $65 million being expended by some 200 scientists and engineers.

Simply stated, MCC sponsors research, the results of which will be available to all participants. Leading the effort is Bobby Ray Inman, the former deputy director of the Central Intelligence Agency and former director of the National Security Agency, who quickly took on John Pinkston of the NSA as his chief scientist.

A good deal of the credit for whatever success there will be at MCC will go to Inman, who is one of the most highly regarded executives in the United States. The reaction of presidential science advisor George Keyworth to the appointment was typical: "The day they picked Bob Inman to head the MCC any concern about its success diminished in my mind."

MCC is at the same time too little and too ambitious for its tasks, and is plagued by what may be the major American shortcoming—a weakness of intercompany cooperation. The group does not include some of the industry heavyweights, such as Cray and, most important, IBM. The funding is inadequate for major tasks, and to date little has come out of the project. At the same time, important antitrust considerations are involved. Clearly MCC could be construed as a combination in restraint of trade if it came up with anything that benefited members and harmed nonmembers, especially if the technology was shared by the insiders.

Furthermore, the companies hardly could be expected to dispatch their most important and innovative scientists to MCC, and would be reluctant to share any knowledge with those from other firms. Participants conceded as much. "These are the problems I guess we had to expect," said Michael McGuire of Harris in the summer of 1984, a year and a half after the project got underway at a campus not far from the University of Texas at Austin, in what has become that region's version of Silicon Valley. "None of us has done anything like this before. But now things are picking up, and we are very encouraged."

Inman personally assembled the staff, rejecting most of the cadres initially sent by the participating companies, as though to signal to them that he had no intention of accepting their second-raters. "We told them they had only one chance to get their best people in the projects," recalled RCA's George Black, who became the MCC vice president for human resources. "All of a sudden we started getting better applicants from the companies." Inman personally hired most of the project directors, several of whom came from nonparticipating firms. Inman also interceded with the Justice Department for exemption from the antitrust laws, and worked with the University of Texas to beef up its computer science program to mesh with MCC requirements. Problems remain, and Inman concedes that the scientists are troubled by what amounts to a dual loyalty. "The key will be a strong sense of ethics," he recently said. "If we find someone pursuing a program he is not part of, we will send him home quickly. They all come with a round-trip ticket."

Under Inman's plan, any company that sponsors research will have exclusive rights to its fruits for three years, after which it can be licensed to others within or outside the consortium. If MCC's effort comes together, the United States will have another defender against the Japanese challenge to go with the aforementioned independent activities centered on the universities and those of IBM.

MCC has four goals: the creation of software, some of which will be along Fifth Generation lines; research into the uses of computers in design and manufacturing; supercomputer design; and the creation of technology to simplify central processing unit structure. Its most ambitious undertakings right now are projects in various areas of computer design and electronics, the most ambitious being ones quite close to Japan's Fifth Generation project, and the development of very large scale integration (VSLI) techniques for assembling new microchips. But without IBM, its possibilities will be limited, since IBM is one of the few companies with both the technological and financial clout required. As Robert Rutishauser put it, "What's required here is a level of investment in some of the advanced technologies that by-and-large only two U.S. companies—IBM and AT&T—have the resources to do. I think the other companies, like Digital Equipment, Motorola, Control Data, collectively could mount such an effort. A $50 million to $100 million investment in the advanced technology is required, on top of the investments the companies have to make in the proprietary technology that they need to stay alive. It's just more than most companies can afford."

The Semiconductor Research Corporation (SRC) is another consortium, this one founded in 1983 by thirteen computer and component firms. Its adherents include several MCC members but also important firms that held back from joining the older group, IBM and Intel among them. SRC does not conduct research on its own, but instead provides grants for new and ongoing projects, most of them at universities. The budget is relatively modest—$12 million in 1983, around $60 million the following year, and $70 million in 1984. Up till now SRC has concentrated on supporting R & D in semiconductors and other electronic components and is not likely to tread in areas that would overlap efforts now concerning DARPA and MCC.

What might come out of all of this remains unknown. Whatever does, however, will redound to the interests of the non-IBM American firms more than to Big Blue. That raises another matter. Will the Japanese attempt to purchase the computer business of a BUNCH firm? It might make sense only after the Japanese obtain an important foothold. We have seen how Matsushita purchased Motorola's Quasar Division in 1974, and how other Japanese firms established manufacturing operations in the United States after obtaining a major slice of the consumer electronics market, and how Toyota, Datsun, and Honda produced cars in the United States when it appeared possible that Congress would enact legislation setting quotas on imports. There has been a takeover in the American auto industry, but not by a Japanese firm. After decades of failing to crack into the market, France's Renault purchased a controlling interest in American Motors, and initially did fairly well as a result.

No one on either side of the Pacific thinks Renault will be a model for the Japanese, however. The acquisition, say, of Honeywell by Toshiba or Univac by Hitachi does not seem in the cards at this writing. Nor does it appear likely that Fujitsu will pour a limitless stream of money into Amdahl. There simply is not any reason to do so. Today the plug-compatible field is dominated by the Japanese; with the failure of Trilogy, only Fujitsu and Hitachi, through Amdahl and NASCO, remain to challenge IBM in the plug-compatible arena, and their prospects hardly are promising.

Equally important are the matters of perception and priorities. Quasar is as much a Japanese company as IBM Japan is an American, but the difference is that Americans have proven more willing to accept foreign products in high tech areas than has MITI. This can be seen in an aspect of the Matsushita-

Motorola deal, which occurred soon after the American firm had initiated discussions with the Japanese firm of Aiwa to sell Motorola TVs in the Japanese market. The price of Motorola's American sets sold in Japan was very little more than comparable Japanese sets sold for on their domestic market. In some cases the American products represented better value. Motorola also knew that the heightened perception of Japanese trade would obviate any attempts to raise tariff barriers against American TVs, for it could lead to retaliation and a trade war that Japan was desperately attempting to avoid. The purchase of Quasar included an agreement by Motorola to cease all manufacture of TV sets, and so removed it as a threat to the Japanese market.

This is to suggest that the prime item on the Japanese agenda is not an assault on the American and European markets, important as those might be in the long run. Rather, the first item of concern is the displacement of IBM Japan as one of the two major computer companies in the domestic market. Not until that is done can we expect the full might of Japan Inc. in world markets.

If then. American's giant corporations have been facing Japanese competition for the past quarter of a century, even though an acute awareness of it is more recent. IBM is unique in not only showing an ability to turn back Japanese information processing companies at the beaches but also to beat them at their own game in the home islands. At this writing, there exists no evidence that this situation will change in the foreseeable future; though given the abilities, ingenuity, and dedication of the Japanese industry nothing is really certain. What is known, however, is that the contest will continue well into the twenty-first century. IBM has won the first round, but there will be others.

SELECTED BIBLIOGRAPHY

That the information processing and distribution industry is among the world's most rapidly changing verges on being a cliché. More than any other industry, today's secrets become tomorrow's commonplace technologies. It has been said by one practitioner that "if you understand it, the knowledge is outdated."

At the same time, we have been inundated with books, articles, pamphlets, special reports, newspaper stories, and television specials on the subject and related ones. One has almost to be living a hermitlike existence in the United States, western Europe, or Japan not to have come across items dealing with the subject regularly.

This is to say that there has been no shortage of materials on the subject. The research problem has been more the sorting, organization, and interpretation of materials than the location of obscure knowledge. Moreover, like many others in the field, I have found practitioners on both sides of the Atlantic and Pacific willing to share nonproprietary knowledge and insights.

For the past half dozen years and more, I have been engaged in studying and writing about this industry; and in the process have come into contact with scores of scientists, managers, salesmen, and others in the field, ranging from top executives at IBM to the fellow who sold me my micro at a small Long Island outlet and instructed me on the more arcane aspects of word processing. To list them all would be impossible; to select the more important ones would be ungracious to those omitted. Suffice it to say that these individuals know who they are and have been thanked for their assistance.

Among the more important published works on the subject are the following. The list is selected with an eye toward future reading and is by no means exhaustive. If the outpouring of materials in the future is anything like it has been in the past, there will be many more items which might be added but were released too late for inclusion.

BOOKS

Abbegglan, James, ed. *Business Strategies for Japan.* Tokyo: Sophia University Press, 1970.

Adams, T. F. M. and Kobayashi, N. *The World of Japanese Business.* Tokyo: Kodansha, 1969.

Allen, George. *A Short Economic History of Modern Japan.* Cambridge: Harvard, 1967.

_____. *Japan as a Market and Source of Supply.* Oxford: Pergamon, 1967.

_____. *Japan's Economic Expansion.* London: Oxford, 1967.

_____. *Japan's Place in Trade Strategy.* London: Moor House, 1968.

_____. *The Japanese Economy.* New York: St. Martin's, 1981.

Allyn, Stanley. *My Half Century with NCR.* New York: McGraw-Hill, 1967.

Auerbach on Small Business Computers. Philadelphia: Auerbach, 1973.

Austrian, Geoffrey. *Herman Hollerith: Forgotten Giant of Information Processing.* New York: Columbia, 1982.

Bain, Joe. *Barriers to New Competition.* Cambridge: Harvard University, 1970.

Balassa, Bela, ed. *Studies in Trade Liberalization: Problems and Prospects for Industrialized Countries.* Baltimore: Johns Hopkins Press, 1967.

Ballon, Robert. *The Japanese Employee.* Tokyo: Tuttle, 1969.

_____. ed. *Joint Ventures and Japan.* Tokyo: Sophia University Press, 1967.

Baranson, Jack. *The Japanese Challenge to U.S. Industry.* Lexington, Ky.: Lexington Books, 1981.

Belden, Thomas and Marva. *The Lengthening Shadow.* Boston: Little, Brown, 1962.

Bell, William. *A Management Guide to Electronic Computers.* New York: McGraw-Hill, 1957.

Benedict, Ruth. *The Chrysanthemum and the Sword.* Boston: Houghton Mifflin, 1946.

Benjamin, Roger and Ori, Kan. *Tradition and Change in Postindustrial Japan.* New York: Praeger, 1981.

Berkeley, E. C. *Giant Brains, Or Machines That Think.* New York: Wiley, 1949.

Bernstein, Jeremy. *The Analytical Engine.* New York: Random House, 1954.

Bieda, K. *The Structure and Operation of the Japanese Economy.* Sydney: Wiley Australasia, 1970.

Boltho, Andrea. *Japan: An Economic Survey, 1953–1973.* New York: Oxford, 1975.

Booth, Andrew and Kathleen. *Automatic Digital Calculators.* London: Butterworth's Scientific Publications, 1956.

Bowden, B. V., ed. *Faster Than Thought: A Symposium on Digital-Computing Machines.* London: Pittman, 1953.

Brock, Gerald. *The U.S. Computer Industry: A Study of Market Power.* Philadelphia: Ballinger, 1975.

Brzezinski, Zbigniew. *The Fragile Blossom: Crisis and Change in Japan.* New York: Harper & Row, 1972.

Chang, C. S. *The Japanese Auto Industry and the U.S. Market.* New York: Praeger, 1981.

Christopher, Robert. *The Japanese Mind: The Goliath Explained.* New York: Simon & Schuster, 1983.

Crosby, Philip. *Quality Is Free: The Art of Making Quality Certain.* New York: McGraw-Hill, 1979.

Crowther, Samuel. *John H. Patterson: Pioneer in Industrial Welfare.* New York: Doubleday Page, 1923.

Davidson, William. *The Amazing Race: Winning the Technorivalry with Japan.* New York: Wiley, 1984.

Denison, Edward and Chung, William. *How Japan's Economy Grew So Fast: The Sources of Postwar Expansion.* Washington, D.C.: Brookings Institution, 1976.

Destler, I. M., Fukui Haruhito, and Sato Hideo, *The Textile Wrangle: Conflict in Japanese-American Relations, 1969–1971.* Ithaca: Cornell University Press, 1979.

—————— and Sato, Hideo, eds. *Coping with U.S.-Janapese Economic Conflicts.* Lexington, Ky.: Lexington Books, 1982.

Diebold, John, ed. *The World of the Computer.* New York: Random House, 1973.

Drucker, Peter. *Adventures of a Bystander.* New York: Harper & Row, 1978.

——————. *The Changing World of the Executive.* New York: Times Books, 1982.

Duncan, William. *U.S.-Japanese Automobile Diplomacy.* Cambridge: Ballinger, 1973.

247

Englebourg, Saul. *International Business Machines: A Business History.* New York: Arno, 1976.

Feigenbaum, Edward and McCorduck, Pamela. *The Fifth Generation: Artificial Intelligence and Japan's Computer Challenge to the World.* Reading, Mass.: Addison–Wesley, 1983.

Fisher, Franklin, McGowan, John, and Greenwood, Joen. *Folded, Spindled, and Mutilated: Economic Analysis and U.S. vs. IBM.* Cambridge: MIT Press, 1983.

_____, McKie, James, and Mancke, Richard. *IBM and the U.S. Data Processing Industry: An Economic History.* New York: Praeger, 1983.

Flint, Charles. *Memories of an Active Life.* New York: Putnam, 1923.

Frank, Isaiah, ed. *The Japanese Economy in International Perspective.* Baltimore: Johns Hopkins, 1975.

_____ and Hirono, Ryokichi, eds. *How the United States and Japan See Each Other's Economy.* New York: Committee for Economic Development, 1974.

Freeman, Christopher. *The Economics of Industrial Innovation.* 2nd edition. Cambridge: MIT Press, 1982.

Frieberger, Paul and Swaine, Michael. *Fire in the Valley: The Making of the Personal Computer.* New York: McGraw-Hill, 1984.

Foy, Nancy. *The Sun Never Sets on IBM.* New York: Morrow, 1975.

Fukeda, Haraka. *Japan and World Trade: The Years Ahead.* Farmborough, U.K.: Saxon House, 1973.

Gibney, Frank. *Miracle by Design: The Real Reasons Behind Japan's Economic Success.* New York: Times Books, 1982.

Gilchrist, Bruce and Wessel, Milton. *Government Regulation of the Computer Industry.* Washington, D.C.: AFIPS, 1972.

Goldstine, Herman. *The Computer from Pascal to von Neumann.* Princeton: Princeton University, 1972.

Greenburger, Martin, ed. *Computers and the World of the Future.* Cambridge: MIT Press, 1966.

Gropelli, Angelico. *The Growth Process of the Computer Industry.* Unpublished Ph.D. dissertation. New York University, 1970.

Hadley, Frank. *Antitrust in Japan.* Princeton: Princeton University Press, 1970.

Haidani, Kanji. *The Japanese Economic System: An Institutional Approach.* Lexington, Ky.: Lexington Books, 1976.

Hall, Robert. *Driving the Productivity Machine: Production and Control in*

Japan. Falls Church, Va.: American Production and Inventory Control Society, 1981.

Harmon, Alvin. *The International Computer Industry.* Cambridge: Harvard University Press, 1970.

Hirschmeier, Johannes and Yiu, Tsenehiko. *The Development of Japanese Business.* Cambridge: Harvard University Press, 1975.

Ho, Alfred. *Japan's Trade Liberalization in the 1960s.* White Plains, N.Y.: International Arts & Sciences, 1974.

Hollerman, Leon. *Japan's Dependence on the World Economy.* Princeton: Princeton University Press, 1967.

Hunsberger, Warren. *Japan and the United States in World Trade.* New York, Harper & Row: 1964.

———. *Japan In United States Foreign Economic Policy.* Washington, D.C.: USGPO, 1961.

———. *Japan: New Industrial Giant.* New York: American-Asian Educational Exchange. 1972.

International Business Machines. *Time to Know: A Brief History of IBM.* New York: IBM, 1967.

Jansen, Marius, ed. *Changing Japanese Attitudes Toward Modernization.* Princeton: Princeton University Press, 1965.

Johnson, Chalmers. *MITI and the Japanese Miracle: The Growth of Industrial Policy, 1925-1975.* Stanford: Stanford University Press, 1982.

Kaplan, Eugene. *Japan: The Government-Business Relationship.* Washington, D.C.: Department of Commerce, 1972.

Komiya, Ryutaro, ed. *Postwar Economic Growth in Japan.* Berkeley: University of California Press, 1966.

Kozaczuk, Wladyslaw. *Enigma: How the German Machine Cipher was Broken, and How It Was Read by the Allies in World War Two.* New York: University Publications of America, 1984.

Lockwood, William, ed. *The State and Economic Enterprise in Japan.* Princeton: Princeton University Press, 1965.

McClellan, Stephen. *The Coming Computer Industry Shakeout: Winners, Losers, and Survivors.* New York: Wiley, 1984.

MacArthur, Douglas. *Reminiscences.* New York: McGraw-Hill, 1964.

Magaziner, Ira and Hout, Thomas. *Japanese Industrial Policy.* Berkeley: University of California, 1979.

Malik, Rex. *And Tomorrow . . . the World.* London: Millington, 1975.

Manchester, William. *American Caesar: Douglas MacArthur, 1880-1964.* Boston: Little, Brown, 1978.

Mannari, Hiroshi. *The Japanese Business Leaders.* Tokyo: University of Tokyo Press, 1974.

Morishima, Michio. *Why Has Japan "Succeeded?"* Cambridge: Cambridge University Press, 1982.

Monroe, Wilbur. *Japanese Exports to the United States: Analysis of "Import Pull" and "Export Push" Factors.* Washington, D.C.: United States–Japan Trade Council, 1978.

Moritz, Michael. *The Little Kingdom: The Private Story of Apple Computer.* New York: Morrow, 1984.

Nomura Research Institute. *Investing in Japan.* London: Woodhead-Faulkner, 1976.

Okimoto, Daniel, ed. *Japan's Economy: Coping with Change in the International Environment.* Boulder, Colorado: Westview, 1982.

———. Sugano, Takuo and Weinstein, Franklin, eds. *Competitive Edge: The Semiconductor Industry in the U.S. and Japan.* Stanford: Stanford University Press, 1984.

Organization for Economic Cooperation and Development. *The Industrial Policy of Japan.* Paris: OECD, 1972.

Ozawa, Terutomo. *Japan's Technological Challenge to the West, 1950–1970: Motivation and Accomplishment.* Cambridge: MIT, 1974.

Patrick, Hugh and Rosovsky, Henry, eds. *Asia's New Giant: How the Japanese Economy Works.* Washington, D.C.: Brookings, 1976.

Phister, Montgomery Jr. *Data Processing Technology and Economics.* Santa Monica: Santa Monica Publishing, 1976.

Pyke, Magnus. *The Science Century.* New York: Walker, 1967.

Pylyshyn, Zenon, ed. *Perspectives on the Computer Revolution.* Englewood Cliffs, N.J.: Prentice-Hall, 1970.

Riley, Robert. *A Case Study in a Differentiated Monopoly: The Computer Time-Sharing Industry.* Unpublished Ph.D. dissertation. University of Cincinnati, 1970.

Rodgers, William. *Think: A Biography of the Watsons and I.B.M.,* New York: Stein and Day, 1969.

Rose, Frank. *Introduction to the Heart of the Matter.* New York: Harper & Row, 1984.

Rosenberg, Jerry. *The Computer Prophets.* New York: Collier-Macmillan, 1969.

Sarnoff, David. *Looking Ahead.* New York: McGraw-Hill, 1968.

Saso, Mary and Kirby, Stuart. *Japanese Industrial Competition to 1990.* Cambridge, Mass.: Abt Books, 1982.

Schoenberger, Richard. *Japanese Manufacturing Techniques: Nine Hidden Lessons in Simplicity.* New York: Free Press, 1982.

Sobel, Robert. *Car Wars: The Untold Story of the Great Automakers and the Giant Battle for Global Supremacy.* New York: Dutton, 1984.

———. *I.B.M.: Colossus in Transition.* New York: Times Books, 1981.

Soma, John. *The Computer Industry.* Lexington, Ky.: Lexington Books, 1976.

Stewart, James. *The Partners: Inside America's Most Powerful Law Firms.* New York: Simon & Schuster, 1983.

Stokes, Henry. *The Japanese Competitor.* London: Financial Times, 1976.

Tasca, Diane, ed. *U.S.–Japanese Economic Relations: Cooperation, Competition, and Confrontation.* New York: Pergamon, 1980.

Tsurumi, Yoshi and Tsurumi, Rebecca. *Sogoshosha: Engines of Export-Based Growth.* Halifax, Nova Scotia: Institute for Research on Public Policy, 1980.

Turck, J. A. V. *Origins of Modern Calculating Machines.* Chicago: Western Society of Engineers, 1921.

Vogel, Ezra. *Japan as Number One: Lessons for America.* New York: Harper & Row, 1979.

———. ed. *Modern Japanese Organization and Decision-Making.* Berkeley: University of California Press, 1975.

Watson, Thomas, Jr. *A Business and Its Beliefs.* New York: McGraw-Hill, 1963.

Wilkins, Mira. *The Emergence of Multinational Enterprise.* Cambridge: Harvard University, 1970.

———. *The Maturing of Multinational Enterprise.* Cambridge: Harvard University, 1974.

Wolf, Marvin. *The Japanese Conspiracy: The Plot to Dominate Industry World-Wide and How to Deal With It.* New York: Empire, 1983.

Wozniak, Stephen. *Digital Deli.* San Francisco: Workman, 1984.

Yamamura, Kozo. *Economic Policy in Post-War Japan.* Berkeley: University of California, 1967.

———. ed. *Policy and Trade Issues of the Japanese Economy: American and Japanese Perspectives.* Seattle: University of Washington, 1982.

Yanaga, Chitoshi. *Big Business in Japanese Politics.* New Haven: Yale University Press, 1968.

Young, Alexander. *The Sogo Shosha: Japan's Multinational Trading Companies.* Boulder, Colo: Westview, 1979.

MAGAZINES AND NEWSPAPERS

Asia and the Pacific
Banker [London]
Barron's
Business Asia [Hong Kong]
Business Automation
Business Week
Byte
Compute!
Computer Decisions
Computer Design
Computers and Automation
Computers and Electronics
Computers and People
Computerworld
Creative Computing
Data Communications
Datamation
Duns Review
Economist
Electronic News
Family Computing
Far Eastern Economic Review [Hong Kong]
Financial Times [London]

Forbes
Fortune
Harvard Business Review
Infosystems
Info World
IBM Data Processor
Industrial Review of Japan
IBM Systems Journal
Japan Economic Journal
Japan Quarterly
Journal of Commerce
Mini-Micro Systems
PC World
Personal Computing
Popular Computing
Think
New York Times, The
Oriental Economist
Softalk/Apple
Survey of Current Business
Wall Street Journal
Washington Post

Index